The
BALLAD
of
TRADITION

To
THE DEVOTED
COLLECTORS WHO IN THE
TWENTIETH CENTURY HAVE
SHOWN THAT FOLK-SONG
THOUGH MORIBUND
YET LIVES

The
BALLAD
of
TRADITION

by

GORDON HALL GEROULD

New York

OXFORD UNIVERSITY PRESS

First published, 1932

Reprinted, 1957

PRINTED IN THE UNITED STATES OF AMERICA

CONTENTS

PREFACE

ONE could not well begin to write a book about ballads without a certain boldness, for the difficulties in the way of studying the subject are apparent to all who have approached it; and one must inevitably finish such a book in a humble state of mind. The difficulties do not vanish when one has coped with them. 'Ballad' has been used as a name for a number of different forms in music and poetry, each of which has as much right as any other to be so called. It is not easy to establish a definition of what we call nowadays the popular or traditional ballad; it is still harder to find how it came into being; and it is quite impossible to make a satisfactory canon of specimens. Yet no one denies the existence of such ballads, and few lovers of music and poetry can resist their charm.

I have been led to attempt a new treatment of this very thorny subject by the unexpected evidence that has come to light within the last twenty-five years. The time has seemed to me ripe for a survey of the whole matter, taking into account what has been learned and pointing out the urgent need of further investigation in a good many different directions. We can no longer ignore, for example, the part that music has played in the history of balladry, and less than ever can we look at ballads as verses printed in books. The field-workers of the past generation have gathered a rich harvest of material, which awaits the attention of other students. I have tried to make a new appraisal of our present knowledge about ballads, and to draw whatever conclusions I could about their history. The reader will note that I have followed the plan of devoting a good many chapters to description and analysis before proceeding to a discussion of theory. I have tried, indeed, to confine my conjectures to a single chapter, although I am aware that statements throughout the book must be coloured by opinion. I must confess that I hold certain opinions strongly, but I hope that I have expressed them without heat, for there is surely no reason why the discussion of ballads should be acrimonious— whatever its reputation in the past. We shall learn a great deal yet, I trust, about the ways of folk-song.

In spite of the collecting done since his time, F. J. Child's *English and Scottish Popular Ballads*, 1882–98, remains the most important repository of texts at the command of students. I have therefore adopted, for ready reference, the device of inserting after the name of a ballad the number it bears in his collection. To other books reference is made in footnotes, while a bibliography will be found at the end of the volume, which may be of service to readers who wish to familiarize themselves with the subject for the first time.

Perhaps a collector of ballads should have written this book instead of a man who has studied them in a library. No one could realize more fully than I the disadvantages under which I have laboured, for no one believes more profoundly that a ballad in print, even when accompanied by a careful musical notation, can never be quite what it was when sung. I can say only this in my behalf: for thirty years I have given ballads at least intermittent attention, and I have here done my poor best to interpret what seem to me their more important characteristics.

It is a pleasure to record my obligations to the officials of the Clarendon Press, and especially to Mr. Kenneth Sisam for his acute and helpful criticism.

PRINCETON,
  October 4, 1931.

Chapter One

THE NATURE OF BALLADS

BACK of all literature stretches an unmapped and immeasurable world of oral tradition. Before men began to write, they made songs and sang them, put together stories and told them. Imagination, memory, and a feeling for rhythm were early human developments, whereas writing, however it began, came later and was an invention quite apart from the much more primitive invention of speech. Literature itself is a far older thing than our forefathers believed. During the last century our knowledge of literary history has been greatly extended; and at the same time we have learned that all races of men, no matter how primitive, possess a store of compositions which cannot be called literature because they have never been written down, but which serve the same ends as literature in that they record action, express feelings or thoughts, and give some sort of pleasure in the hearing. Since it has been demonstrated that folk without writing know the art of composition in language, and preserve the memory of what they have thus composed, it is a fair inference that all peoples, since the very dawn of human intelligence, have made songs and stories, and transmitted them to their children.

There is no way by which we can penetrate the shadowed region beyond history that we conjecture, nor is there much profit in speculation by students of literature about what was made, and how, by the earliest singers and story-tellers. We need merely to remember that before the word was written it was spoken, and that throughout the ages since writing was invented a very great part of what man has uttered for his pleasure and edification has been recorded by memory rather than by the pen. We need to remember this because of the constant and inevitable influences that have played, and still to some extent are playing, back and forth between literature and oral tradition. The lyric poet, the story-teller in verse or prose, and the dramatist may at any moment find an image, a phrase, a situation, a theme for his use in something he has heard; and conversely something one man has written and many men have read may float away on the tide of memory to undergo strange adventures.

In our day, when even the uneducated have the habit of reading, when most of us get our impressions rather more through the eye than through the ear, it is hard for us to comprehend that any product of the imagination, with a pattern in its warp and woof, can exist in an oral state only. We think of the written symbols of words instead of the words themselves, and half-con-sciously regard the printed representation of a poem as the thing itself. So far have we gone on this road, in-deed, that the maker of literature must have a pen in his hand while his imagination is at work, and his audi-ence can scarcely appreciate the beauty he has created except by reference to the printed page. The drama is the only one of our literary categories which escapes to any considerable extent from this bondage to the symbol; and we have all met persons who prefer to read plays rather than to see and hear them.

Yet the phenomenon which is to be the subject of the present study is a completely oral one. The popular ballad, the ballad of tradition as I believe we may more justly call it, has no real existence save when held in memory and sung by those who have learned it from the lips of others. In saying this I am not ignoring the difficult question of its origin, which we must in due course consider, but merely emphasizing the primary condition of its being. Strictly speaking, the ballad as it exists is not a ballad save when it is in oral circulation, and certainly not until it has been in oral circulation. In this respect it is like the folk-story, or *Märchen*, and like other folk-songs that are not ballads.

For the ballad is a folk-song, and is subject to all the conditions of production and transformation peculiar to folk-song, though it is distinguishable in respect of content and purpose. Defined in simplest terms, the ballad is a folk-song that tells a story. Whatever may be added to this statement is by way of amplification, to explain and clarify merely, since the whole truth of the matter is in it. What we have come to call a ballad is always a narrative, is always sung to a rounded melody, and is always learned from the lips of others rather than by reading. Folk-song is a term of more general application, covering not only narrative songs but others that tell no story, although we may use it without confusion in a restricted sense for songs of the latter sort, to distinguish them from ballads, provided we always keep in mind that they have developed under the same conditions and are simply different manifestations of the same art. Nothing can properly be called folk-song that has not been submitted to the moulding processes of oral transmission, nor is any song a traditional ballad, whatever its origin and content may be, unless it has been formed or transformed by popular tradition. In other words, an imitation of the ballad style by a lettered poet and a schooled composer, whether made in the fifteenth century or the nineteenth, does not belong to the *genre* we are considering, though it may be absorbed into the *genre* by processes of re-creation that will be studied in due course.

Although our immediate concern is the ballad of tradition as it has developed among singers to whom some form of English speech is native, we must never forget that the cultural phenomenon we are studying is common to many peoples; and we should be careful, in defining it, not to limit our inquiry to the songs of a single race. Widely though they differ in form and content from English ballads, the ballads of Spain, for instance, belong in the same category and must be considered if one wishes to get at the real nature of such songs and to understand their curious and interesting history. To frame a definition that should take into account merely English and Scottish ballads, and to say that such formal characteristics as the refrain or the normal couplet, with its haunting succession of full stresses and half stresses, are essential to the ballad, would be misleading and would almost certainly keep us from recognizing the far more significant traits common to the folk-narratives of many countries. We must, at least, be wary of accepting general conclusions about the balladry of one race without checking them by the practice of other lands.

The plain fact is that collectors and students of ballads, whether the material of their special interest be Scottish, Scandinavian, or Spanish, somehow always recognize that they are dealing with the same kind of thing. Not only can many ballad themes be traced from land to land, but there is a similarity in the way the song-stories are told which marks them as belonging to the same *genre*. A ballad is a ballad, whether it be called *vise*, or *romance*, or *bolina*. Some common factors there are, it is evident, apart from the primary ones of story-telling in song and completely oral development. Such factors, and such factors only, may safely be added to the definition we are framing.

One of these constants is stress on situation, rather than on continuity of narrative or on character as character is presented in heroic poems or prose sagas. Not only are all ballads stories of action, but they are stories in which the action is focused on a single episode. Sometimes, to be sure, a whole series of events in the past is revealed by the incident which is the subject of the narrative, but only by reference. Thus the tragic predicament of the two young men in *Bewick and Graham* (211), who fought to the death through the folly of their fathers, was conditioned by the oath of blood brotherhood that they had taken at some earlier day, but the ballad begins with the quarrel of the fathers over their cups. More commonly the past is ignored altogether, or is implied rather darkly, and the situation is presented for itself alone. We are not told why the outlaw brother of *Babylon* (14) had become a 'banisht man', though his long absence is necessary to the outcome of the story: instead, we have the stark encounter of the three ladies with him. The adventures of *Thomas Rymer* (37) begin only when he meets the elf-queen, and the trials of Fair Ellen when she confesses to the hero of *Child Waters* (63) that her child is his.

This way of telling a story in terms of its crucial or concluding incident, to the neglect of the chain of events that precedes it, and of permitting the action to interpret itself with the minimum of comment and descriptive setting, is quite as characteristic of ballads on the Continent as of those sung in England and Scotland. This is strikingly illustrated by Spanish ballads, the material of which is derived from earlier, extended narratives. The ballads themselves are completely centralized, episodes no longer, but stories of a single dramatic situation briefly but independently developed. They have, as Menéndez Pidal has well said, 'the totality of their being in themselves',[1] for they are not fragments, but gain their effect of unified completeness by their concentration on one point. What goes before and comes after is of importance only with reference to the central situation.

[1] *Flor Nueva de Romances Viejos*, 1928, p. 11.

Even the heroic ballads of Scandinavia, which not infrequently show a tendency to greater elaboration of incident than is usual, cannot properly be classed as embryonic epics any more than can *A Gest of Robyn Hode* (117). Whether or no there were lays before there were epics, the most loosely woven ballads that we know do not seem to be on the road towards the epic. Their structure is as fundamentally different as is their style; the compressed and centralized episode is their unit.[1]

Action, then, and action centred on a single situation, which may be either the culminating point in a larger series of events or an isolated happening of sensational value, is the first constant discoverable in the ballads of European nations. The second constant is closely related to it, and is, I believe, even more clearly established by the facts. Whatever the matter of a ballad may be, and whatever the manner of presentation in other respects, there is always a marked tendency to tell the story dramatically. The brevity of the narrative has much to do with this, no doubt, but it does not explain everything, since a short poem may well be entirely without dramatic quality. Ballads, however, are not merely short: they are compressed. The series of events is seized at its culminating point and is envisaged in terms of the action which then takes place; nothing matters except the action; the characters speak because they have thoughts to express about what is taking place. Little as the dialogue of ballads has to do with the talk of actual life, it has at its best a trenchant pertinency not to be matched except in highly developed drama. Con-

---

[1] The importance of situation in balladry was admirably shown by F. B. Gummere, *The Popular Ballad*, 1907, pp. 85–90. A discussion of the matter will be found hereafter, in Chapter V, where the question of ballad and epic is also considered. For purposes of definition, the generalized statement need not be modified.

sider the treatment of the tragic theme in *Edward* (13),
or the beginning of *Fair Annie* (62 A):

'It's narrow, narrow, make your bed,
     And learn to lie your lane;
For I'm ga'n oer the sea, Fair Annie,
     A braw bride to bring hame.
Wi her I will get gowd and gear;
     Wi you I neer got nane.

'But wha will bake my bridal bread,
     Or brew my bridal ale?
And wha will welcome my brisk bride,
     That I bring oer the dale?'

'It's I will bake your bridal bread,
     And brew your bridal ale,
And I will welcome your brisk bride,
     That you bring oer the dale.'

'But she that welcomes my brisk bride
     Maun gang like maiden fair;
She maun lace on her robe sae jimp,
     And braid her yellow hair.'

'But how can I gang maiden-like,
     When maiden I am nane?
Have I not born seven sons to thee,
     And am with child again?'

We must not say that the dialogue produces the dramatic
effect, because the dialogue is so obviously the result
of the vivid intensity with which the situation is seen.
Ballads are dramatic because they present action, because
—as far as it may be done in a narrative form—they
represent action; and dialogue has its inevitable part in
this.

Every ballad-lover is familiar with the dramatic handling
of story-themes—so familiar with it indeed that the full
significance of the phenomenon has not been realized.
We have taken it for granted, and have failed to recognize,
as it is so easy to do with the simple and obvious, how

truly amazing is the fact. The makers and singers of popular narative, throughout Europe, have somehow and at some time worked out a technique of story-singing that not only emphasizes action rather than other elements, but prevailingly casts the action in semi-dramatic form. There would be nothing very surprising in this uniformity of treatment if it were true of the Latin nations only, or if it held true only for ballads among peoples with a large admixture of Germanic blood; but it may well appear both surprising and exceedingly important when it is found to be the case with the ballads of such distant stocks as the English and the Slavic. It is all the proof we need that the ballad exists as a *genre*, and it must be included as a factor of primary importance in any definition of the ballad.

Less completely typical, perhaps, is another characteristic, which is nevertheless so general that it may be regarded as a third constant in balladry. This is the impersonal attitude to the events of the story that is at least the rule among ballad-makers. The story is told for the story's own sake, while the prepossessions and judgements of the author or authors are kept for the most part in the background. In English and Scottish songs, to be sure, there is the occasional use of a formula, containing an 'I', by way of gambit; but this is nothing more than an attempt to increase the sense of present actuality when the ballad is sung,[1] as if to bring the events of the tale closer to audience and performer. In certain instances there is even an attempt to tell the story in the first person, which fades out after a few stanzas into the normal objectivity of the third.[2] The impersonal quality is not destroyed, as a matter of fact, even when the 'I' appears. *The Wee, Wee Man* (38) is not different in effect from *Thomas Rymer* (37), though the first person

[1] See Gummere, *The Popular Ballad*, pp. 66–7.
[2] See W. M. Hart, *Ballad and Epic*, 1907, pp. 50–1.

is used throughout; and a spirited Negro version of *Lady Isabel and the Elf-Knight* from Texas[1] is not injured as a ballad because the narrative is turned, according to a common habit with the coloured race, into direct discourse.

Ballad impersonality does not mean that sympathy is not aroused for the victims of mischance or cruelty or injustice. Maker, singer, and audience have doubtless always had strong feelings about the course of events in their stories, even though sometimes extraordinarily tolerant of violence; but they have been content to let the facts, dramatically presented, speak for themselves. The tragic pathos of *The Wife of Usher's Well* (79) lies not in anything that is said about the mother's yearning for her shipwrecked sons, but in the appearance by her fireside of the ghosts who have been called back at her desire. No words are wasted in *The Twa Brothers* (49) to emphasize the horror of the incident: the slaying of brother by brother and the speech of the dying victim are all that we need. The narrator of *Child Maurice* (83) makes no comment when the husband unwittingly kills his wife's bastard son; the cry of the mother makes other attempts at heightening quite superfluous:

> 'I never beare no child but one,
> And you have slaine him trulye.'

Even ballads with a grim background of deadly feud like *Johnie Cock* (114) and ballads of the Border, which must have been made and sung by folk who were intensely partisan, to say the least, are singularly restrained in their expression of disapproval, singularly objective in manner. Some of them, it is true, distort historical fact and are very unjust to this person or that, as in *Captain Car* (178), which accuses Adam Gordon of atrocities during an attack at which he was not even present.[2]

[1] D. Scarborough, *On the Trail of Negro Folk-Songs*, 1925, pp. 43–5.

[2] On this point see A. Keith in Gavin Greig's *Last Leaves of Traditional Ballads and Ballad Airs*, 1925, pp. xxxviii–xxxix.

Others, like *The Rising in the North* (175) and *The Fire of Frendraught* (196), use such words as 'treason' and 'false traitor'. Yet partisan feeling does not prevent objective treatment. It is the infant heir in *Johnie Armstrong* (169 A) who vows to be revenged on the 'treacherous Scots' for his father's death, and Lady Margaret in *The Bonnie House o Airlie* (199) who says of her sons:

> 'Although I had an hundred more,
>   I would give them all to Prince Charlie.'

As a rule, that is, strong feeling is shown by persons taking part in the action, but not by the makers themselves.

Throughout the English and Scottish ballads this dramatic impersonality of handling is evident, and it has been little disturbed even in versions that have been tampered with by printers of broadsides. It appears to be common also in the balladry of other lands, though with certain exceptions. Wherever it does not occur, the cause may be found, I suspect, in a perfectly natural proximation to lyric folk-song.[1] No category can ever be absolutely exclusive: there are frontier zones where characteristics intermingle. Yet objectivity of approach to ballad themes is certainly one factor helpful to a definition of the *genre*. The epithet that Menéndez Pidal applies to Spanish ballads may be used of them all; they have what he finely terms 'realistic austerity'.[2] In no respect is this more apparent than in the pronounced tendency to let events furnish their own commentary.

We may, then, safely amplify our original definition by adding to it the statement that in at least three respects all European ballads are alike, and that by virtue of these common qualities we recognize them to be ballads. We may say that a compressed and centralized episode is the ordinary narrative unit, that dramatic presentation of

[1] See Menéndez Pidal, *op. cit.*, p. 23, for the *serranilla*, classed as a ballad.
[2] *Op. cit.*, p. 28.

action is the ordinary narrative method, and that impersonality of approach to the theme is the ordinary narrative attitude. A ballad is a folk-song that tells a story with stress on the crucial situation, tells it by letting the action unfold itself in event and speech, and tells it objectively with little comment or intrusion of personal bias.

When we consider that a definition of ballads, stated somewhat like the one just framed, is equally applicable to the story-songs of Denmark and Sweden, of Russia and Serbia, of Italy and Spain and France and Great Britain, we cannot fail to conclude that we are studying a cultural phenomenon rather than waifs and strays from primitive ages beyond recall. Leaving unquestioned for the time the insistent problems connected with their origins and looking only at the songs themselves, the words and tunes which have been gathered from the lips of those who have learned them and held them in memory, we see that we have to do with a distinct species of poetry and music, which has developed along common lines in a great many countries, yet quite without the control of writing.

We must recognize that these songs have the power to give aesthetic pleasure not only to the simple folk who have sung them, but to persons of more sophisticated taste who have formed their standards and developed their appreciation with reference to the music and poetry of canonical art. Such persons, it is worthy of note, can enjoy the tunes and the words of ballads separately, which the original possessors of them are almost invariably incapable of doing. Musicians with little knowledge of poetry find delight in folk-melodies, and suggestions for use in their own composing; while poetry-lovers, even though they may be incapable of musical appreciation, get keen joy from the texts. This state of things makes evident the aesthetic worth of ballads both as music and as poetry, and the need of studying the two elements together if we are to understand the origin of the *genre* and its place in cultural history.

The investigation of the folk-lore of ballads, though it has very great value by way of showing the persistence of racial memory, tends perhaps to obscure the nature of the songs. They show traces, to be sure, of immensely old custom and belief; but they should not be regarded primarily as fossil-beds, for they are much more important and even more interesting as products of a traditional art, which is only now dying. We have, in English, ballads like *Johnie Cock* (114), with its apparent reminiscenses of a time when there were wolves about, when a sister's son was a man's closest relation, and when one drank the hot blood of the slain deer; and we have likewise most admirable ballads, like *Captain Car* (178) or *The Baron of Brackley* (203), which deal with events of the later sixteenth century and contain no memories of an earlier age. Although one kind serves the folk-lorist as the other does not, they are equally important in balladry and equally useful in defining the status of the art.

Similarly, the study of the poetry of primitive races does not get us far towards an understanding of the ballad as it has been cultivated in recent centuries, and may even lead us astray on the trail of false identifications, though it is of the utmost value in helping us appreciate the mental processes and the emotional reactions of simple folk. Ballads are very far from being primitive poetry, indeed; they are rather the flower of an art formalized and developed among people whose training has been oral instead of visual. Unlettered the makers have been, simple of mind and heart, but not without moulding traditions perpetuated through many centuries and not without some contact with their superiors in the social and educational scale. Primitive music and primitive poetry could not come from them any more than it can come from the composers and poets who practise a more sophisticated and conscious artistry. They have had an art of their own, a double art of melody and verse, distinct from that of their betters but by no means unworthy, oddly enough, to stand beside it. Indeed, to trace the connexion between the two in the same lands and periods is of more importance to an understanding of the formal qualities of ballad music and ballad stories than to search for analogies among backward races.

Art of a sort there is, even among peoples who are backward in development. Research during the past generation has shown quite clearly that the history of art is exceedingly long and its ramifications co-extensive with man; but the art of the unlettered portions of European peoples is in another case from that of Bantu tribesmen. They have always formed parts of nations in which artists more or less nourished on conscious aesthetic tradition have at the same time been working. This state of things undoubtedly makes the study of ballads, to mention only the instance with which we are immediately concerned, much more difficult than it would be if ballads were phenomena with a less complicated environment. Yet it cannot be too strongly urged that we should keep the true state of things in mind and use with discretion analogies from the verse and music of primitive races.

There is no real antithesis between folk-music and folk-poetry on the one hand, and the poetry and music of art on the other, though it has been so often stated that we are in danger of accepting it unthinkingly. A contrast exists, it is true. The phrase is useful by way of indicating differences in attitude on the part of makers and wide differences in conditions of production; but it is misleading, because it suggests that folk-song is not art. Folk-song has developed orally, without consciousness of the aesthetic principles according to which it is moulded; but the principles are there. Folk-song has seemingly developed also without the kind of individualistic effort that goes to the production and reproduction of poetry and music among the lettered classes. The literate artist cannot wholly escape, no matter how hard he may try, from the effects of critical theory; and the history of literature and music proves, we should probably all agree, that in such bondage he has thriven. The Martha of criticism has been a most useful sister to the Mary of creation. The processes of folk-song have been different. Forces of which the makers have been almost unconscious have often shaped it to beauty, taste acquired through the long-continued practice of a traditional art has directed imagination; but there has been no effort at intellectual control, which is probably why the art of the folk, with all its vitality and vigour, has been a somewhat ragged thing, amazingly lovely sometimes, almost always interesting, but curiously uneven in execution.

Into the processes of folk-song as they have operated in the particular domain of the ballad we propose to inquire in the present volume, and specifically as to ballads the words of which are English. There can be no harm in thus limiting our field of study if only we keep in mind that this oral, traditional art has been confined to no one people. Certain features of English and Scottish ballads are peculiar to themselves, but the art of which they are representative has been widespread throughout Europe at least. Having defined the nature of balladry, let us try, in the next place, to see our English and Scottish specimens in their international relations.

Chapter Two

BRITISH BALLADS AND THEIR
CONTINENTAL RELATIONS

IN his great thesaurus of English and Scottish ballads Child included 305 specimens in as many varying forms as came to his hand, wishing, as he said in his preface,[1] to have 'at command every valuable copy of every known ballad'. As has become increasingly evident since the great editor finished his work, his noble purpose could never have been accomplished, even though he had been granted twice the span of an ordinary lifetime, since collecting need never come to an end while ballads are still sung. He brought together, however, so large and so representative a collection of texts that the student requires no further illustration either of the subjects treated or of the manner in which the stories are told. Only in respect of ballad melodies does Child's work fail to provide an adequate body of material for an understanding of the form as it has developed among English-speaking folk, and only by the magnificent Danish collection of Grundtvig and Olrik[2] has it ever been rivalled in scope.

The qualities for which we most honour the labours of Child, as well as those of Grundtvig and Olrik—their indefatigable industry, their wide learning, and their keenness of judgement—have in a way exaggerated the importance of British and Scandinavian ballads at the expense of those sung elsewhere in Europe. There has been careless speaking and writing to the effect that our ballads, together with those of Scandinavia and possibly Germany, somehow surpass in number and quality those

---

[1] *English and Scottish Popular Ballads,* i, vii.
[2] *Danmarks Gamle Folkeviser,* 1853–1920.

of other lands. The great editors I have just mentioned never, of course, gave such an impression intentionally. Grundtvig and Child were indeed pioneers in the comparative study of ballads, for they saw the art of folk-song as a possession common to many races, and examined each of their specimens to see whether it should be regarded as indigenous or had been transplanted from without. No one has yet studied the international relations of so many ballads as did those two great scholars. The work they began is still far from complete, but not because they failed to see the importance of it and to advance it immensely by their own efforts.

In no country is the ballad an isolated phenomenon. As we have already seen, there are marked resemblances in form among all European ballads; and quite as remarkable is the way the same stories have been used in their songs by the folk of many different lands. Although it is true that several important groups of English and Scottish ballads, like those dealing with Robin Hood and with Border feuds, appear to be quite independent of any continental relationships, a very large number are closely akin to ballads found in various parts of Europe. This does not mean merely that the same themes have furnished material for song—the ageless heritage of story—but something more than that; it means that the same ballads have been circulated on both sides of the Channel, with only such changes as might be expected after translation into other tongues and adaptation to the particular habits of song in this region or that. In other words, any given ballad may quite well have been carried across the face of Europe, and may belong equally to the repertory of a singer in Piedmont or in Shropshire. It cannot be said to be English any more than Danish, or possibly Polish, since in most such cases the country of its origin cannot be accurately determined.

Consider the famous instance of *Lord Randal* (12), which has been found as far east as Czecho-Slovakia and Hungary, as far north as Scotland and Sweden, and as far south as Calabria. More than three hundred years ago an Italian professional singer, advertising his wares in easy verse on a broadside printed at Verona,[1] quoted three lines which unmistakably belong to *L'Avvelenato*, as that ballad has been found in circulation up and down the peninsula within the last half-century; and *L'Avvelenato* is so close in form and content to our familiar *Lord Randal* that certain versions might be taken as paraphrases of one another.

> 'Where supped you yestereve,
> Dear son mine, noble and wise?'
>   'Oh, I am dying,
>   Ohimè!'
> 'Where supped you yestereve,
> My noble knight?'
> 'I was at my lady's;
>   I am sick at the heart,
>   How sick am I!
> I was at my lady's,
> My life's at an end.'
> 'What supper did she give you,
> Dear son mine, noble and wise?'
>   'Oh, I am dying,
>   Ohimè!'
> 'What supper did she give you,
> My gentle knight?'
> 'An eel that was roasted,
>   Mother, dear mother;
>   I am sick at the heart,
>   How sick am I!
> An eel that was roasted,
> My life's at an end.'

[1] A. d'Ancona, *Poesia popolare italiana*, 2nd ed., 1906, p. 124; Child, i. 152.

The lines roughly translated above were taken down by D'Ancona[1] in the country near Pisa some sixty years ago; and the opening is almost identical with that quoted in the Veronese broadside of 1629. Compare them with the first three stanzas of a Scottish version of *Lord Randal* (12 A), which was copied out in the eighteenth century:

'O where ha you been, Lord Randal, my son?
And where ha you been, my handsome young man?'
'I ha been at the greenwood; mother, mak my bed soon,
For I'm wearied wi hunting, and fain wad lie down.'

'An wha met ye there, Lord Randal, my son?
An wha met you there, my handsome young man?'
'O I met wi my true-love; mother, mak my bed soon,
For I'm wearied wi huntin, an fain wad lie down.'

'And what did she give you, Lord Randal, my son?
And what did she give you, my handsome young man?'
'Eels fried in a pan; mother, mak my bed soon,
For I'm wearied wi huntin, and fain wad lie down.'

Detailed comment is superfluous. It is not a question of different songs with the same theme, but of the same ballad in circulation over wide areas. In spite of translation from language to language, there are similarities of phrase that establish the identity, which is furthermore shown by the marked likeness in the way the story is introduced and developed. The mother questions the son, who has come back to her mortally ill after eating what seemed to be eels, but were probably snakes; and she learns, as the dialogue progresses, the horrid truth. The amazing coincidence between the Italian and English forms, it is fair to say, does not extend to all the European versions of *Lord Randal*. Although they keep the general outline of the story unaltered, the actors vary greatly: the young man with a vindictive sweet-

[1] D'Ancona, *op. cit.*, pp. 124-5.

heart becomes a child with a wicked step-mother, a girl with a murderous aunt, or a boy with an unnatural grandmother. The English versions themselves, indeed, illustrate the ease with which tradition plays upon such changes, for they are by no means consistent in the persons whom they introduce. In short, there is quite as much reason for believing that the very same ballad exists in all the European forms as there is for gathering the English and Scottish versions of the story under the single heading of *Lord Randal*.

It need occasion no surprise, nor should it arouse any scepticism about what has just been said, that the migrations of what we may for convenience call *Lord Randal* cannot be traced as it has passed from land to land. Only to a very limited extent have the movements of ballads within a given area of speech been studied as yet; and possibly the attempt to establish definite routes of exchange over larger areas may never be completely successful, though the matter deserves far more research than has been given to it. Certainly it is odd that in the case of *Lord Randal* the nearest approximation among the various forms should be between those found in Italian and English,[1] whereas no French version—as far as I know—has been collected; yet in our present state of ignorance about the methods and means of diffusion we can do no better than to say humbly that we cannot tell whether the song travelled by land or by sea, nor yet whether it travelled from Italy to Great Britain instead of in the opposite direction. There may have been unrecorded French versions, for anything we know, and the earlier record of the ballad in Italy by no means

[1] D'Ancona's belief (see *Poesia popolare italiana*, 2nd ed., 1906) that most of Italy's folk-songs originated in Sicily, and were diffused through Tuscany, is very insecurely based, though often quoted. His admission (p. 136) that a large number of narrative songs came in from the north shows the fragility of his argument. The importance of Provence as a distributing centre has not been sufficiently stressed, it would appear. The matter deserves study.

proves that it originated in the South. All we can be certain of is the identity of the song.[1]

Something a little more definite may perhaps be said about the migration of certain other ballads, though always with considerable diffidence. *Lady Isabel and the Elf-Knight* (4) is a good example. Its ramifications have been thoroughly studied by Grundtvig,[2] as well as by Child,[3] who says of it: 'Of all ballads this has perhaps obtained the widest circulation.'[4] A later examination of the material by Doncieux[5] resulted in no important modification of the views Child had expressed, but furnished a well-ordered tabulation of the versions, which erred only in being too precise. Child was content to say that 'Dutch tradition has kept the capital features best of all',[6] while Grundtvig with equal caution expressed the belief that the ballad had its original home either in Scandinavia or the Netherlands.[7] Doncieux derived all the forms from the Dutch *Halewijn*, but did not prove his case satisfactorily. It is clear, however, that the drift of the ballad across northern continental Europe was from west to east, and that the English and Scottish versions must have come either from Denmark or Holland. It is equally clear that the special form developed in Great Britain gave rise to the very popular French ballad *Renaud le Tueur de Femmes*. Beyond that point we shall be wise to refrain from too exact a statement as to the routes by which it spread. Everywhere, however, the story is essentially the same. A young woman, who has been decoyed away by a stranger (who

---

[1] See Martinengo-Cesaresco, *Essays in the Study of Folk-Songs*, 1886, pp. 214–27.

[2] *Op. cit.* iv. 1–32.

[3] i. 22–54, ii. 496–8, iii. 496–7, iv. 440–2, v. 206–7, 285.

[4] i. 22.

[5] G. Doncieux and J. Tiersot, *Le Romancéro populaire de la France*, 1904, pp. 351–65.

[6] i. 54.

[7] iv. 29.

must originally have been a supernatural creature), saves herself by her ready wit and prompt action from the fate of her several predecessors, or else is saved by the opportune appearance of her kinsmen. Although this simple theme has undergone numberless transformations in detail, which make its wanderings difficult to trace, the entity of the ballad throughout cannot be questioned. Call it *Lady Isabel and the Elf-Knight*, or *Halewijn*, or *Gert Olbert*, or any other name, the song is always one. Such complications as that by which most of the Polish versions approach the English and French[1] in placing the scene of the murderous attack beside a river or the sea, whereas in both Great Britain and Poland the more customary forest is also known, illustrate the extraordinary fluidity of the material; but they need not lead us to doubt the actual migration of the ballad from the undiscovered land of its origin into the many countries where it came to be a part of native tradition.

Similarly, *Clerk Colvill* (42) has interesting relationships, which can be traced with some confidence, although one cannot be quite sure where it began its course. Clearly the hero has been the lover of a water-sprite of sorts, and has broken with her to marry a mortal woman. He cannot resist the temptation to return to the mermaiden, and thus meets the doom his unfaithfulness deserves. A comparison of versions collected in Brittany (with eighteen variants) and in Scandinavia (with sixty-nine variants) makes it probable, though not certain, that the ballad began among Celtic-speaking folk, whether continental or insular, whence it spread to the north and had great popularity.[2] In Great Britain it was either never generally known, despite its merits, or died out

[1] See Child, i. 39, 42.

[2] So Grundtvig concluded, as the result of his exhaustive study. See *op. cit.* ii. 109–19, 663–6, iii. 824–5, iv. 835–74. Doncieux, *op. cit.*, pp. 84–124, adopted the view that the Breton song derived from the Scandinavian.

before collecting began, since only Child's three Scottish versions have been found. The wide variation among these three leads me to believe that the latter alternative probably represents the truth, and that we cannot safely assert their provenience from a Scandinavian rather than a Celtic source. We can be sure, however, that the ballad spread from Brittany through France, where it has been enormously popular, in a somewhat abbreviated form, most frequently under the title of *Le Roi Renaud* or the like. In his elaborate study of the ballad Doncieux listed no less than sixty-seven variants from France and Piedmont, and traced its course in Italy and Spain. In the latter country at least forty-five variants have been collected, and it has been found in Portugal. Somehow it was also carried along the Baltic from Scandinavia, and thence it travelled as far south as Czecho-Slovakia.

An interesting problem in migration is presented by our *Lord Thomas and Fair Annet* (73), which in one form or another has been very widely known both in Scotland and England. In the words of Child,[1] 'the Scottish traditional copy is . . . one of the most beautiful of our ballads, and indeed of all ballads'. Perhaps because of its very excellence and popularity, it suffered through early printing as a broadside and the consequent diffusion of an inferior version; but it did not perish on that account, as is witnessed by the many variants recovered of late years in the United States as well as Great Britain, usually under the title *Lord Thomas and Fair Eleanor*. In the uncompounded forms the story is this: a young man, truly in love with a young woman, is persuaded by his family to give her up for another. Whether he pays her a farewell visit, or she learns by some other means of the impending marriage, she comes in state to the wedding and is stabbed by the jealous bride. The young man then kills the bride and falls on his own

[1] ii. 180.

sword. Except when it has absorbed the conclusion of *Fair Margaret and Sweet William* (74), the ballad keeps to this general outline through all its many variants in Great Britain, Ireland, and America.

It so happens that both the Scandinavian and French forms, which are numerous, not only vary greatly among themselves, but diverge in two different directions from the British specimens. The former[1] do not indicate why the lover abandons his mistress, and they supply almost too many endings, pathetic or violent. In none is the fate of the three characters so clearly marked as in the Scottish and English versions. The French ballad, on the other hand, has the young man give up his love at the bidding of his father, but is singularly feeble in its conclusion. The only element which remains constant throughout is the fact that the forsaken mistress comes to the wedding in most gorgeous raiment. It seems probable that the ballad migrated from Great Britain to the North, there to undergo one set of variations, and again to France, where it suffered another transformation.[2] In other words, the evidence points to diffusion from a British source.

The illustrations I have given will perhaps suffice to show not only that certain ballads have migrated from country to country, but that the versions of them form an intricate network even more difficult to study than the interrelations of poems belonging to literary rather than oral tradition. Constantly shifting in form and to some extent in content, constantly subject to re-creation in the imagination of individual singers and equally subject to addition or decay through faulty memories, they baffle

---

[1] See Grundtvig, *op. cit.* iv. 212–20.

[2] Grundtvig, *op. cit.* iv. 213, refers to the English-Scottish ballad as a 'shoot' of the Scandinavian, but wrongly, I believe. Doncieux, in turn, *op. cit.*, p. 347, thinks that the Scottish form came from the French, but he is less likely to be right than Child, who says (ii. 181): 'A Southern ballad has something of the outline of the English and Norse, and sounds like a thin echo of them.'

any one who tries to plot their course; but they are even more amazing in their unity than in their diversity. The errant ballad stubbornly persists and is often recognizable when found very far from its source. In such cases, despite its millions of adventures—and this is not to exaggerate the possibilities—it has kept its identity. In other cases, no doubt, it has perished either through complete transformation or through forgetfulness; but so many ballads have endured the good and evil chances of diffusion through various lands among peoples speaking various tongues that we are justified in regarding not only the species but the individual specimen as an international phenomenon.

Our English and Scottish ballads are not, then, to be considered something peculiar to a single island, but are to be viewed as manifestations of a culture common to European folk as a whole. There are indications, indeed, that they belong to a still wider domain extending into Asia, though knowledge is yet too fragmentary to permit anything more than vague guesses about the outer boundaries of ballad diffusion. Studies in both melodies and texts will have to be pushed much farther than they have been up to our time before we can be sure how the currents of migration have set and to what limits they have gone.

It is quite certain, however, that between eighty and ninety of the ballads in Child's collection are not specifically and peculiarly British, in that versions of them have been found on the Continent. My own count is eighty-five; but this is probably somewhat too low a figure and will doubtless be raised as studies in the problem go on. At all events, we are safe in saying that between a quarter and a third of the 305 ballads that Child printed can already be shown to belong to the treasury of international folk-song rather than to Great Britain alone. Some of them, such as *Lord Thomas and Fair Annet*, doubtless originated in England or Scotland, and were thence diffused; others drifted over from the mainland and were adopted by insular singers. The balance between the two cannot be struck in the present state of our knowledge, and possibly may never be accurately determined. The only thing that can be asserted as a fact at present is the identity of a large number of our ballads with similar folk-songs of the Continent.

The orderly study of folk-music has not yet proceeded far enough to give us warrant in saying that the migration of tunes has followed precisely the same lines as the migration of texts; but such investigations as have been made[1] point to the conclusion that they have moved with at least equal freedom. *A priori* one would expect this to be so, since the transference from country to country would be attended by no difficulties of language; and, as will be shown in more detail in a later chapter, the melody is an integral part of every ballad. It must be remembered, however, as will also be shown, that melodies are in some respects more difficult to trace than themes in words, since they may be transformed phrase by phrase, leaving no trace of the original tune, whereas the central idea in a story acts as a kind of preservative against total obliteration. The tale a ballad recounts is likely to serve as a conservative influence, but a tune has no such inner check. None the less, we shall see that the melodies of some British ballads have survived distant migration and a total change in environment when brought to America, and we have the right to surmise that the same thing has been true throughout the realm of balladry.

It need occasion no surprise to discover that within the realm I have just mentioned there appear to be provinces

[1] See L. E. Broadwood, *Journal of the Folk-Song Society*, v. 237–8 (1915), who shows the likeness between the tune of a Westphalian version of *The Maid Freed from the Gallows* (95) and one sung in Cumberland, noting that in Elizabeth's reign Germans developed copper mines at Coniston, with smelters at Keswick.

—regions which because of contiguity, similarity of speech, or likenesses in culture and social organization have large stores of ballads in common. Great Britain before the Union, Germany as well as Italy (both of them politically united only a couple of generations ago), Provence with Piedmont and Catalonia, and the Scandinavian countries all furnish examples of such conditions. Within each of these regions ballads have evidently circulated with the greatest freedom, and versions of any individual specimen may be expected to occur here and there throughout the entire province. The collectors of the English Folk-Song Society, it is worthy of note, have shown in our time that many ballads, once thought to be peculiarly Scottish, belong equally to England. Quite possibly even larger districts than those I have sketched should be mapped out, which have either shared a common heritage of song or have exchanged their songs to an uncommon extent, although my own knowledge is not sufficient to determine what they should be. For example, the interchange of ballads between Great Britain and Scandinavia seems to have been unusually extensive, which is what one would expect,[1] considering the maritime habits of the two peoples. Child found Scandinavian forms of twenty-five specimens in his collection for which he discovered no other continental versions; and no one, as far as I am aware, has come upon anything since his time to upset these figures. In other words, towards a third of the British ballads that have had international circulation appear to be shared only with the Scandinavian countries. The evidence, however, is not conclusive, for

[1] The extent to which Great Britain and Scandinavia traded with each other between the twelfth and fifteenth centuries can be seen by going through the documents summarized in D. Macpherson, *Annals of Commerce*, 1805. England's commercial relationship was closer than Scotland's, and the greatness of Yarmouth as a port largely depended upon it. For various reasons, the trade declined in importance in the sixteenth century. A monograph on this subject is needed.

we must always bear in mind that the well-ordered and exhaustive collection of Grundtvig and Olrik has made comparison with Northern ballads far easier than with those of other regions. We know all too little as yet about the sectional distribution of folk-songs and their international relations.

But our English and Scottish ballads, whether first composed on the island or derived from foreign sources, have a life of their own, like the ballads of all other peoples. If we do not forget their European relationships, we may safely consider them by themselves in our effort to learn more about their characteristics as a manifestation of popular and traditional art. To begin with, however, we ought to inquire what sort of stories are told in them and what estimate can be made as to their number. Let us consider the second question, first of all, in order to get some clear notion of the material to be studied.

It will be recalled that Child began his work, as he stated in his preface, with the ideal of not printing until he had 'at command every valuable copy of every known ballad'.[1] Although he must have become increasingly aware, as time went on, of the difficulties that beset an editor who aims to include everything of a given sort, he kept valiantly to his purpose and evidently regarded his 305 ballads as a complete *corpus*. But he never made clear the standard by which he ruled out or included a given specimen;[2] and his friends and pupils—a notable group of scholars—have never succeeded in explaining his procedure. He printed *Kinmont Willie* (186), for example, but excluded *Auld Maitland*[3] despite the protest of so

---

[1] i, vii.

[2] For an admirable summary of his views see W. M. Hart, *Publications of the Modern Language Association*, xxi. 755–807 (1906). Even the publication of the correspondence of Child with Grundtvig by S. B. Hustvedt, *Ballad Books and Ballad Men*, 1930, does not clarify the matter.

[3] Scott, *Minstrelsy of the Scottish Border*, ed. T. F. Henderson, 1902, i. 244–57; Lang in *Folk-Lore*, xiii. 191–7 (1902). Lang later changed his mind

shrewd a judge as Andrew Lang. Most illuminating as to the quandaries in which he found himself is the confession in his introduction to *Young Ronald* (304):[1] 'In this and not a very few other cases, I have suppressed disgust, and admitted an actually worthless and a manifestly—at least in part—spurious ballad, because of a remote possibility that it might contain relics, or be a debased representative, of something genuine and better. Such was the advice of my lamented friend, Grundtvig, in more instances than those in which I have brought myself to defer to his judgement.'

Grundtvig's opinion, in this matter, was certainly sounder than that of his friend, since it is obvious that the principles of selection, whatever they were, had proved inadequate in practice. With very good reason, Child was not content to print only such ballads as he could definitely prove to have been in oral circulation, since that would have ruled out *A Gest of Robyn Hode* and a great many other pieces found in print or manuscript; and he was not content to accept whatever had been in oral circulation merely by reason of that fact. Yet he had to take every precaution he could against admitting fabrications to his list. In other words, he found it impossible to include 'every known ballad', since even he—the greatest master of British balladry who has lived—could not always decide what was worthy to appear in such a collection as he was making. Gummere put the matter well when he wrote: 'For the matter of wheat and chaff, of good and bad, any selection of genuine ballads must be an affair of purely subjective judgement.'[2]

It is evident, then, that Child's thesaurus cannot be, even apart from certain unexceptionable specimens derived from folk-singers since his day, a complete and definitive

and regarded both *Auld Maitland* and *The Outlaw Murray* (Child, 305) as 'literary imitations'. See his *Sir Walter Scott*, 1906, p. 33.

[1] v. 182.   [2] *The Popular Ballad*, p. 317.

collection of all the traditional ballads in English, for 'subjective judgement' was necessarily used in making exclusions, while confessedly dubious pieces were admitted.[1] Professor Kittredge showed less than his ordinary caution when he wrote of the collection that it 'comprises the whole extant mass of this material'.[2] Gummere, similarly, was ill advised in connecting a canon of ballads with the question of how they came into being, which led him into a very hazardous position. If his definition by origins were correct, he put it, he could 'deal with a definite subject', as critic and historian of balladry, and base his work 'upon compact and complete material,—the collection of Professor Child'.[3] Otherwise, he felt, 'all boundaries of the subject are obscured, the material is questionable, and a haze at once fills the air'. One has to admit, I fear, the dubiety of much of the material, whether it be within Child's collection or outside, and one has to deal as best one can with songs that fall in grey zones and are hard to classify. Certainly one cannot hope to have a complete array of the material while ballads are alive in popular tradition at all, as the experience of the past thirty years has shown. Any absolute canon, in short, has never been attainable, and doubtless never will be, even after the last ballad has been sung by the last singer. How many there are, or have been, we shall never know.

It might not be worth our while to delay over this matter, were it not for the fact that certain scholars have shown a tendency of late years to distinguish between what they call 'Child ballads' and ballads of another sort, not in any careful way defined.[4] Although this is a tribute

---

[1] See *Robin Hood and the Tinker* (127), *Auld Matrons* (249), *The Kitchie-Boy* (252), *Willie's Fatal Visit* (255), *The New-Slain Knight* (263), *The Knight's Ghost* (265), *Child Owlet* (291), *Young Ronald* (304).

[2] Sargent and Kittredge, *English and Scottish Popular Ballads*, p. xiii.

[3] *The Popular Ballad*, p. 29.

[4] See, for example, Louise Pound, *Poetic Origins and the Ballad*, 1921, *passim*.

to the admirable quality and inclusiveness of Child's collection, it is a wholly arbitrary and quite indefensible distinction. A ballad is either a ballad because it conforms to a certain definition as to form and transmission, or it is not a ballad at all. Its inclusion in Child's volumes has nothing to do with the matter beyond the fact that his vast learning and critical acumen enabled him to sift with amazingly few errors of judgement the spurious imitation from the real ballad of tradition. I hope I have made sufficiently clear my veneration for Child's performance, and I yield to no one in my admiration for his two greatest followers, Professor Gummere and Professor Kittredge. I believe, however, that harm has been done by too rigid an insistence on the authoritative completeness of Child's collection. Gummere's plea that 'all boundaries of the subject are obscured' unless we base our studies on Child's list, and nothing more, must be admitted; but the admission need not disturb us. Child found the boundaries impossible to mark with certainty, and nothing is to be gained by an unjustified simplification of any problem. It should be remarked, furthermore, that no one has done more than Professor Kittredge to stimulate the study of ballads either unknown to Child or for some reason excluded by him.

For the reasons we have been discussing, nothing like an exact census of English and Scottish ballads can be made. Probably no two scholars would ever quite agree about all specimens, though they might be in complete accord as to definitions. In literary criticism it is notoriously difficult to make categories that will fit all cases, and it is even harder when one is dealing with the anonymous fluctuating stuff of folk-song. The border-line between narrative and purely lyrical pieces, for one thing, is a very wavering one, while still other complications are introduced by the interference of printing with the even course of oral tradition. We do well to place

among ballads such riddling songs as *The Elfin Knight* (2),
Riddles Wisely Expounded (1), and *Captain Wedderburn's
Courtship* (46), since in all of them the encounter of wit
solves a human situation. We do well, likewise, to include
A Gest of Robyn Hode (117), even though it is not a ballad
at all in its extant form, because it was certainly made
up from ballads. Similarly the English forms[1] of *Geordie*
(209), as distinguished from the Scottish, must not be
omitted, though the narrative element is slight; and the
same thing may be said with even more emphasis of such
favourites as *Bonny Barbara Allan* (84), *The Bonny Earl
of Murray* (181), and *Bonnie James Campbell* (210).

The excellence of a ballad according to literary standards, I think we must agree, or its total lack of such
excellence, has nothing directly to do with its status as
a ballad. Unless we accept this principle, we shall be
for ever begging the question about the source of the
aesthetic appeal and the way it came to be. We have no
right to rule out narrative songs the words of which do
not make good literature, and then base theories of origin
and development on the residue. It is safer for us to
hold to the generalized definition we have already formed:
to say that a ballad is a folk-song that tells a story with
stress on the crucial situation, tells it by letting the action
unfold itself in event and speech, and tells it objectively
with little comment or intrusion of personal bias. We
need not then be troubled though some specimens have
come to us through the hands of printers and editors with
little conscience about meddling with words and phrases;
and we need not be troubled though a good many could
never serve as poetical models to a Scott or a Keats. The
'boundaries of the subject' will be vague, to be sure;
this or that set of verses will be hard to place; some

---

[1] See L. E. Broadwood, *English Traditional Songs and Carols*, 1908, pp. 32–3;
Journal of the Folk-Song Society, i. 164–5 ; Sharp and Marson, *Folk-Songs from
Somerset*, 1st ser., 1904, no. 2, p. 5; *J. F.-S. S.* ii. 27–8.

ballads will give us keen pleasure, some almost none at all; no satisfactory catalogue of specimens can be made. On the other hand, we shall find that various general qualities run through them all, certain ways of telling a story, certain ways of accommodating verse to melody, certain ways of intensifying emotion by rhetorical devices. By accepting the situation as it is, we shall be able to study the phenomena of origin, development, and change with more hope of arriving at the truth.

No one, it seems to me, ought to dispute, even though he hold very firmly to the tradition of Child, the acceptance as ballads of a great many songs that are not to be found in our monumental collection. Gummere received *The Bitter Withy*[1] without question[2] when it came to light, and he has been unhesitatingly followed by other scholars. The collectors and editors of the Folk-Song Society, as well as their valiant colleagues in America, have been content to garner and study sets of words and melodies without troubling themselves overmuch about definitions; and they have done wisely, for they have not only demonstrated the facts that ballads have remained alive down to our own generation, but that a surprisingly large number of those not included by Child are quite as interesting and valuable as very many which he put into his volumes. *The Blind Beggar of Bednall Green*,[3] for ex-

[1] See F. Sidgwick, *Notes and Queries*, 29 July 1905 (reprinted *J. F.-S. S.* ii. 300–2). Other versions : *Folk-Lore*, xix. 190–200; *J. F.-S. S.* ii. 205, iv. 29–47, viii. 31–3 ; E. M. Leather, *Folk-Lore of Herefordshire*, 1912, pp. 181–7. See also Gerould, *Publications of the Modern Language Association*, xxiii. 141–67, and Barry, *Journal of American Folk-Lore*, xxvii. 79–89. In my opinion *The Holy Well*, though it has a different ending, should not be listed as a separate ballad or carol. Versions : W. Howitt, *Rural Life in England*, 1837 (reprinted *J. F.-S. S.* ii. 306, in 2nd ed., Philadelphia, 1841, p. 395) ; W. Sandys, *Christmas Carols Ancient and Modern*, 1833, pp. 149–52; J. Sylvester, *A Garland of Christmas Carols*, 1861, pp. 32–5; W. H. Husk, *Songs of the Nativity*, 1884, pp. 91–4; C. S. Burne, *Shropshire Folk-Lore*, 1883–6, pp. 567–8 ; F. Sidgwick, *Popular Carols*, 1908; *J. F.-S. S.* iv. 26–7, v. 1–6.

[2] *The Popular Ballad*, pp. 227–8.

[3] See Hales and Furnivall, *Bishop Percy's Folio Manuscript*, 1867–8, ii. 281–9;

ample, is as well authenticated—if not so widely circulated —as *The Bailiff's Daughter of Islington* (105). *The Seven Virgins*[1] has as much right to appear as *The Cherry-Tree Carol* (54). *The Shooting of his Dear*, or *Molly Bawn*,[2] from childish recollections of which Jamieson wrote his absurd *Lord Kenneth and Fair Ellinour*, has been proved to have an elaborate traditional history, though no version can be praised for its beauty. It cannot be denied a place in the category. On the other hand, *The Lyke-Wake Dirge*[3] ought not to be included despite its charm, because it has no narrative element whatever. Again, the very lovely *Over Yonder's a Park* or *Corpus Christi*[4] is truly a ballad, for it pictures an intensely dramatic situation and does so altogether in the manner of the *genre*. Similarly I can

Percy, *Reliques*, 2nd ed., 1767, ii. 160–74; J. H. Dixon, *Ancient Poems, Ballads, and Songs of the Peasantry*, 1846, pp. 60–71 (reprinted R. Bell, *Ancient Poems, Ballads, and Songs of the Peasantry*, 1857, pp. 51–9); W. Chappell, *Popular Music*, 1855–9, i. 158; C. J. Sharp, *English Folk-Songs*, ii. 37–9; Broadwood, *J. F.-S. S.* i. 202–3; A. Williams, *Folk-Songs of the Upper Thames*, 1923, pp. 255–6.

[1] See J. Sylvester, *op. cit.*, pp. 71–3 (whence Husk, *op. cit.*, pp. 105–7; A. H. Bullen, *Carols and Poems*, 1886, pp. xxiii–xxiv; Quiller-Couch, *Oxford Book of English Verse*, no. 382; F. Sidgwick, *More Ancient Carols*, 1906, pp. 20–2); C. S. Burne, *op. cit.*, pp. 566–7; E. M. Leather, *op. cit.*, pp. 187–8, from *J. F.-S. S.* iv. 49–51; F. Sidgwick, *Popular Carols*, 1908, pp. 21–3; Sharp, *J. F.-S. S.* v. 21–3, viii. 34; Gilchrist, *J. F.-S. S.* vii. 283–6.

[2] See R. Jamieson, *Popular Ballads*, 1806, i. 193–9; P. W. Joyce, *Old Irish Folk Music*, 1909, p. 220; S. Baring-Gould, *Songs of the West*, rev. ed., 1905, pp. 128–9; Sharp and Marson, *Folk-Songs from Somerset*, 1st ser., 1904, no. 16, pp. 32–3; *J. F.-S. S.* ii. 59, vii. 17–21; *Journal of the Irish Folk-Song Society*, iii. 25; Campbell and Sharp, *English Folk-Songs from the Southern Appalachians*, 1917, pp. 159–60; J. H. Cox, *Folk-Songs of the South*, 1925, pp. 339–41; A. P. Hudson, *Specimens of Mississippi Folk-Lore*, 1928, pp. 36–7; *J. A. F.-L.* xxii. 387, xxx. 358–60.

[3] See F. Sidgwick, *Popular Ballads of the Olden Time*, 2nd ser., 1904, pp. 88–91, 238–44; Quiller-Couch, *Oxford Book of English Verse*, no. 381.

[4] MS. Balliol. Coll. 354, ed. E. Flügel, *Anglia*, xxvi. 175; F. Sidgwick, *Notes and Queries*, 10th ser., iv. 181; Chambers and Sidgwick, *Early English Lyrics*, 1907, p. 148. For other versions from tradition see *Notes and Queries*, 3rd ser., ii. 103 (whence *N. and Q.*, 10th ser., iv. 181; Chambers and Sidgwick, *op. cit.*, p. 357; *J. F.-S. S.* iv. 53–4); R. Vaughan Williams, *J. F.-S. S.* iv. 63–4.

see no reason for excluding *The Bold Fisherman*,[1] which is quite clearly a ballad, and one of very picturesque quality. As for *Bruton Town* or *The Bramble Briar*[2] (to use only two of the several titles by which it is known), Professor Belden showed long since that it is a poor relation of a distinguished family, but eminently respectable in its own way. If we regretfully exclude the interesting *Twelfth Day*,[3] found in the same manuscript as the thirteenth-century *Judas* and in the same hand, it must be because it lacks the proper narrative manner, for the movement of the verse suggests balladry. Its importance can scarcely be exaggerated, for we must agree with its discoverer, who wrote: 'I am not sure that a thirteenth-century literary imitation of a popular ballad may not possess even greater interest than the genuine article.'

This is not the place to list or to attempt a valuation of all the waifs and strays of tradition that might, on one score or another, be classified as ballads. Later we must return to some of them, and notably to certain songs of American origin which are interesting for the light they throw on processes of development and transmission. For the moment my concern is rather to emphasize than to minimize those uncertainties of boundary that Gummere feared. Only by avoiding artificial limitations can we get a just notion of the material we have to study. The characteristic qualities of such songs are plain to see.

---

[1] See Broadwood and Fuller-Maitland, *English County Songs*, 1893, p. 110; C. J. Sharp, *English Folk-Songs*, ii. 32–3; Sharp and Marson, *Folk-Songs from Somerset*, 3rd ser., 1906, no. 69, pp. 42–3; *J.F.-S. S.* i. 138, v. 132–5, vii. 36–40.

[2] See H. W. Belden, *Publ. Mod. Lang. Ass.* xxxiii. 327–95; Sharp, *English Folk-Songs*, i. 4–5; Broadwood, *English Traditional Songs and Carols*, 1908, pp. 28–9; Sharp and Marson, *Folk-Songs from Somerset*, 1st ser., 1905, no. 12, pp. 24–5; A. E. Gillington, *Songs of the Open Road*, 1911, p. 10; *J. F.-S. S.* i. 160–1, ii. 42–3, v. 123–7; Campbell and Sharp, *op. cit.*, pp. 151–3; Cox, *op. cit.*, pp. 305–7; W. R. Mackenzie, *Ballads and Sea Songs from Nova Scotia*, 1928, pp. 90–1; *Sewanee Review*, xix. 222, 321; *J. A. F.-L.* xx. 259, xxix. 169.

[3] MS. Trin. Coll., Cambridge, B. 14. 39, ed. W. W. Greg, *Mod. Lang. Review*, viii. 64–7 (1913), ix. 235–6 (1914).

We have found that they share certain traits with their kindred on the mainland, and we shall discover in a later chapter various other ways by which they may be recognized. It is not important that we should be able to agree as to the status of every specimen, for those in debate will always be those that depart most widely from a norm about which there ought to be no serious dispute. The norm will appear, I hope, when we examine more minutely the structure of ballads and the conditions under which they exist.

Chapter Three

BALLAD STORIES

WE ought to observe, before proceeding to any detailed analysis of ballad structure, what the stories are that ballads tell. What are they about? Is their content of a special sort or the mere common currency of fiction? The choice of themes and the management of them will certainly tell us something about the habits and tastes of the people who have made and sung them, and help us to understand the problem in cultural history which they present.

In the first place, since they depend for their appeal, as we have already seen, upon action, and somewhat concentrated action at that, any striking situation will serve for material. The range is wide. It is limited only by the quality of the human drama they present, which is—and must of necessity be—simple, elemental, unshaded. No subtleties of emotion, no great delicacy of perception can be looked for in songs that have their being on the lips of ordinary folk. Intensity of passion, justice of feeling, wise understanding of the common lot there may well be, which is one reason why a great many ballads are so moving to persons of every degree; but there is frequently displayed an insensitiveness to suffering that appals nerves more finely drawn, an impassivity in the face of life's worst outrages that reveals the equilibrium of a childlike and healthy race. Vices and virtues, in so far as they motivate ballad stories, are the vices and virtues of rather primitive folk; the strong sensations that animate them are what would be needed to move their simple hearts.

Child's collection is so extensive that we are quite safe in regarding the contents of it as representative of ballad themes which have been in circulation for at least the past hundred and fifty years; and probably it gives us a fair notion of the subjects that appealed to still earlier generations, though we have no right to assume that fashions have never changed. We may conjecture, indeed, that certain subjects now seldom appearing were once more common, but we cannot be sure of this.

It is odd, for instance, that only one ballad, *Sir Hugh* (155), should be definitely traceable to the vast store of exemplary anecdote current in the Middle Ages;[1] and perhaps even more curious that not one specimen is known to be extant which derives from the legends of the saints. Considering the part once played by such tales in the consciousness of English folk, we must suppose that the Protestant generations have gradually obliterated them from memory. We have a scanty handful of ballads, however, based on themes drawn from the New Testament and the apocryphal gospels, one of which (*Judas*, 23) was scribbled down in the thirteenth century and another (*St. Stephen and Herod*, 22) in the fifteenth. Neither of these has been found by modern collectors; but four others,[2] printed by Child, have been in circulation in recent times, three of them within the present century. Two ballads unknown or ignored by Child, it should be noted in passing, fall into this category: *The Bitter Withy* and *The Seven Virgins*. On the whole, such themes are not well represented, though the specimens preserved incline one to the belief that there must have been a great many more of them at some time in the past.

Very much the same thing is true of the fund of secular story which found expression in medieval literature.

[1] In *Brown Robyn's Confession* (57) the hero is saved from the sea by the Virgin, but this is merely an echo of an anecdotal commonplace, as is Robin Hood's speech in *A Gest of Robyn Hode* (117, st. 271).

[2] *The Maid and the Palmer* (21), *The Cherry-Tree Carol* (54), *The Carnal and the Crane* (55), *Dives and Lazarus* (56).

Unlike the Spanish and Scandinavian peoples, which have wonderfully preserved in ballad form the heroic tales of their past, the British stock has lost almost all such material from popular memory. Although traces of it survive in songs like *Earl Brand* (7), which can be vaguely connected with the *Hildesaga*, they could not be recognized except for the Scandinavian ballads which preserve the same themes. A dozen ballads or so embody stories otherwise known through romances of the medieval period, whether or not they are actually founded on the literary productions they resemble; yet since a third of these are known only by the seventeenth-century copies in Bishop Percy's famous manuscript, and since few variants of the others have been gathered by modern collectors, it appears that they represent at best a fading tradition. In other words, the connexion between British ballads, as we know them, and the traditional tales out of which were fashioned medieval heroic and romantic narratives is very slight indeed. We must later consider this state of things more fully; for the present we need only note that the subjects of nearly all our ballads are singularly free from any earlier literary associations whatever.

Of the 305 specimens printed by Child, by far the largest number have to do with what may be called private and personal affairs rather than with matters that concern the larger social units of clan or nation. Even when the latter are in question, the emphasis of the story is usually on the adventures of one or more individuals; but more commonly the ballad-singer is interested in the fates of men and women in the common relationships of life. During the past two centuries at least, one is safe in saying, he has been prevailingly satisfied with the drama which overtakes men and women in the restricted group of family and personal friends or enemies.

One is not surprised to find the theme most commonly recurring that of sex. More than a third of the ballads are love-stories of one sort or another. If those be included in which crimes of violence take place on account of sex, nearly one hundred and fifty fall into the category. They run the gamut of feeling and behaviour that would be understood among people essentially simple and inhibited only by custom and the loyalties apt to arise from the bond of the flesh. They are frank in their recognition of desire, and untroubled by the ruthless satisfaction of it. In *Willie's Lyke-Wake* (25), for example, the lover lures the maiden to his bed by pretending death, and that is the whole of the story. In *Crow and Pie* (111) a casual rape is treated in humorous vein. In *The Jolly Beggar* (279) the animalism is equally frank, though the attitude of the young woman is not above reproach. In *The Broom of Cowdenknows* (217) and *The Wylie Wife of Hie Town Hie* (290) the completely fortuitous encounter is matched by the equally fortuitous return of the man and his decision to marry the girl. Even more romantic is the story of *Gil Brenton* (5), in which a man, now become a very monster of vicarious virtue in dealing with a succession of unfortunate wives, marries without knowing it the victim of his earlier lust. It matters not at all for our present inquiry that the chastity of the seven wives has been magically tested, and found wanting, or that the last bride protects herself from discovery by substituting her maid in the marital bed. The plot of the ballad, baldly stated, is what I have set down. *The Knight and the Shepherd's Daughter* (110) and *The False Lover Won Back* (218) give a different turn to the theme, laying no emphasis on the seduction, but telling how the lover was dogged by a persistent mistress until he married her. It should be noted that maidens sometimes baffle the attempts on their virtue, either by magic as in *The Broomfield Hill* (43), or by mother-wit as in *The Baffled Knight* (112) and that very facetious ditty, *The Friar in the Well* (276).

But the balladist has always been ready to acknowledge the love of woman for her man when she has made her choice. Whatever her fears and scruples, the heroine is willing to elope if necessary. There are at least eighteen such escapes recorded in Child's volumes. In one of these, *Brown Robin* (97), the maiden coolly disguises her lover as one of her attendants.

> The gown she pat upon her love
>   Was o the dainty green,
> His hose was o the saft, saft silk,
>   His shoon o the cordwain fine.
>
> She's pitten his bow in her bosom,
>   His arrow in her sleeve,
> His sturdy bran her body next,
>   Because he was her love.

'Because he was her love', the heroine of *Katharine Jaffray* (221) deserted her bridegroom with no ado for the man she preferred; in the same way, quite simply, the primitive creature in *Earl Brand* (7) fled with her proud and loyal lord; and just as whole-heartedly the heroine of *The Gypsy Laddie* (200) ran away from her husband to go with Johnny Faa.[1] The elopement in *Leesome Brand* (15) is of another sort—an escape on the part of the lovers from punishment for their illicit relationship, with results so terrible that they have been partially obliterated in the extant form; but the determination of the 'gay lady' is like that of all the scores of women in the ballads who love with consuming passion, and love till death.

Such love is shown by the stories like *Fair Annie* (62),

[1] Apart from those mentioned above, see *Erlinton* (8), *The Fair Flower of Northumberland* (9), *Bonnie Annie* (24), *Willie o Douglas Dale* (101), *Willie and Earl Richard's Daughter* (102), *Christopher White* (108), *Bonny Lizie Baillie* (227), *Richie Story* (232), *The Duke of Gordon's Daughter* (237), *Lord William, or Lord Lundy* (254), *The Beggar-Laddie* (280), *Dugall Quin* (294), *Young Peggy* (298).

Child Waters (63), and *Thomas o Yonderdale* (253), in which the devotion of women is rewarded in the end after subjection to tests beyond those of Griselda. It is shown in *The Rantin Laddie* (240), when the extremely neglectful Earl of Aboyne responds to the message of his distressed mistress and comes to rescue her at the head of five hundred men.

> As they cam in thro Buchanshire,
> They were a company bonie,
> With a gude claymor in every hand,
> And O but they shin'd bonie!

Both faithful and bold are the ladies of *Young Beichan* (53), *The Bailiff's Daughter of Islington* (105), and *Robin Hood and Maid Marian* (150), who go adventuring in search of their lovers and happily find them. There is a pair of such brave girls in *Rose the Red and White Lily* (103), whose cruel stepmother separates them from their lovers, her sons by an earlier marriage. Their amazing adventures combine the tests of childbirth and swordplay, but have a happy outcome. Equally loyal and quite as dauntless are the Lady Margaret of *The Laird o Logie* (182) and the Annie of *The Bent sae Brown* (71), who plead successfully for the lives of their lovers, or the unnamed heroine of *The Gay Goshawk* (96), who, like Shakespeare's Juliet, drank 'a sleepy draught' in order to join her mate. Of less resolute nature, but of equal devotion, is the weeping damsel of *John of Hazelgreen* (293), who is curiously rescued from her woe by the father of the young man she adores, and by him escorted to her love.

Almost never are the women of balladry capable of such unfaithfulness and treachery as lurks in the background of *Lord Randal* (12), where the mistress poisons her lover for some reason that we do not learn. On the other hand, they are on occasion exceedingly dangerous when ill treated, for not all of them have the devoted patience of Ellen in *Child Waters*. In *Young Hunting* (68) a woman whose lover is forsaking her kills him with her own hand, and in *The Duke of Athole's Nurse* (212) an equally vengeful mistress sends her brothers to slay the recreant—though he is saved by the ready wit of another woman. The tragedy of *Lord Thomas and Fair Annet* (73) is motivated by the bridegroom's faithfulness to his old love, who attends the wedding and is stabbed by the bride. Lord Thomas waits only to kill the jealous girl before burying a dagger in his own heart. Lady Erskine of *Child Owlet* (291) is utterly merciless when her husband's nephew refuses her advances: she has him torn to pieces by four horses on Darling Moor. Similarly the queen in *The Queen of Scotland* (301) treacherously sends Troy Muir to lift a stone under which is 'a serpent that lang wanted meat', and she is baulked of her revenge only by the casual appearance of a maid who cuts off one of her breasts to heal the young man.

Sometimes there are lovers who are equally faithful to one another in life and death. *Tom Potts* (109) tells how one such pair was married, and *The Holy Nunnery* (303) how another couple came together somewhat picturesquely in a convent after a separation of seven years. The pathos of *Andrew Lammie* (233) lies in the successive deaths of the maiden and her faithful trumpeter of Fyvie.

> O Andrew 's gane to the house-top
>   O the bonny house o Fyvie,
> He 's blawn his horn baith loud and shill
>   Oer the lawland leas o Fyvie.

In *The Suffolk Miracle* (272) the devotion of the separated lovers is emphasized by the young man's return as a ghost and the girl's unquestioning acceptance of his invitation to ride with him. The poignancy of the tragedy in *Glasgerion* (67) rests upon the same passion and understanding between the lovers: the princess kills herself unhesitatingly when she finds she has been tricked by the page who has intruded on her bed, and Glasgerion himself follows her example as soon as he has killed his treacherous servant.

Although men are more often represented as fickle than are women, even they are shown as remorseful in the end for their unfaithfulness. In *Fair Margaret and Sweet William* (74), *Lord Lovel* (75), and *The Lass of Roch Royal* (76) there are developed three appealing variants of this same theme. In one form of *Burd Isabel and Earl Patrick* (257 A), and that the most satisfactory, the recreant lover comes to a very bad end indeed because of his falsity.

> The hundred evils enterd him,
> And he fell oure the brim.

A less catastrophic but very correct punishment overtakes the fickle lover of *The Brown Girl* (295), for the deserted maiden scorns him in turn as he lies on his death-bed, repentant, and grimly promises to dance above his grave 'a whole twelvemonth and a day'.

Yet men are not only eager in pursuing the girls of their choice, as is shown by the stories of seduction already mentioned, but often chivalrous and generous as well. In *King Estmere* (60), *Sir Cawline* (61), *Johnie Scot* (99), and *Tom Potts* (109), heroes of very different degrees, from sovereign to serving-man, win their ladies in fair fight. *Robin Hood and the Prince of Aragon* (129) might be added to this list, save that after the great battle the princess has to choose among three champions and takes Will Scaddock rather than either Robin Hood or Little John. The ever-popular *Willie o Winsbury* (100) is a curiosity in that the hero wins the favour of the princess's father, as he has already won her love, by his extreme good looks. Such lovers as the two Willies of

Rare Willie Drowned in Yarrow (215) and *The Mother's Malison* (216) prove their devotion by riding through dangerous waters at the risk of their lives in order to keep their trysts, in the latter case defying a mother's fatal curse to do so. There are lovers, too, who die because their ladies are unkind, as *Bonny Barbara Allan* (84), *Lady Alice* (85), and *Alison and Willie* (256) bear witness. It is significant of the balladists' view of love that these cruel ladies die of remorse, as do their male counterparts in such songs as *Lord Lovel*.

Despite the not uncommon brutality and the even commoner lack of any restraint in the satisfaction of physical appetite, love appears in the ballads not only as the chief source of romance, but as its own excuse for being. Love awakens love in *Glenlogie* (238), for instance, where the nobleman marries Jeanie, whose heart is set on him, though he has earlier been 'promised away'. The singers have liked to believe in stories like that of *The Kitchie Boy* (252)—the low-born youth returning in prosperity to claim the 'lady of birth and fame'. They have liked to play at least with such strange wooings as that of *Kemp Owyne* (34), whose three kisses transform a hideous monster of the sea to her natural shape as a fair maiden. They have liked to imagine such talismans as those of *Hind Horn* (17) and *Bonny Bee Hom* (92), which change colour with danger or misfortune. Although there are plenty of cases, as we have seen, in which cruelty and unfaithfulness in love have a just reward, and plenty of cases in which true lovers come to sad ends, very seldom indeed does even illicit love bring punishment, unless the jealousy of a husband is aroused or the family honour must be avenged. The sympathy is almost invariably with the lovers, whatever they do. *The Clerk's Twa Sons o Owsenford* (72) is exceptional in that the two youths are executed by process of law for their 'dear-bought love', and even here the mayor who pronounces sentence upon them is the father of the girls they have seduced. The implication is that he was not justified, any more than was the father in *Willie and Lady Maisry* (70) for killing his daughter's lover, who has won through to her bower by slaughtering (in one version) thirty-two men-at-arms and her brother! She is as inconsolable as May Margaret of *Clerk Saunders* (69), whose brothers rush in and slay her lover.

Somewhat curiously, I think, stories of physical violence on the part of lovers are extremely rare. There is *Young Johnstone* (88), who barbarously killed the mistress who had been protecting him from his pursuers—and she the sister of the man he had just slain. But Johnstone is scarcely to be matched except by *Jellon Grame* (90), who kills either his mistress because he fears the discovery of the baby that 'maun shortly see the light', or in other versions the woman who has rejected him for another. Most of the lovers are more gentle in their behaviour as lovers than they are in other circumstances of life.

Apart from tales of love-making that is preliminary to marriage or frankly illicit, no less than seventy-five of the ballads in Child's collection, as I count them, have to do with family relations of one sort or another. Nearly half of these, it is interesting to note, bring in manslaughter. In the others a considerable variety of themes is developed, although three-quarters of them concern husbands and wives. Themes involving parents and children, except as fathers object to the marriage of daughters, occur very seldom. There is the knight in the first 'fytte' of *A Gest of Robyn Hode* (117) who has impoverished himself to save his son; and there is the father of *The Laily Worm and the Machrel of the Sea* (36) who rescues his son and daughter from the spell cast upon them by their stepmother; but such cases are few. In view of their general ill-repute, it is odd that the wicked stepmother just mentioned is matched by only three others in the whole collection: the witch of *Kemp Owyne* (34), who bespells her stepdaughter; the woman in *Rose the Red and White Lily* (106), from whom the two heroines escape to a life of splendid adventure; and the evil creature of *Lady Isabel* (261), who accuses the maiden of incest and poisons her.[1]

Married life furnishes much more drama to the ballad-makers, comedy as well as tragedy, than do the relations of parents and children. There are the tales of stolen brides, to begin with, all but two of which are unsuccessful from the point of view of the intending husband. In *Rob Roy* (225) the Highland chieftain has no other purpose than to get a lady to 'haud his house in order', and he accomplishes that end. So, presumably, does the hero of the dashing fragment *Charlie MacPherson* (234 A), but he was less the abductor than the rescuer, we make out. In *Eppie Morrie* (223) the girl is so well able to take care of herself that she awaits with composure the coming of her true love; and she is matched by the heroines of *Walter Lesly* (296) and *Broughty Wa's* (258), both of whom run away from their captors. Less bold, but quite as re-calcitrant, *Bonny Baby Livingston* (222) sends an appeal for help to her lover, who comes in haste, though, as the matter is reported in some versions, too late to save her from death.

Other dramatic situations follow marriage. Two ballads, for example (*Lizie Lindsay*, 226, and *Glasgow Peggie*, 228), turn on the bride's discovery that her new husband is a far more prosperous person than she had supposed. In other cases the husband rescues his wife from peril: in *Willie's Lady* (6) from his mother's magic, which prevents her from bringing forth her child; in *King Orfeo* (19) from enthralment by the King of Fairyland; and in *Brown*

---

[1] A wicked stepmother appears also, but more casually, in *The Marriage of Sir Gawain* (31). In some versions of *Lord Randal* (12), one ought to add, a stepmother, rather than a mistress, poisons the hero.

Adam (98) from a seducer who is at the moment just
flashing his sword, having failed to tempt her with rich
gifts. The counterpart of these is *Geordie* (209), where
the faithful wife pleads for her husband so affectingly
that the bystanders make up his ransom. The lady in
The Baron of Leys (241) is another magnificent instance
of wifely devotion: when she hears that her foolish lord
has entangled himself with a woman, she wishes to hold
his bastard child in her arms, and sell her jointure-lands
to pay off the mistress. Loyalty under other conditions
is shown by the wife in *The New-Slain Knight* (263), whose
husband tests her by disguising himself and pretending
to have seen her lord lying dead, for she refuses his somewhat inopportune proffer of marriage and declares that
she will father her bairn on the King of Heaven, 'since
my love's dead and gane'. More moving, because less
fantastic, is the tale of *The White Fisher* (264), at least as it
appears in the Aberdeenshire versions collected by Greig.[1]
When the husband finds that his bride of a month is with
child by a serving-man or priest in her father's castle, who
has ravished her, he not only conceals the fact, but at her
bidding takes the infant at birth and pretends to throw
it into the sea. On his return, he finds his wife sorely
lamenting what she has done, but comforts her with the
tidings that he has really given the child to his mother to
rear. His conduct is in violent contrast to that of *Jamie
Douglas* (204), who repudiates his wife on a false accusa-
tion of adultery, and to that of *The Earl of Aboyne* (235),
who insults his lady when she welcomes him home and
leaves her to die of a broken heart. Unworthy, too, of
a faithful wife is the husband in *The Twa Knights* (268),
who pledges his wife's constancy and permits her to meet
the difficult situation alone—a plot that belongs to the
large family from which one element in *Cymbeline* also
derives. The husband just mentioned is even more repre-

[1] *Last Leaves*, pp. 207–10.

hensible, indeed, than the brother in *Redesdale and Wise William* (246), who wagers his head that his sister's honour cannot be successfully assailed, for Wise William has the grace to inform her of what he has rashly done.

The sorrows peculiar to women serve the ballad poets, not at all surprisingly, for some of their most poignant moments. Seldom do they fail to make the most of a lamentation for the husband or lover who is dead. In *The Bonny Earl of Murray* (181) the widow is in the background, mourning, despite the unfaithfulness of her lord; and the equally lovely *Bonnie James Campbell* (210) is nothing but a threnody, with the stricken wife in the centre of the picture.

> My meadow lies green,
>   and my corn is unshorn,
> My barn is to build,
>   and my babe is unborn.

So, too, with the dangers attending childbirth, which are seldom mentioned except incidentally, but in *The Death of Queen Jane* (170) are made the theme of a lachrymose ballad. *Fair Mary of Wallington* (91) tells a more tragic story, for the doom of dying in childbirth is upon the seven sisters, if they marry, and the doom must be fulfilled. Equally terrible is the story of *Fair Janet* (64), who is married just after she has given birth to a child by her lover, and dies while dancing at the wedding in order to conceal her state.

Not all wives are faithful or kind. For some reason that probably lies deep in social custom, marital unhappiness is almost always lightly treated in the ballads unless it ends in homicide. Neglecting for the moment tales of the latter sort, we ought to note a group of graceless stories like *Our Goodman* (274), in which the wife tries vainly to hide her lover, and *The Farmer's Curst Wife* (278), which tells how the devil returned a shrewish woman to her husband. The same mocking spirit occurs in *Burd Ellen and Young Tamlane* (28) with its quarrel about who shall rock the cradle, in *Get up and Bar the Door* (275) with its decisive victory for the bride in a battle of wits, and in *The Wife Wrapt in Wether's Skin* (277), where the husband is both ingenious and brutal. Cruel, too, is the comedy of *The Earl of Errol* (231), which tells how Kate Carnegie's accusations of her lover were proved false by the event. Perhaps the quarrel of the pair in *Earl Crawford* (229) is the most curious of all, in that the wife started the trouble by a mocking speech, as if jealous of the attention her husband has paid their little son, and in the end died before the proud lord came to beg for a reconciliation. This story is true tragedy, because the love of the couple for one another is made very clear.

Domestic tragedy of a violent sort is common enough in the ballads. A husband kills a wife, together with her lover, in *Old Robin of Portingale* (80), in *Little Musgrave and Lady Barnard* (81), and *The Bonny Birdy* (82), in the two former cases repenting of the deed as soon as it is done. In the grim tale of *The Laird of Wariston* (194) a wife murders the husband she does not love, but likewise repents immediately. Only once does a father kill his son (in *Child Maurice*, 83), and then ignorantly, believing him to be his wife's lover. Equally terrible are the two instances in which a son kills a father: *Edward* (13 B) and *Jellon Grame* (90 A). In the former Edward has evidently been urged by his mother to the evil deed, and in the latter the son is avenging his mother, who has been killed by Jellon Grame, her lover, at the time of the child's birth. In only one ballad is a mother guilty of murdering a son or daughter of mature age: *Prince Robert* (87), namely, where the mother poisons the son because she is jealous of his wife; but there are two cases of infanticide, in both of which just retribution comes quickly. *The Cruel Mother* (20), which has had a wide circulation in Great Britain and America, tells how an unfortunate girl killed her baby in order to hide her guilt, and was then haunted by the ghost of the child; *Mary Hamilton* (173) is the story of the proud mistress of the king, who was tried and executed for the murder of her new-born infant.

The relations of brothers and sisters with one another furnish themes for other ballads. In all the versions of *Edward* (13), save the one mentioned above, the crime is fratricide as the result of a foolish quarrel.[1] In some versions of *The Twa Brothers* (49) one brother kills the other by accident, but in what was probably the older tradition[2] there is a quarrel over a girl. There is essentially the same situation in *Lord Ingram and Chiel Wyet* (66), although the setting of the quarrel is more elaborate. In *Bewick and Graham* (211) two young men who are not related by blood but have taken the oath of blood brotherhood are forced into a fatal duel by a silly quarrel of their fathers'. So deep is the affectionate loyalty between them that the tragedy is one of the most poignant in all balladry. Only in *The Twa Sisters* (10) do we find an instance of a quarrel between sisters that leads to murder.[3] As one would expect, it is jealousy that makes Ellen push her younger and preferred sister into the stream. There are four ballads, to conclude our enumeration of such crimes, in which a brother is responsible for the death of a sister. *The Cruel Brother* (11) tells a savage story of

[1] One wonders whether the copy furnished Percy by Lord Hailes (Child B) does not preserve the earlier form of the story, despite the concurrence of the Scandinavian and Finnish ballads with the other versions. It will be noted that the continental versions say nothing about the mother's guilt, which is an essential feature of *Edward*, though rather senseless if the brothers quarrel suddenly about some trifling matter.

[2] See Barry, Eckstorm, and Smyth, *British Ballads from Maine*, 1929, pp. 100–6.

[3] Two versions of *Sheath and Knife* (16 D, E) have transformed another theme into something of the same sort.

how a brother stabbed his sister on her wedding-day because the lover had failed to ask his consent to the marriage. The three other ballads of the sort are not less primitive, and all involve at least the threat of incest. In *Sheath and Knife* (16) and *Lizie Wan* (51) the brother kills his sister when he learns that she is pregnant by him. They are gruesome tales, but not more so than is *Babylon* (14), in which an outlaw brother meets his three sisters and kills two of them for resisting his proposals before discovering from the third their identity.

Incest appears in four other ballads, one of which (*Lady Isabel*, 261) has already been noted in connexion with the guilty stepmother, who first accuses the heroine falsely of having unlawful relations with her father, and then poisons her. *Brown Robyn's Confession* (57) verges on the absurd, or would do so if the theme, of throwing a guilty man overboard to save a ship, were not so seriously treated:

> For wi my mither I had twa bairns,
> And wi my sister five.

In *The Bonny Hind* (50) and *The King's Dochter Lady Jean* (52) the tragedy is Aeschylean: a brother meets a sister, from whom he has been separated, and has his will of her before they discover their relationship. The girl dies in each instance, in most versions killing herself, and seemingly the brother perishes in turn.

In addition to these themes involving acts of violence within the inner circle of the family, there are other cases of homicide, equally personal and private, which have to do with an outer fringe of persons. We have seen that a husband sometimes kills his wife along with her lover: in other instances, naturally enough, only the lover is slain. Such is the affecting story of *Young Waters* (94), where the hero is guilty only of inspiring a casual word of admiration on the part of the queen; a similar story lies behind the elegiac fragment of *The Knight of Liddesdale* (160); and the king is certainly responsible for the death of *The Bonny Earl of Murray* (181), though the over-zealous Huntly actually commits the deed. In only one ballad, strangely enough, does a rejected lover kill his successful rival (*Lord Livingston*, 262), and he does so in a fair fight. There is a hotter fire of jealousy behind the action ot the bride in *Lord Thomas and Fair Annet* (73), who stabs her rival at the wedding, but the jealousy is justified by the dazzling and ostentatious splendour of Annet.

> And whan she cam into the kirk,
>   She shimmerd like the sun;
> The belt that was about her waist
>   Was a' wi pearles bedone.

The relations of lovers and husbands with the fathers and brothers of their ladies supply the themes for a half-dozen other tales of violence. In *Willie and Lady Maisry* (70) the father came upon the lovers after the hero had won through to Maisry's bower by his sharp sword, and killed him as he slept; and in *Lady Diamond* (269), which tells Boccaccio's story of *Guiscardo and Ghismonda*, the lady's royal parent slaughtered her 'kitchen-boy' lover and sent his heart to her in a cup of gold. In *Clerk Saunders* (69) it was May Margaret's seven brothers who killed the lover whom they found sleeping with her, while in *Young Benjie* (86) three brothers avenged the death of their sister, whom her 'false true-love' had drowned. In the background of *The Braes of Yarrow* (214) there doubtless lurks a feud, but the subject of the lovely ballad is the ambush laid for a husband by his brothers-in-law, and the wife's heart-breaking grief. There is a feud, too, in *The Bent sae Brown* (71), already mentioned in connexion with the successful plea

of the heroine for the life of her lover. The hero, discovered by the girl's mother, was beset by her three
brothers while riding away, and valiantly killed them
all—a deed for which he was later haled before the
king.

Treachery, as well as a long-continued feud, motivates
Fause Foodrage (89), which ends with the killing of a
murderer by his victim's son, who releases his imprisoned
mother. A companion piece to this is one form of *Jellon
Grame* (90 B), in which a villain, who has killed a woman
out of jealousy just at the time when she gives birth to
his rival's child, is punished with death by the son when
he approaches man's estate. Unique in the story it tells
is another ballad of private vengeance, *Lamkin* (93).
Lamkin, angry because he has not been paid for the work
he has done as a mason, conspires with a nurse and kills
the mistress of the castle and her little child.

From these stories of personal violence we may properly
turn to tales of fights and forays, battles on land and sea,
sieges and feats of arms, which are more numerous than
any other ballads except those that have to do with love-
making. Nearly sixty of Child's 305 have themes of this
kind. There is, first, that notable group (183–190), including *Willie Macintosh*, *The Lads of Wamphray*, *Dick o
the Cow*, *Kinmont Willie*, *Jock o the Side*, *Archie o Cawfield*,
Hobie Noble, and *Jamie Telfer in the Fair Dodhead*, which
celebrate wild exploits along the Border by small groups
of marauders. To name them is to get a whiff of moor-
land air, for they embody the free spirit of the region
whence they sprang, with its stalwart virtues as well as
its somewhat barbaric manners. Differing only in its
point of view, which is that of the raided rather than the
raiders, is *Rookhope Ryde* (179), an excellent 'minstrel'
piece. Along with such tales should be ranged two, of
which horse-thieves are curiously the heroes: *Hughie Grame*
(191) and *The Lochmaben Harper* (192). In the former

the robber is caught and hanged despite his valour and his high-born friends; in the latter the blind harper succeeds by a trick in stealing King Henry's Wanton Brown.

Separable from these ballads, in a rough classification, are nearly a dozen in which the emphasis is on feats of arms. *Robin Hood and Guy of Gisborne* (118) is of this sort, as are *Robin Hood and the Monk* (119) and *Robin Hood and the Prince of Aragon* (129). So are the delightful *Gude Wallace* (157) and *Johnie Armstrong* (169), ballads of the Border. It matters not at all that in the latter the hero dies in the valiant attempt to escape from the trap into which he had been decoyed by the king, for he died,

> Saying, Fight on, my merry men all;
> And see that none of you be taine;
> For I will stand by and bleed but awhile,
> And then will I come and fight againe.

Hugh Spencer's Feats in France (158) is another tale of courage and skill in arms, and it is matched by the latter part of the somewhat rambling *Earl of Westmoreland* (177). Less good specimens of such feats of arms are *Lord Delamere* (207) and *Young Ronald* (304). We should remember also in this connexion those ballads in which ladies are won by the martial prowess of the heroes: *King Estmere* (60), *Sir Cawline* (61), *Johnie Scot* (99), and *Tom Potts* (109), as well as *Robin Hood and the Prince of Aragon*, which has just been mentioned.

A more sinister side of feud-fighting is shown in such ballads as *Johnie Cock* (114)—though Johnie is unquestionably a poacher—and *The Death of Parcy Reed* (193), the former as primitive a specimen as we possess, the latter of much later invention. The point of the story in each is the attack on a sleeping man by his enemies, with a fight to the death when he wakes. Not less savage is *The Fire of Frendraught* (196), in which Lord John and Rothiemay were burned to death by their treacherous host. Presumably there is a feud, too, behind the curious *Robyn and Gandelyn* (115), which recounts how Robyn is shot from ambush and how Gandelyn takes immediate vengeance for his death. We know that the very affecting *Lord Maxwell's Last Goodnight* (195) is certainly based on a feud: the hero has killed his ancient enemy and must go into exile, but he promises vengeance on his return. Another aspect of the old feuds is shown by the tales of attacks on houses. The first episode of *Adam Bell* (116) concerns the assault on William of Cloudsley's house in Carlisle, which is fired in order to compel the outlaw to surrender—which of course he does not do. There is a similar attempt in *Captain Car, or Edom o Gordon* (178), where the brave defence by the lady is the theme of the whole ballad. That dauntless lady is one of the great heroines of folk-song, though equalled in courage by Lady Margaret of *The Bonnie House o Airlie* (199). Almost their match is the sister in *Redesdale and Wise William* (246), whose final trial is her escape from a burning house, defying Redesdale to the last. They are of a different stripe from the treacherous woman in the equally stirring *Baron of Brackley* (203), who sends out her husband to certain death under the walls of the beleaguered dwelling. In *James Grant* (197) the hero is more fortunate and wins away. *Sir John Butler* (165) and *The Slaughter of the Laird of Mellerstain* (230) are merely cases of assassination, though they involve the taking of a house and may therefore be mentioned here.

To be differentiated from such ballads as we have been considering, though not sharply, are those which have a more political cast. In two cases, the fragmentary *Thomas Cromwell* (171) and *Lord Derwentwater* (208), the story consists simply of the arrest of an alleged traitor; in two others, *Earl Bothwell* (174) and *Northumberland Betrayed by Douglas* (176), there is political intrigue and betrayal;

while *The Rising in the North* (175) and *King James and Brown* (180) recount tales of conspiracy and rebellion. These purely political ballads are far less vigorous, as one would expect, than the set of battle pieces, some of which have been deservedly famous for centuries. The list includes the following: *Durham Field* (159), *The Battle of Otterburn* (161), *The Hunting of the Cheviot* (162), *The Battle of Harlaw* (163), *Flodden Field* (168), *Musselburgh Field* (172), *Bonny John Seton* (198), *The Battle of Philiphaugh* (202), *Loudon Hill* (205), and *Bothwell Bridge* (206)—ten in all. Although the view they give of historical events is far from accurate, they are among the most precious songs that have come down to us. Less interesting, but not to be forgotten, are *King Henry Fifth's Conquest of France* (164) and *The Rose of England* (166), which narrate respectively the campaigns culminating in Agincourt and the triumph of Henry Tudor over Richard III.

It is difficult, at first sight, to understand why Great Britain, always an island of sailors, should have produced so few tales of the sea among her ballads, or at least so few that have been enshrined in Child's collection. Some of the reasons for this state of things will develop when we examine how ballads have been made, but for the moment let us be content with remarking that there have been far more narratives of the sea in circulation than would appear from looking through our great thesaurus.[1] The pieces there included, though not representative quantitatively, are nevertheless admirable in quality. The gallant fight in *Sir Andrew Barton* (167) has deserved its long life in popular tradition up to the present day, whether in its earlier form or in the truncated version listed by Child as *Henry Martyn* (250). *The George*

---

[1] See C. H. Firth, *Naval Songs and Ballads*, 1908, which contains a good many things that have been in traditional circulation, as does J. Masefield, *A Sailor's Garland*, 1928. Everything in J. C. Colcord, *Roll and Go, Songs of American Sailormen*, 1924, has been orally derived.

Aloe and the Sweepstake (285), *Captain Ward and the Rainbow* (287), and *The Young Earl of Essex's Victory* (288) are all vigorous narratives of fights at sea, and all have been widely known. Robin Hood's battle with the French ship of war in *The Noble Fisherman* (148) is another good story of the same sort, though the outlaw is useful on the sea only through his shooting. Why *John Dory* (284) should have died out of traditional memory it is impossible to say, for it is an excellent ballad and was very much sung in the seventeenth century. Perhaps the only rival to *Sir Andrew Barton* in popularity has been *The Sweet Trinity, or the Golden Vanity* (286), which does not celebrate a battle, but the exploit by which a sailor scuttled the enemy ship that had captured his own. The most famous of all sea-ballads among readers, however, has always been *Sir Patrick Spens* (58) with its haunting suggestions of a catastrophe beyond the power of speech. The variant published by Bishop Percy in his *Reliques* would of itself have been enough to give his book its great place in English poetry. It illustrates the odd chances of oral transmission that the tale of shipwreck known to singers of our time should be, not *Sir Patrick Spens*, but *The Mermaid* (289), which is attractive but comparatively insignificant.

But the ballad-makers ranged more widely for their material than would be indicated by the themes we have been reviewing. There is a large residue of stories that do not fall into the categories we have been using, though they are equally tales of adventure. Some act of prowess, some trick of man or fate, furnishes the memorable action for them, and the spirit of comedy generally prevails. Most of the Robin Hood ballads belong in this somewhat makeshift group, which is only a group at all in that such ballads illustrate a tendency to imaginative playfulness, which is not often apparent in the tales that have to do with the relationships and accidents of ordinary life. Some of the love-stories give evidence of the same stretch of fancy; but otherwise we must turn to the miscellaneous ballads of adventure, to the Robin Hood set, to the riddles and tricks, in order to appreciate that folksingers have not been altogether solemn and serious in cultivating their art.

A favourite theme of the sort is the one so often recurring in connexion with Robin Hood: how the brave and wily outlaw is bested by a potter (121), a butcher (122), a friar (123), a pound-keeper (124), a tanner (126), a tinker (127), a Scotchman (130), a shepherd (135); by pedlars (132, 137), by beggars (133, 134), by foresters (131, 136), by Little John (125), and by Young Gamwell, his nephew (128). Of the same stamp are *Jock the Leg and the Merry Merchant* (282) and *The Crafty Farmer* (283), though in the latter there is no sword-play, while several good ballads not included by Child might be added to the list. In other cases, outlaws are represented as outshooting supporters of the king, as in the latter part of *Adam Bell* (116), in one episode of *A Gest of Robyn Hode* (117), and in two less interesting specimens of the woodland cycle (139, 152). The rescue of a comrade by the robbers, which appears as the second theme of *Adam Bell*, and again in *Robin Hood and Guy of Gisborne* (118) and *Robin Hood Rescuing Will Stutly* (141), recalls such Border ballads as *Jock o the Side*, but without the wild excitement of those pieces. The necessities of their profession compel Robin and his men to thievery, but robbery is never the real subject of a song. Either the outlaws take money from a monk to restore it to a knight, as in the *Gest*, or their wit is emphasized, as when Robin deals with the two lusty priests in *Robin Hood's Golden Prize* (147), or moral lessons are administered to bishops (143, 144) or to beggars (142), with purses mentioned very lightly. So many imaginations played about the career of Robin Hood himself, and eventually he became so real a figure, that any action attributed to him made a story. If one counts separately the successive episodes of the *Gest*, the cycle of his deeds includes no less than forty-three tales. So he becomes a match-maker, as in *Robin Hood and Allan a Dale* (138), he becomes a lover himself, as in *Robin Hood and Maid Marian* (150), he goes to court, as in *Robin Hood and Queen Katherine* (145). There are even ballads about his birth and breeding (149) and about his life as a whole (154), while twice we are given accounts of his death (120, 153).

Some of the exploits of ballad heroes have much in common with the extravagances attributed to the knights of medieval romance. *Sir Lionel* (18) is a case in point, with its tale of giant-killing and the rescue of a lady. Other themes like those of romances, though they cannot be connected with any literary works we know, are *Sir Aldingar* (59), which tells how the treachery of a false steward was foiled and how the good queen was saved, and *The Boy and the Mantle* (29), which describes a test of chastity at Arthur's court. *The Marriage of Sir Gawain* (31) and *King Henry* (32) recount the story of the Loathly Lady, which was old when Chaucer put it into the mouth of the Wife of Bath. The boasts of the kings and knights in *King Arthur and King Cornwall* (30) come from the same ancient fund of story, as do the adventures in *John Thomson and the Turk* (266).

Of a more homely growth is *James Hatley* (244), though it has a background of chivalry in that the hero is able to prove his innocence of the charge of theft by a duel with his accuser. Another oddment is *The Heir of Linne* (267), which tells the old and widespread story of the spendthrift who recovers his estate by means of a hidden treasure left by one of his parents. It is curious, too, in another way, that we should have three ballads which tell how women go adventuring. *Rose the Red and White Lily* (103) has already been noticed in connexion with stepmothers, but the central fact in the plot is that two girls disguised themselves as youths and went to seek their fortunes. Fair Elise in *The Famous Flower of Serving-Men* (106) was a widow when she set out on the adventure that was to make her a queen, and we learn that she was driven forth by her broken heart. Blancheflour in *Blancheflour and Jellyflorice* (300), on the other hand, sought to better her condition and took service without disguise in the castle of which she was destined to become, after some trials, the honoured lady. Another ballad concerning womankind is *Bessy Bell and Mary Gray* (201), the story of which is quite unlike anything found elsewhere. Two girls fled from the pest, but were caught by it none the less and died in their 'bower on yon burn-brae'. The pathos of their tale is far removed from the jollity of *The Bonny Lass of Anglesey* (220), who had a ballad made about her because she outdanced fifteen lords at the king's court.

As I have already said, riddles and tricks serve as material for a considerable group of narratives. Their appeal is natural, since the kind of wit and humour they embody can be understood by the simplest folk. Of *Riddles Wisely Expounded* (1) there exists one variant from the fifteenth century, which consists simply of a dialogue between a devil and a maiden. By answering his riddles as he propounds them, she escapes his threat of abduction. In other variants the questioner is a knight in search of a wife, but not always so innocent as he seems, for sometimes he shows his cloven hoof before the end of the conversation. Another turn of the same theme, with amusing differences, occurs in *King John and the Bishop* (45). The Bishop or Abbot of Canterbury must answer certain questions in order to keep his head, and he finds a ready-witted shepherd to serve as his vicar. In *Captain Wedderburn's Courtship* (46) a wooer has to solve a series of riddles before he can win the lady of his sudden desire ;

and in most versions of *Proud Lady Margaret* (47) the same kind of colloquy takes place, though the ostensible lover reveals himself before the end of the song as an avenging ghost. *The Elfin Knight* (2) turns the contest another way : the maiden is set an impossible task, which she counters with another for the man. Perhaps the strangest of all such ballads is *The False Knight upon the Road* (3), in which a young boy has to find ready replies to the questions put to him or be carried off, presumably by the devil. The necessity of answering a riddle is also found in *The Marriage of Sir Gawain* (31), though the dominant motive in such stories of the Loathly Lady type is of course unspelling rather than wit.

How greatly quickness of wit has been esteemed is shown in still other ballads, where there are no riddling questions. It becomes the point of the story in *The Twa Magicians* (44), for the wizardry of the blacksmith and the lady would be useless without the ability to think of the next move. Of a similar tendency are the expedients by which lovers avoid the lie direct or the broken promise, as in *Clerk Saunders* (69) and *The Bent sae Brown* (71), where the man is carried from door to bed in order that his mistress may be able to swear that he never trod her bower. Another joke of which balladry has never wearied is that illustrated by *King Edward and the Tanner of Tamworth* (273) and by a similar episode in *A Gest of Robyn Hode* (117, vii-viii). The encounter of a king with a humble person who does not recognize him has not failed to excite good-natured mirth since the story of Alfred and the cakes was invented.

There remain to consider only those ballads motivated by superstition, of which there are some twenty-five. We shall do well to postpone to a later chapter our discussion of the survival of primitive belief and custom, which is a matter of great interest in itself, confining ourselves for the present to specimens in which there would be no

story except for the superstition. Among these is *Thomas
Rᵥmer* (37), which recounts how the hero rode away with
the Queen of Elfland. In *The Queen of Elfan's Nourice*
(40) and *Hind Etin* (41) a woman was carried off by a
supernatural being, in the latter instance to be his wife.
The extant Scottish versions of *Hind Etin* obscure the
nature of the abductor, which is quite clear in the Scandinavian and German forms of the ballad, but they have
not lost the point that she still longed for her home after
having borne seven children to her lord. There is another
journey to Fairy Land in *The Wee Wee Man* (38), the
plot of which indeed is simply and solely such an expedi-
tion. Sometimes a mortal has the advantage of a supernatural being, as we have seen is the case in the riddling
ballads. The same thing is true of *Lady Isabel and the
Elf-Knight* (4), in which the lady by her wiles managed
to kill the monster into whose power she had fallen. Her
luck was better than that of the hero of *Clerk Colvill* (42),
who was killed by the mermaid with whom he had un-
wisely entered into relations. Equally ill-omened was the
love-affair chronicled in *The Great Silkie of Sule Skerry*
(113) between a mortal woman and a selchie, or seal,
who was a merman.[1] The selchie took their child with
him into the sea and was later shot by a ' gey good
gunner ', who had meanwhile married the woman.

A happier set of stories are those that deal with unspelling and rescues from wizardry. *Willie's Lady* (6)
tells how a wicked mother-in-law sought to obstruct the
delivery of the heroine, but was eventually baffled, under
the direction of Belly Blind—evidently a household spirit
—by counter-spells of superior force.

> And now he's gotten a bonny young son,
> And mickle grace be him upon.

[1] A version printed by F. Sidgwick, *Popular Ballads*, 2nd ser., pp. 235–7,
gives the story much more clearly than does Child's.

In *The Laily Worm and the Machrel of the Sea* (36) the father of the enchanted son and daughter compels the evil stepmother to restore them to their proper shape. *Kemp Owyne* (34) narrates the heroism of the king's son who dares kiss three times a horrible sea-monster, thus undoing a spell (again worked by a stepmother) and bringing back to her rightful form 'as fair a woman as fair could be'. The very beautiful and appealing *Allison Gross* (35) emphasizes equally the enchantment accomplished by the witch and the release of the man by the Queen of the Fairies from his hateful bondage—a feature not found elsewhere in northern tradition. The Fairy Queen plays a different role in *Tam Lin* (39), for the fairy folk have bewitched the heroine's lover, who is saved at the last because she holds him in her arms while he turns into a succession of terrifying shapes. In *The Earl of Mar's Daughter* (270), finally, the lover is a dove by day and a young man by night, having been bespelled by his mother. Only after living with his lady for seven years is he compelled, on the advent of another wooer, to carry her away to his own land.

Some ballads are ghost stories. In *The Cruel Mother* (20) the woman is haunted by the babes she has slain, and in *Proud Lady Margaret* (47) a brother returns to warn his sister against pride. Such monitory ghosts are surpassed by the ghost, or vampire, whatever she may be, who meets the hero of *Willie's Fatal Visit* (255) and rates him soundly for his sinful life, before tearing him to bits. Seldom is a supernatural visitant so inane as the creature in *The Knight's Ghost* (265), who comforts his widow indeed by telling her that she shall join him in heaven, but tactlessly adds that in the meantime she will remarry and have nine children! There is exquisite poignancy, on the other hand, in *The Unquiet Grave* (78), which shows that the lover cannot rest in his grave because of the excessive grief of his mistress.

> You crave one kiss of my clay-cold lips;
>> But my breath smells earthy strong;
> If you have one kiss of my clay-cold lips,
>> Your time will not be long.

Somewhat similar is *The Wife of Usher's Well* (79), although the mother who has lost her three sons does not, except in weakened versions, either pray for their return or bring them back by excessive sorrow. There is, rather, a kind of pagan spell about her words in that most famous variant which we owe to Sir Walter Scott :

> I wish the wind may never cease,
>> Nor fashes in the flood,
> Till my three sons come hame to me,
>> In earthly flesh and blood.

In *Sweet William's Ghost* (77) the dead lover comes back to his mistress to ask that she give him back his ' faith and troth ', since death has separated them.

> Gie me my faith and trouthe again,
>> And let me fare on my way.

His behaviour is very different from that of the other wooer in *James Harris* (*The Daemon Lover*) (243), who returns as a ghost after his beloved has married, and carries her away to a watery death.

> He strack the tap-mast wi his hand,
>> The fore-mast wi his knee,
> And he brake that gallant ship in twain,
>> And sank her in the sea.

It should, however, be added that James Harris, though rationalized as a sailor, must have been a devil when first conceived. One of the most appealing of all these ghost stories is *The Suffolk Miracle* (272), of which there is unfortunately no version in English with poetic merit. When the lover appears to his betrothed, who has not heard of his death, she does not suspect from anything about him that he is a ghost, and rides away with him without question. The humanity of this puts it into a very special category.

The intelligent behaviour of ships, whether helpful to human beings or malevolent, is the only other superstition that serves as the theme of a ballad. Perhaps it is going too far, indeed, to say that the 'comely coug' in *Young Allan* (245), which responds so nobly to the promise of gold, furnishes a plot; but certainly we are led to understand that the efforts of the ship saved the crew alive. There can be no hesitation about *Bonnie Annie* (24) and *Brown Robyn's Confession* (57). In each case a ship definitely misbehaves out of repugnance to the sinfulness of a passenger, who has to be thrown overboard accordingly.

In reviewing the range of ballad material, as we have been doing, we ought in conclusion to observe that certain themes common in fiction and drama are either wholly absent or little stressed. Filial ingratitude, for example, does not appear as a motive, or the jealousy that age feels of youth. Just why there should be this particular omission I do not know, or why avarice should not be used as an impelling force, since stories based upon these weaknesses of human nature are very ancient. It is easier to understand why vaulting ambition should not come in, and why tales of doubt and hesitation do not occur. The folk who have sung ballads for a long while past, at least, have been simple of mind and station. Action, for them, has been limited by circumstance, but it has not been inhibited by 'thinking too precisely on the event'. Apparently they have seldom been moved to envy of their betters, since envy is not a motive used. Personal jealousy, like personal pride, is common enough; but dissatisfaction with the scheme of things does not appear. Even the outlaws object only to injustices of administration. Similarly absent are tales of discouragement and failure : man's reach is not beyond his grasp, and he accepts without repining whatever comes. Sloth, which gave the medieval church such concern, has not troubled the ballad-singer, perhaps because the sin does not lend itself to dramatic incident.   Another conspicuous omission is of stories that turn on sacrifice for the sake of persons outside family or clan. There are plenty of heroic deeds, but they are prompted either by self-interest or by devotion to some one within a narrow circle.   Quite as we should expect, the ballad-makers have not been interested in drama which recognizes man's relationship to humanity in the mass. They are the work of people whose knowledge of the world has usually been limited to the parish or the county, and they show men acting either individually or in small groups—seldom with consciousness of anything beyond. The range of their themes reveals to us the preoccupations, emotional and intellectual, of common folk during the past few centuries. This in itself would warrant the collection and study of them as social documents. Fortunately they are much more than that, as we must never forget : they are narrative poetry, and they are music.

Chapter Four

BALLAD TUNES

SINCE ballads of the traditional sort were first collected and popularized by scholars whose chief interest was poetical and antiquarian, it is not strange that ballad tunes were long neglected. Bishop Percy was well aware that the minstrels, to whom he devoted an introductory essay in the *Reliques of Ancient Poetry*, had harps and chanted to that accompaniment, but he seems to have been wholly incurious as to their music and to have supposed that ballads might quite as well be recited as sung. Indeed, the earlier successors of Percy, who like him were eager compilers and editors rather than collectors at first hand, got their copies of ballads in most cases from the recitation of educated persons, who were able to carry in memory sets of words apart from their melodies. We owe a great debt to Mrs. Brown, at Falkland, who could both repeat the text of ballads and sing the tunes of many of them ; but obviously the editors who profited in the first instance by her memory cared very little about the melodies she knew. Scott in 1802–3 and Jamieson in 1806 published none, although Ritson between 1783 and 1794 had printed a certain number of airs in his compilations. Ritson, indeed, appears to have been the only one of the early editors who was aware of the importance of melody to the study of ballads. In retrospect, it does seem at first sight unaccountable that Sir Walter Scott should not have recognized how closely dependent on one another are words and music; but this is to be wise after the event.

At the end of the eighteenth century, and during the earlier part of the nineteenth, scholars and men of letters had but newly grasped the fact that in folk-poetry there existed treasures of great aesthetic and antiquarian value. Upon this their minds were engaged. We cannot rightly blame them for not seeing that James Johnson, who began the publication of *The Scots Musical Museum* in 1787, was doing after his own fashion something of equal importance. His aim was a practical one : to preserve and disseminate the popular songs of his country, no matter what their origin or their character. The enthusiasm of Percy and his successors was for the romantic past. Only Ritson seems to have had any inkling that folk-melodies were worthy of serious study, and he was not the kind of man to recommend his personal discoveries to his contemporaries, for his manners were inferior to his scholarship. Scott and his friends, like the men of similar mind on the Continent, were satisfied with the rich mine of poetry they had opened. In the state of musical studies at the time, furthermore, it could not have been expected that the importance of folk-melody would be understood.

Only very gradually, indeed, did the artistic worth of the musical accompaniment of folk-song come to be understood. Long after drawing-rooms and concert-halls were resounding with sentimentalized and enfeebled arrangements of traditional airs, long after composers had learned to look for inspiration to snatches of folk-song, the proper and methodical collection of melodies from the lips of singers was delayed, and consequently any adequate study was impossible. In Germany and Denmark the necessity for such collecting and investigation was understood much earlier than in English-speaking lands, but rather by professional musicians than by students of the ballad. Grundtvig, it is clear, had no notion that anything greatly mattered except the words when, in 1852, he began to publish his magnificent *Danmarks gamle Folkeviser*, which was to become a model for all countries as a collection of texts.

As for England, a historian of music could write,[1] as late as 1879 : ' It seems rather singular that England should not possess any printed collection of its national songs with the airs as they are sung at the present day; while almost every other European nation possesses several comprehensive works of this kind.' He went on to say that the opinion, held by some, that ' the country people of England are not in the habit of singing . . . would probably be found to be only partially correct if search were made in the proper places '. When such ignorance of the real state of things could be shown by a man so enthusiastic and so learned as was Engel, poetry-lovers can be forgiven for having continued to neglect melodies, or to give them very secondary consideration. What slight attention was paid to ballad music down to the very end of the nineteenth century is fairly indicated by the few pages devoted to it in Child's monumental *English and Scottish Ballads*. Indefatigable in industry and omnivorously curious about everything concerned with balladry as he was, that great editor provided an ' index of published airs ' and appended fifty-five tunes, or variants of tunes, from manuscript sources ; but this was all by way of appendix. The thing that mattered to him —the ballad itself—was still the text, just as had been the case a century earlier.

Deplorable though it is that ballad tunes were not collected from singers while the art was still in its best estate, we may take what comfort we can from the knowledge that most of the earlier notation of the songs was inadequate, and gave a false impression of the music. Collectors of airs were even slower than collectors of texts in learning that only what the singer uttered should be set down, and, withal, precisely what the singer uttered. The late Cecil Sharp, who did more to promote the study and understanding of English folk-song than any other

[1] C. Engel, *The Literature of National Music*, p. 32.

man who has worked in the field, wrote in 1907 as
follows :[1] 'In conclusion, we must once again warn the
student of folk-song not to search for his material amongst
the printed and manuscript music of the past, nor in the
numerous collections of "Old English Songs". He must
either go direct to the peasant singers themselves, or
to those publications which contain songs that have been
taken down from their lips by competent musicians.' In
an appendix Sharp listed [2] seventeen publications which
he regarded as fulfilling the conditions he had laid down,
among them being the three volumes at that time issued
of the *Journal of the Folk-Song Society*. The complete
adequacy of his list is of no moment, nor the fact that he
included only one volume with songs from Scottish
sources. What is noteworthy is this: that with the exception of a little group of Sussex songs privately printed
for John Broadwood in 1843, he saw fit to pass as representing the actualities of folk-song no volume issued
before 1877, and that most of the volumes he mentioned
were published after 1890. Nothing could demonstrate
more clearly how belated were the attempts to collect and
to set down truthfully the music of ballads, as well as
other folk-songs.

Sharp's own herculean labours until his death in 1923,
which are comparable only with those of Child in editing
the texts of ballads, together with the almost equally remarkable work of Miss Lucy Broadwood and other devoted enthusiasts on both sides of the Atlantic, have gone
far during the past forty years to make good the neglect
of earlier generations. They have shown that the ballad,
far from being dead, has lived on into the age of news-
papers and widespread primary education. Probably the
collectors have had the good fortune to catch the last
generation of English and Scottish ballad-singers with

[1] *English Folk-Song: Some Conclusions*, 1907, p. 118.
[2] *Op. cit.*, pp. 142–3.

whom the art can be wholly traditional, since even twenty-five years ago the singers were chiefly old men and women ; and no doubt the mountaineers, the maritime folk, and the Negroes of the United States and Canada will forget their ballad-singing ere long ; yet even now it cannot be said with truth—so surprising have been the discoveries during the past three decades—that ballad-singing is a ' lost art ', as Professor Kittredge wrote of it[1] twenty-five years ago. Moribund it is, but it has survived long enough to furnish a great body of material for study. Without attempting to reckon the precise amount of this, and without comparing it with the ballad-music collected in other lands, one can say unhesitatingly that it not only demonstrates the unity of melody and words in folk-song, but furnishes a rich harvest of tunes to set beside the poetry that has been garnered during the last century and a half.

One may reasonably question, however, whether this body of music that has escaped oblivion by so slight a margin of time represents the art at its best in any adequate way. We know that ballad verse, for instance, has deteriorated in the past seventy-five years. What has happened to it will be shown in a later chapter. Comparatively few of the variants collected during the last fifty years are so good, from the point of view of the poetry lover, as the average of the better versions gathered from oral circulation a century and more ago. May it not be that the melodies have suffered in similar fashion, and for similar reasons ?

To this question it is impossible to give an answer with absolute certainty. It is easy enough to say, and undeniably true, that the tunes collected in our day on both sides of the Atlantic are more interesting than those of earlier record ; but it is not at all fair to compare the two, since all competent musicians agree that the notation

[1] Sargent and Kittredge, *English and Scottish Popular Ballads*, p. xiii.

of the older specimens was very faulty. Beauty evaporated in the process, no doubt, just as it disappeared in the texts that Percy and his successors sought to 'improve'. Yet the probability is that melodies have suffered very much less in the last hundred years than have ballad texts. The conclusion of Cecil Sharp about this may well be quoted, since it was the matured opinion of a man with the widest experience and the soundest taste: 'The causes, whatever they may have been, which led to the decadence of the words have, happily, operated upon the tunes to a much smaller extent.'[1] More recent studies, particularly in connexion with melodies preserved in America, appear to confirm this judgement. Even though we cannot be quite sure, there is every reason to believe that ballad tunes have kept up to our own day the qualities that so moved Sir Philip Sidney when he heard ' the old song of Percy and Duglas '.

There is evidence for this, certainly, in the state of the ballads collected in such extraordinary numbers among our American mountaineers. Very seldom do the words have the magic of phrase and of subtle rhythm that is characteristic of the ballad at its best. Structurally they are often very good, by which I mean that the stories are well told, but the texture of the verse is in general rather thin and poor. The melodies, on the other hand, are often exceedingly beautiful, and so multiform in their variations that one cannot fail to see in them the traditional art of the singer unaffected by passage of time or pioneer emigration. It is as if uprooting the stock from the old country and moving about from place to place before it came to rest, subjecting it to new experiences and a strange environment, had greatly injured taste and the power of good individual variation, as far as the words are concerned, whereas the art of musical accompaniment, less easily affected by new influences,

[1] Sharp, *op. cit.*, pp. 120-1.

had kept the qualities developed by many generations of singers on the other side of the sea.

American tunes, moreover, as we shall have occasion to notice in another connexion, appear to be somewhat more archaic in their technique than the English melodies gathered of late years. That is, the prevalence of hexatonic and pentatonic scales, and of irregular time, indicates that the singers have been extremely conservative in carrying on the musical tradition brought to this country by their ancestors. Yet the English tunes have equal beauty, though following a somewhat newer fashion, and they are of course often close variants of the melodies found in America. In short, neither from Great Britain nor from the United States is there evidence of any deterioration in ballad music during the past century and a half. Changes there have been, to be sure, for neither poetry nor musical phrase continues unvaried in oral tradition, but no degeneration that need make us regret too sharply the neglect of British and American folk-song until the close of the nineteenth century.

In studying the music of ballads, a matter of primary importance is the relationship of the tune to the verse. Ballads are narrative poems with well-defined characteristics, as we have seen, yet they are also songs. The melody is as indispensable as the words. One might suppose that they would therefore be inseparable, a given tune for ever mated with a given poem, and that the music would come first in the estimation of the singer. All the evidence, however, runs counter to this, which will not surprise us when we remember why ballads have been made and sung. They are stories, after all, though stories narrated in rhythmic patterns and, I believe, moulded to a very marked degree by the musical accompaniment to which they have been set. They are stories, and are sung as stories, which explains why their melodies are usually subordinated to the words, and why close variants of the same ballad are found to have completely different tunes.

The case has been admirably stated thus by an experienced collector: ' Habitual singers of these songs do not regard them merely, or even mainly, as music. They often cannot hum the air without the words.... All this points to the fact that in folk-songs the music has always been a mere vehicle for the words.' [1] This was written about English singers, but there is testimony to the same effect from other races. Scotch Highlanders are said to be ' frequently almost unaware what tune they are using '.[2] Tiersot, whose experience with French folk-song was both intimate and profound, puts it that the melody remains ' subordinated to the poetry, from which it takes its form '.[3] The statement of Sharp, made after hearing both English and American singers, seems to be true everywhere : ' So far as I have been able to comprehend his (that is, the singer's) mental attitude, I gather that, when singing a ballad, for instance, he is merely relating a story in a peculiarly effective way which he has learned from his elders, his conscious attention being wholly concentrated upon what he is singing.' [4]

Under conditions such as these, it is not strange that the same ballad should be sung to more than one tune. The individual singer ordinarily knows but one melody for each of the ballads in his repertory, and the same tune is sung to the same words over very wide areas; yet

[1] B. M. Cra'ster, *J. F.-S. S.* iv. 76 (1910).

[2] L. E. Broadwood, *op. cit.* iv, no. 16, ix (1911).

[3] J. Tiersot, *Histoire de la chanson populaire en France*, 1889, p. 324.

[4] Campbell and Sharp, *English Folk-Songs from the Southern Appalachians*, 1917, p. x. Alexander Keith in Greig, *Last Leaves of Traditional Ballads*, 1925, pp. xlii–xliii, reports that Greig found singers ' who used their melodies as an aid to the recollection of their ballads', and disputes the conclusions of Sharp. It appears, however, that Greig's experience was really not very different from that of other collectors. Keith concludes that 'folk-poetry and folk-music are essentially and intimately related', which is the main point. The mating of words and melody is not indissoluble, though it is indispensable.

singers living only a few miles apart may have completely different airs for slightly varying sets of words. One cause for this state of things, where it occurs among folk to whom printed ballads have penetrated—and in one way or another the dissemination of such pieces has been very widespread—is undoubtedly the use of tunes already learned traditionally for words that have come to the singers through some one's reading. A broadside ballad, if it got into oral circulation, as many such uninspired poems certainly did, might be sung to any air that happened to fit it; it might be used with half a dozen different airs perhaps, in spite of the directions at the top that it should be sung to the tune of so-and-so. A good example of this is *The Golden Vanity* (286), which without much doubt began its career as the invention of some broadside writer, and is sung to several distinct melodies.[1] There need be no question that the tunes are traditional, as the words have long come to be, and quite possibly some of them far antedate the words of the ballad, though that is a matter about which there is no evidence.

Another reason, however, why different airs are found for the same ballad is the variation that constantly takes place in the melodies themselves. They are no more static than the verse—less so, indeed, since the individual singer is much more likely to change musical phrases than the words with which he is familiar. Probably the blind man in Somerset, of whom Sharp wrote,[2] was exceptional in this, as he was in other respects, but he furnishes an admirable illustration of what may happen. 'He will habitually vary every phrase of his tune in the course of a ballad. I remember that in the first song that he sang to me he varied the first phrase of the second verse. I asked him to repeat the verse that I might note the variation. He at once gave me a third form of the same phrase.'

[1] See P. Barry, *J. A. F.-L.* xxiii. 445 (1910).
English Folk-Song: Some Conclusions, p. 21.

Although it is true that folk-singers are amazingly accurate in the reproduction of tunes they have learned,[1] and will sometimes sing a melody identical in every note with one recorded from the lips of another singer, the general rule is quite different. Identical copies are rare, as is becoming more and more evident with the latter-day multiplication of records; and variations are infinitely diverse. Quite apart from changes of phrase, what is essentially the same melody may be sung with differences of time and of scale. In short, there is no more fixation of tune than there is of verbal phrase. Just as in the case of the words, each copy of an air is likely to be a variant, and the variants in turn can be grouped in more widely differing sets, which are still versions of the same tune.[2]

When we say versions of the same tune, however, we cannot mean, if we are thinking clearly, that the multiform variants are departures from a fixed standard. Each variant, though one may be very interesting and one very unimpressive, has the same authenticity as every other. The melody exists in all of them alike. Not that it is a composite of the versions, for the changes introduced are often far too many and too delicate even to be codified and catalogued.[3] It is rather more like a botanical species, though the comparison is of course inexact. The status of these melodic variants is precisely like that of the sets of words that constitute a ballad, each one, as we shall see, a variant and each one as authoritative as any other. It would not matter though the melody, in a given case, could be proved to go back to a tune composed by some one trained in conscious art, which had strayed into oral tradition:[4] the variants would be of the same sort and

[1] See, for instance, the case recorded by Sharp, *op. cit.*, p. 17.

[2] See the valuable study of *Lord Randal* by Barry, *J. A. F.-L.* xxiii. 443–4 (1910).

[3] See G. O. Arlt, *Modern Philology*, xxvii. 147–54 (1929).

[4] See J. Meier, *Kuntslied in Volksmunde*, 1906, pp. 18–32; C. Engel, *An Introduction to the Study of National Music*, 1866, pp. 12–18.

would have the same standing as the variants of a tune developed by folk-singers unaware of any theory or any rules. Slowly, phrase by phrase, there would be such alteration that the original tune might wholly disappear.

Though the origin of melodies may be diverse, there can be no doubt, I think, that one source of them is precisely this: variation carried so far that nothing is left of the tune that was, and the birth of an entirely new air, which in turn becomes subject to change. Thus certain ballads may well be sung to different melodies because the tune originally attached to them has varied itself out of existence. Such was the conclusion of Tiersot about French folk-songs. 'Sometimes the alterations are so many that only a little fragment of the first version remains; and if this fragment disappears in turn, who will say whether the melody so formed comes from a primitive type or whether it has been independently composed?'[1] We cannot be certain in a given case that alteration so complete as this has taken place, but we can follow a tune through its variations up to the point of disappearance, which makes the transmutation satisfactorily clear.

It must not be thought that the variations we have been discussing are wholly fortuitous—mere whimsies on the part of individual singers. Sharp summed up the causes for such changes as five,[2] to which may perhaps be added a sixth of at least equal importance. Some gifted singers, he shows, constantly invent new phrases, much as a schooled musician composes, only more spontaneously and unconsciously, thus furnishing fresh material for selection by more conservative performers. The bold variations of such men appear to be made without forethought and ordinarily to be unremembered, much as suggestions come into the mind of the writer of imaginative

[1] *Op. cit.*, p. 358.   [2] *Op. cit.*, pp. 23–8.

literature or of the composer while at work, who then selects from among the possibilities the one that seems to him best. The inventive folk-singer does not consciously select: his is music of the moment, and he is careless of survival. But some at least of his changes are sure to win the approval of others. When they do so, and are adopted by his neighbours, new versions of melodies get into circulation all at once.

Most variations, however, are less striking. They may be due to a love of ornament, which finds its expression in trills and turns, though English singers are less inclined to such embellishment than the Irish, for example, or the Scottish Highlanders.[1] They may be due to a change of mode, since some singers have a fondness for a particular mode and make free transpositions of tunes accordingly, with resulting alterations in cadence. Again, the adaptation of a familiar air to a new set of words is almost certain to bring about changes, either because of slight metrical differences or differences in feeling that demand musical expression. Or the faulty memory of a singer may lead him to substitute verbal changes that are metrically irregular and require him to invent musical phrases to correspond, which often produces interesting variations in the melody. Last of all, and not mentioned by Sharp, any change in the words of a ballad, even though it does not involve irregularities of rhythm but merely a shift of phrase within the limits of the pattern, is sure to produce some variation in the melody, since, as we have seen, the air is a musical accompaniment and must respond to the cadences of the verse.

Ballad airs, like all folk-song, are thus ever shifting, ever renewing themselves. They may be exceedingly old, since oral memory is powerful and sometimes clings to far-off things with amazing tenacity. They may, on the other hand, resolve themselves through bewildering com-

[1] *J. F.-S. S.* iii. 3–38 (1908).

plexities into something quite different from what they were in earlier times. Even less easily than the words of ballads can they be dated, because they contain no allusions to event or custom. Whatever their date, however, the art they represent is assuredly an old one, the unconscious product of countless generations of singers, who developed both invention and taste while they sang. Only on this assumption can one explain the continuance of the power of excellent variation down to the present day. If folk-song were the mere wreckage of such music as was formerly composed by the sophisticated and literate, the collectors of our time might indeed have found beautiful things; but they would certainly not have found beautiful things in the making, variants so good that they deserve perpetuation, melodies so much alive that they are still leading singers to experiment and change.

The art is still alive, though surely moribund; and we know that it is old because it still preserves patterns and technical means discarded by musicians of the schools with the development of harmony at the end of the sixteenth century. On this account the folk-songs collected in America are of the very greatest importance, since they are prevailingly more archaic in form than those found in Great Britain.

It must be borne in mind, to begin with, that folk-music is made upon a variety of scales rather than in the two modes, major and minor, which are used in modern music. The minor is indeed found very infrequently, as evidence not only from Great Britain and America, but from continental countries as well, goes to show. The notion that such 'plaintive numbers' as those Wordsworth heard from the lips of the Highland girl were in the minor key is a popular error to be discarded. The major scale is employed much more often than any other in England, but only as one of five modes which have equal standing, though used with varying frequency. The mountain singers of America, on the other hand, avoid the major scale for the most part and indeed add a sixth mode to the possibilities. According to Sharp's testimony,[1] they do not for the most part employ a seven-note scale at all, but one of five or six notes, with either two or one of the semitones omitted. Such 'gapped' scales, while common in Gaelic music, have been encountered with relative infrequency among Lowland Scottish and English singers.

The nature of the modes[2] may best be understood by beginning with the diatonic scale, which may be heard by playing the white notes of a piano. In going from any note to its octave above, we pass through a series of seven unequal intervals. This succession of so-called natural notes is an octave of the diatonic scale, and each octave consists of five tones and two semitones. The position of the semitones will of course vary from octave to octave, depending on the note with which we begin; but every octave will include five full tones and two semitones.

A mode is a scale based upon one of these natural notes as its tonic, and the tonic must be felt throughout a melody that is composed in a given mode. Generally speaking, the tonic stands at the conclusion of the tune. Since there are seven natural notes, A to G, each of which may be used as a tonic, there are seven modes, which are named from their supposed accordance with the musical system of Greece, although Greek music, using the tetrachord rather than the octave as the unit of its scale, had nothing quite like them. The names themselves date from the sixteenth century only. Modal music, as we

---

[1] Campbell and Sharp, *English Folk-Songs from the Southern Appalachians*, 1917, p. xv.

[2] A clear explanation of these matters is given by William Pole in Grove's *Dictionary of Music, sub* 'Scale'. If read in connexion with this article, Sharp's chapter in *English Folk-Song: Some Conclusions*, pp. 36–53, will be better understood.

know it, appears to have been a development of the earlier Middle Ages and to have been connected with the rise of plain-song, although the latter took a course of its own, branching out into complexities that do not concern us.

Each mode is distinguished by the points at which the semitones occur, whereby it possesses a character of its own, for the sequence of intervals varies from mode to mode. Let us begin with the Dorian, with D as its tonic:

In this the semitones fall between the second and third and between the sixth and seventh notes. The Phrygian mode has E as its tonic, with the semitones falling between the first and second and between the fifth and sixth notes. And so on. The Lydian has the tonic of F, the Mixolydian of G, the Æolian of A, the Locrian of B, and the Ionian of C. The last named is of course the major scale of modern music, while the Æolian has affinities with the minor scale, though the two should not be confused.

Of these modes, English singers use the Ionian prevailingly, as I have said, but employ as well the Æolian, the Dorian, the Mixolydian, and—rarely—the Phrygian. Among American singers the Lydian has also been found. As already intimated, however, the thing that shows most clearly what traditional conservatism has prevailed in the folk-music on this side of the Atlantic is the existence of 'gapped' scales. Without going into the question as to whether scales omitting one or both of the semitones everywhere preceded the heptatonic, we can be assured that they are technically more primitive than the latter and quite inexplicable as a phenomenon of degeneration. In other words, American folk-singers use five- and six-tone scales because their ancestors were accustomed to sing after that fashion, and they have been satisfied to follow in the old ways.

An admirably clear explanation of the pentatonic and hexatonic systems has been given by Sharp,[1] to which the reader may be referred. It should perhaps be said for the benefit of those who have never observed the tunes made on these scales that the lack of the semitones does not imply musical poverty. A pentatonic variant of a ballad melody may be quite as delightful an accompaniment as one in which all the tones of the octave appear. The same tune, we must remember, may be sung in different versions according to different modes; and it may sometimes be hexatonic, sometimes pentatonic, and sometime heptatonic. This is quite at the option of the singer, who, without being aware of musical terms or musical technicalities, knows by his inherited art how to transpose from key to key and from scale to scale.

One further phenomenon of folk-music must be mentioned before we pass on to an examination of ballad texts. This is the mixed time in which melodies are often sung. A tune will sometimes begin in 3/2 time, for example, will change to 2/2, will switch back to 3/2, and will end with 2/2. Or sometimes a single measure of irregular length occurs. As Sharp remarked,[2] this habit, which makes some melodies look less simple and natural when set down on paper than they really are, serves the same purpose as the irregular barring to which the modern composer has recourse on occasion. Traces of the practice have been found in German dance melodies and in Danish ballads,[3] while it is apparently as common in France[4] as

[1] Campbell and Sharp, *op. cit.*, pp. xv–xviii.

[2] *English Folk-Song: Some Conclusions*, pp. 81–2.

[3] See J. C. H. R. Steenstrup, *The Medieval Popular Ballad*, trans. E. G. Cox, 1914, pp. 165–6. Steenstrup recognized the importance of the phenomenon with reference to verse.

[4] See J. Tiersot, *op. cit.*, p. 334.

among people of British stock. It is also a well-known phenomenon in the music of so-called primitive races.[1] As we shall see in connexion with the rhythm of ballad poetry, the matter is of considerable importance and deserves more thorough investigation than has yet been given it.

Indeed, an adequate account of folk-music in its relations with folk-poetry cannot yet be written, because at so many points where the two impinge upon one another there is need of further study by scholars with a technical knowledge of music such as I, unfortunately, do not possess. In this brief chapter I have tried to do no more than sketch the elementary facts about ballad tunes and to stress their importance for an understanding of the subject.

[1] See, for example, W. Matthews, *Navaho Legends*, 1897, p. 255, in a note by J. C. Fillmore.

Chapter Five

BALLAD CHARACTERISTICS

IT is time for us to turn from the stories embodied in our English and Scottish ballads, and from the melodies that accompany them, to the texts themselves. We must see what distinguishing characteristics they have as narrative poems, what peculiar qualities of structure and texture give them their place apart. We have already discovered that they share with the ballads of other lands, some of which are close relatives, certain ways of story-telling that enable us to define them as a *genre*. All European ballads seem to be marked by a tendency to focus the tale on a central situation, and to relate it in terms of dramatic action, as a rule quite objectively and impersonally. By such habits of narrative we recognize their kinship, even when both in theme and manner they have otherwise little in common.

In a particular examination of British ballads we must, of course, bear in mind these general characteristics, and indeed scrutinize them more closely, in order to see just what they have to do with the effect, so easy to recognize, so difficult to analyse, and so impossible for the sophisticated poet to imitate, that we may call the ballad style. We shall find, however, other qualities of structure and poetic handling which have to be studied with equal care, although they appear with less complete regularity. Some of these conventions are by no means confined to the balladry of Great Britain, but can be found in the narrative songs of various other countries as well, some are more peculiarly products of the traditional art of England, Scotland, and their immediate neighbours. In establishing our ideas of the ballad on its formal side, we shall do well to consider all well-marked characteristics, whether they appear quite generally over a wide area, or whether they are more fluctuating and more limited geographically. In defining a *genre* we may safely disregard whatever is peculiar to this or that specimen or group, but in the description of it we have to take into account all the phenomena that are available.

With this in view, we must resist the temptation to set up an *eidolon* of the ballad, fashioning it according to our preconceived notions and ignoring or minimizing whatever does not square with them. We have no right to say, of songs which have obviously been a century or two in oral circulation, that this one has the proper hall-mark and that one is base metal—if not altogether spurious. Any specimen culled from printed sources, whether from a broadside or from a collection made in the days before editors learned to leave their texts 'unimproved', is to some degree suspect, to be sure, because we can never be quite certain to what extent we have the words as they were actually sung; and folk-memory sometimes operates so well that a wretched poetaster's verses may survive some generations of singing with comparatively slight changes. Our material must accordingly often be used with great caution. Yet we must, I repeat, look with unprejudiced eyes at everything that has the warrant of tradition behind it, whether or not it seems to us 'good' according to any theory of origins or our sophisticated standards of aesthetic taste. If we do otherwise, we shall run grave risks of suppressing evidence and of finding ourselves in a hopeless bog.

I. BALLAD STRUCTURE

It is not safe to argue, for example, that those ballads which seem to point back to beginnings in chorus and dance are the most authentic and ancient, for among the eighty or ninety specimens in Child that carry out the action almost wholly through dialogue a good many cannot have been made before the sixteenth or seventeenth century.[1] In other words, this method of telling a story was a continuing fashion in balladry, and should be so considered, irrespective of the question of choric origins which we must in due course consider. Before trying to decide how ballads took their rise in a somewhat distant past, we must see what they became in process of time— what their attributes have been since they began to fall into the hands of collectors.

It will be well for us to look, first of all, at the tendency, already remarked, to focus a story on a central situation, which is a phenomenon common throughout Europe. This means something more, I believe, than a lack of ability on the part of untutored poets to tell a long story in verse. Everything goes to show, as a matter of fact, that long verse narratives have developed early among all peoples. The epic is admittedly the most ancient of literary *genres*, and the epic is something with a large canvas. The ballad, on the other hand, wherever we find it, is concentrated; the action is so massed that we do not get the effect of a skeletonized long story, but of a unified short story, a story complete in itself, not infrequently implying events before and after but always fairly well centred on a single main event. Whatever be the truth about the way epics developed, the manner of presenting a tale in the ballad is different, and it has persisted through the centuries down to our own time. Art of a sort there must be in this, an art of structure, no matter how unconsciously acquired.

It is not enough to say that ballads have had to be short in order to keep the attention of listeners, and have therefore become forcible and vigorous, for some of them have

[1] See *Northumberland Betrayed by Douglas* (176), *Captain Car* (178), *King James and Brown* (180), *The Death of Parcy Reed* (193), *Lord Maxwell's Last Goodnight* (195), *The Gypsy Laddie* (200), *The Baron of Brackley* (203), *Loudon Hill* (205), *Lord Derwentwater* (208), *Richie Story* (232), *Andrew Lammie* (233), *The Baron o Leys* (241).

been popular though ungainly in structure and longer than need be. Concentration of emphasis is the rule, however, and their most captivating attribute as stories. That the habit of fitting them to melodies, or of fitting tunes to verses—put it how you will—has had much to do with this concentration of emphasis cannot well be doubted. Neither in Great Britain nor in any other European country, so far as I know, are ballads sung to a non-melodic accompaniment; and there is accordingly a constant repetition of the tune. Generally speaking, though not invariably, the melody of our ballads terminates with each stanza, beginning again with the next stanza. The musical form is lyrical; it is a song. Under such conditions the tendency to focus the story rather sharply on some central point is easy to explain. A sweep and flow of narrative is held in check by the musical iteration. In order to get the story told at all, it has to be told at not too great length; and in order to get it told effectively, non-essentials have to be eliminated. The nature of his musical setting has forced the folk-singer, in other words, into habits of narrative to which Boccaccio and Chaucer and Maupassant attained, being men of genius, by trying along the lines of literary tradition to make the most of their story material. More or less successfully, the story in our ballads is concentrated about a single situation, and as little else is told as may be.

The centralization, as well as certain other structural qualities, can be seen in *Johnie Cock* (114). In nearly all the versions the story begins with the morning of the hero's fatal hunt. Let us look at the well-known copy sent to Percy by Miss Fisher of Carlisle in 1780 (A). Johnnie's mother, afraid of what the seven foresters of Pickeram may do, begs him to stay at home. Keener than ever for the warning, he goes out and pursues the 'good dun deer' to the death, whereupon he and his hounds gorge themselves on the flesh and the blood, and fall asleep. An unexplained and inexplicable palmer (or an equally intrusive old man, in half a dozen of the variants) hastens to tell the seven foresters, who recognize Johnnie from the description they get. The resulting fight is amazingly syncopated, yet very vivid:

> O the first y stroke that they gae him,
>   They struck him off by the knee;
> Then up bespake his sister's son:
>   'O the next'll gar him die!'

Like the pilgrim, this nephew (who appears in two other versions, with traces in a third: D, E, H) is quite unexplained. There follow three stanzas of defiance, stirring and yet pathetic, after which:

> He has killd the Seven Forsters,
>   He has killd them all but ane,
> And that wan scarce to Pickeram Side,
>   To carry the bode-words hame.

Two stanzas more complete the ballad. First Johnnie speaks:

> 'Is there never a boy in a' this wood
>   That will tell what I can say;
> That will go to Cockley's Well,
>   Tell my mither to fetch me away?'

> There was a boy into that wood,
>   That carried the tidings away,
> And many ae was the well-wight man
>   At the fetching o Johny away.

All this conveys the effect of continuity because of the extreme swiftness with which events move. Actually the scene shifts at one point from Johnnie to the abode of the seven foresters, but not in such a way as to destroy the unity of the tale. It does not break the unity any more, that is, than does the discontinuous method by which the whole story—like most ballad stories—is presented to us. There is nothing irrelevant, but there is a good deal left unexplained. The events burst out in a series of flashes, each very sharp and each revealing one further step in the action. What lies before and after remains in darkness, and can be learned only by inference. There is unity because the flashes are all directed on what is essential to our imaginative and emotional grasp of a quite simple situation. No method of narration more direct and effective, within its limitations, could be desired. It would not serve for a tale of elaborate action or for one in which subtlety of feeling might be required, but it is excellent in its kind. Imposed by the desire of the unknown makers to tell a straightforward tale, and conditioned by the habit of fashioning that tale in brief stanzas to the accompaniment of a recurrent melody, the art of such poems became the admirable thing it is.

In this process the audience would have its part, for we must not think of the group listening to a ballad as separable in spirit and training from singer or singers. Most of the listeners would themselves have a repertory of songs, and they would certainly be so steeped in the tradition of singing that their approval or disapproval of a ballad's content and form would be effective. Their criticism would doubtless not be expressed in speech; it would more probably result in their subconscious avoidance, in later renditions, of the phrases that offended taste, or in the disappearance of the ballad altogether. The judgement of the group would be final, at least in so far as a particular locality was concerned. But I have never seen any evidence that singers consciously make alterations on account of dissatisfaction felt by themselves or by others.

We may postpone, until we have finished our examination of ballads as they are, any theorizing about how they came into being, and how the art of them developed.

Our present concern is with the qualities they display. It should be obvious to every one that the structural method of such a piece as *Johnie Cock* has merits to which the critic need not condescend. Although the execution may be faulty in some particulars, as is almost always the case in ballads, the method itself merits high praise. This must be strongly emphasized, since even such a stout champion as Gummere [1] conceded that 'the way in which the story is told ... is not narrative art at high pitch'. What I wish to show now is precisely that the basic structure of the ballad does in point of fact show narrative art 'at high pitch', and that this structure depends on the habit of presenting the central situation in such a series of flashes as we have been observing.

The method is apparent in those pieces of the simplest possible construction, like *Riddles Wisely Expounded* (1), *St. Stephen and Herod* (40), *The Maid Freed from the Gallows* (95), *Lord Randal* (12), or *Edward* (13), which consist of a single dialogue. Such ballads have often been used to illustrate theories of communal origin, brilliantly and with discretion by Professor Kittredge,[2] less wisely by some of his followers. *Edward* will serve well as an example of these ballads, which appear at first sight to have no more narrative structure than those other folk-songs—serenades, or *aubades*—which are purely lyrical and altogether static, as far as action goes. Yet every one remembers the fine dramatic quality of *Edward*, not a little of which is preserved even in those American versions which have changed the point of the story, in that they do not implicate the mother in the murder.[3] The version that Lord Hailes sent to Percy (Child B)

---

[1] *The Popular Ballad*, p. 69.

[2] Sargent and Kittredge, *English and Scottish Popular Ballads*, pp. xxv-xxvii.

[3] See Davis, *Traditional Ballads of Virginia*, 1929, pp. 120-4.

does not differ in this respect from the others, though it has a tragic power of its own:

> 'Why dois your brand sae drap wi bluid,
>> Edward, Edward,
> Why dois your brand sae drap wi bluid,
>> And why sae sad gang yee O?'
> 'O I hae killed my hauke sae guid,
>> Mither, mither,
> O I hae killed my hauke sae guid,
>> And I had nae mair bot hee O.'

Each question by the mother and evasive reply by Edward form a separable scene, if one chooses to look at them in that way, and each pair of speeches moves forward towards the terrible and unsuspected conclusion, when the revelation comes that the parricide (or, in other versions, fratricide) was committed with the connivance of the mother. Our progressive enlightenment is accompanied by an increase of emotional tension, which is brought to a climax by the despairing truculence of the hero in the last two stanzas:

> 'And what wul ye leive to your bairns and your wife,
>> Edward, Edward?
> And what wul ye leive to your bairns and your wife,
>> Whan ye gang ovir the sea O?'
> 'The warldis room, late them beg thrae life,
>> Mither, mither,
> The warldis room, late them beg thrae life,
>> For thame nevir mair wul I see O.'
>
> 'And what wul ye leive to your ain mither deir,
>> Edward, Edward,
> And what wul ye leive to your ain mither deir?
>> My deir son, now tell me O.'
> 'The curse of hell frae me sall ye beir,
>> Mither, mither,
> The curse of hell frae me sall ye beir,
>> Sic counseils ye gave to me O.'

Surely this way of telling a story by constantly advancing stages, with nothing said that can be supplied equally well by the imagination, shows art of no mean order. We shall see presently that it has disadvantages, since something left in the deep shadow may occasionally be necessary to a clear understanding of what took place in the light; but we can be sure that a large part of the fascination exercised by ballads on countless generations of illiterate or imperfectly literate country-folk, and equally on newer generations of poetry-lovers, is due in great measure to their narrative structure. They are not formless things, but are formed on a perfectly adequate principle, which is apparently the first law of their being.

Let us look at a couple of specimens, by way of contrast, where dialogue is very little used. *Kemp Owyne* (34 A) will serve for one, grim tale of the supernatural that it is. It begins with two plain stanzas of introduction, which state in almost so many words that Isabel's stepmother, 'the warst woman that ever lived in Christendom', threw her into the sea. The next stanza consists of the stepmother's curse (or boast) that Isabel shall lie there till Kemp Owyne comes over the sea and 'borrows' her with three kisses. Then—

> Her breath grew strang, her hair grew lang,
>   And twisted thrice about the tree,
> And all the people, far and near,
>   Thought that a savage beast was she.

Thus far we have not come to the main situation, but in the very next stanza we meet it. Kemp Owyne, far beyond the sea, heard the news and hastened to look on the savage beast. Everything is foreshortened, that is to say, in order to bring into sharp focus the crucial scene between the rescuer and the horribly enchanted maiden. She utters her challenging invitation to him : ' Come to Craigy's sea, and kiss with me ', offering him in turn a belt, a ring, and a sword, alike invincible. Each time, as he accepts the gift, he kisses her, until with the third kiss:

> Her breath was sweet, her hair grew short,
> > And twisted nane about the tree,
> And smilingly she came about,
> > As fair a woman as fair could be.

Quite as in the case of *Johnie Cock* and *Edward*, the story is not only concentrated on a central episode, but it moves to its appointed end through a series of definitely marked stages. These stages are indicated, it will be observed, as they are in *Edward* but not in *Johnie Cock*, by an interesting rhetorical device for which Gummere coined the apt term 'incremental repetition', making it 'the touchstone and test of original ballad structure'.[1] Into the nature of this repetition we must later examine. I take it to be rather different in kind and in function from what Gummere believed, but I should not wish to minimize in any way the importance of his observations regarding it. In ballads made like *Kemp Owyne* or *Edward* it is certainly structural, quite as Gummere pointed out with reference to *Babylon*,[2] though only because in such cases the stages of progression are accomplished by means of this rhetorical expedient rather than by other devices.

Any such method of story-telling has its disadvantages, as I have suggested above. Vivid and emotionally arresting as are the momentary glimpses or the cumulative speeches out of which the narrative is built up, they furnish little opportunity for explanation. We never learn why Kemp Owyne's name is uttered in the stepmother's curse; we are not told how the summons to action reached the hero; there is no plausible account of the magical objects offered by the bespelled maiden. Such a minor ambiguity as the line about the mermaiden's hair:

> And twisted thrice about the tree,

[1] *The Popular Ballad*, p. 117.   [2] *Op. cit.*, pp. 111-14.

is not organic, but merely one of those sayings half-way between nonsense and high romantic poetry with which folk-verse abounds. Dark spots there are, however, as is the case in most ballad versions, which come of necessity from the attempt to tell a story very briefly, but very vividly in stanzaic form.

We come to our second specimen, which may as well be *Katharine Jaffray* (221), Scott's model for *Lochinvar*. It is a ballad of quite another sort from *Kemp Owyne* : a tale of the Border, with lords and lairds and the manners of a more sophisticated if still rather violent world. The different versions—Child knew twelve, and half a dozen others have since come to light [1]—vary among themselves most interestingly, not simply in detail but in the whole conduct of the story. One of the Aberdeen-shire variants (Greig B) will serve us for analysis. It was learned by the man who sang it, we are told, in the middle of the nineteenth century :

> Lochnagar cam fae the West
> > Into the low countrie,
> An' he had coorted Katharine Jaffray,
> > An' stole her heart away.
>
> Hame he cam, ane Amosdale,
> > Cam fae the north countrie,
> An' he has gained her father's heart,
> > But an' her mother's tee.
>
> A bridal day it then was set,
> > An' the bridal day cam on,
> An' who appeared among the guests
> > But Lochnagar himsel?
>
> A glass was filled o good red wine,
> > Weel drunk between them twa:
> Said he, 'I'll drink wi you, bridegroom,
> > An' syne boun me awa.

---

[1] See Greig, *Last Leaves*, pp. 158–61; Sharp, *English Folk-Songs*, i. 40–1 ; Barry, Eckstorm, and Smyth, *British Ballads from Maine*, pp. 400–6.

'A few words wi your bridesmaiden
  I hope you'll grant me then:
I'm sure before her wedding day
  I would have gotten ten.'

Out spoke then the first groomsman,
  An' an angry man was he,
Says, 'I will keep my bonnie bride
  Until the sun gae tee;

Until the sun gae tee,' he said,
  'Until the sun gae tee,
An' deliver her ower to her bridegroom,
  Which is my duty to dee.'

But he's taen her by the middle jimp,
  An' never stoppit to ca',
He's taen her by the milk-white han'
  An' led her through the ha'.

He leaned him ower his saiddle-bow
  An' kissed her cheek an' chin,
An' then he wissed them a' good nicht,
  An' hoised her on ahin.

He drew a trumpet fae his breist,
  An' blew baith lood an' shrill;
A hunner o weel-airmed men
  Cam Lochnagar until.

A hunner o weel-airmed men,
  Wi milk-white steeds an' grey,
A hunner o weel-airmed men
  Upon his wedding day.

Horsemen rode an' bridesmen ran,
  An' ladies in full speed,
But you wadna hae seen his yellow locks,
  For the dust o his horse' feet.

She turned in the saiddle-bow,
  Addressed her late bridegroom,
Says, 'The compliments I got fae you,
  I'll return them back again.'

> So Katharine Jaffray was mairriet at morn,
> An' she was mairriet at noon;
> She was twice mairriet in ae day,
> Ere she keest aff her goon.

The rivalry of the two suitors is here explained in a couple of undistinguished stanzas, such as we so often find at the beginning of a ballad. At some time or other the usefulness of a bald statement about the situation has been felt, and it has been supplied. Immediately thereafter, however, we reach the bridal day and the real action. Lochnagar drinks with the bridegroom and demands speech of the bride. There follow in our text two stanzas concerned with the best man's intervention, of which there is no hint elsewhere except in one of the versions from Maine.[1] In the next stanza Lochnagar is leading the lady through the hall; in the next he is already mounted, and catches her up behind him; in the next he blows his trumpet to summon his hundred followers. Each, it will be observed, finds the action one step farther on. The method is that of progressive scenes, just as it is in the seemingly more primitive ballads previously examined. There follows, in the next quatrain, one of those purely lyrical passages familiar to the ballad-lover, which add nothing to the tale save feeling, but serve that purpose admirably. Again, in stanzas 12 and 13, there is another swiftly formed picture—as swiftly dissolving— of the chase. The literary critic may regret the banality of the bride's taunt, as she turns in her saddle, but it is justified structurally, for the story needs some such closing scene. Doubtless, too, the sententious final stanza pleased the simple folk whose hearts had been stirred and cheered by what had gone before.

There is another structural quality in ballads, which ought to be considered at this point because it depends, I believe, upon the narrative method we have been

[1] B. P. 404.

observing: that of brief, sharply illuminated scenes or the equivalent of them. Not infrequently a startling effect is produced by ellipsis or under-statement—something that would be accomplished by the conscious artist through rigorous excision. All that is given of the culminating scene of *Sir Patrick Spens* in Percy's famous version (58 A), for instance, is this:

> O our Scots nobles wer richt laith
> To weet their cork-heild schoone;
> Bot lang owre a' the play wer playd,
> Thair hats they swam aboone.

Or consider the simple effectiveness of *Bonnie James Campbell* (210) in any of the extant versions, Scottish or American.[1] We see the gallant gentleman ride out, we see his riderless steed come home, we hear the laments of his sisters or mother and of his wife. That is all, but it suffices to tear the heart. *Willie Macintosh* (183) has the same power, attained by the same means.[2] The two versions of *The Bonny Earl of Murray* (181), which differ so widely from one another that they have only a single stanza in common—the king's speech berating Huntly for killing the earl instead of bringing him in a prisoner—furnish another excellent illustration of what I mean. Neither leaves any doubt as to what took place, yet each does little more than hint at the story. This was one of the ballad characteristics that Keats caught supremely well in composing *La Belle Dame sans Merci*. His genius seized upon the device and made clear for all time the artistic virtue of something the makers and refashioners of folk-poetry doubtless stumbled upon because of the way they were accustomed to sing their tales.

[1] The notes of Mr. Barry in Barry, Eckstorm, and Smyth, *op. cit.*, pp. 279–84, are indispensable for a knowledge of this ballad. His reconstructed version should be noted.

[2] The admirable variant of Scottish origin, collected in New Brunswick, should be studied. See Barry, Eckstorm, and Smyth, *op. cit.*, pp. 264–6.

But it is time for us to turn from such ballads as we have been examining, in which events are very briefly related, to longer pieces. Were their structure fundamentally different, we could not be right in the contention that the first law of balladry is the presentation of a story in a series of clearly marked stages, whether of little scenes or of their equivalent in dialogue. It will not do to lay down a principle like Gummere's 'incremental repetition is the fundamental fact in ballad structure',[1] only to find that in the case of the Robin Hood ballads the principle will not serve.[2] The evidence of chronology is too scanty to enable us to determine what was earlier and what was later; and we have no right to assume that the Robin Hood ballads and their like are 'far gone in epic',[3] simply because their pattern is not in all respects like that of *Babylon* (14) or *The Maid Freed from the Gallows* (95). As a matter of fact, *Judas* (23), which was written down in the thirteenth century and is therefore actually the earliest documentary record we possess by about two centuries, comes as close in structure to *Robin Hood and Guy of Gisborne* (118) or *The Hunting of the Cheviot* (162) as it does to *Edward* or *Lord Randal*. In other words, we must not assume an inner circle of balladry and then exclude from it, because of preconceived theories of origin, some of our most famous specimens.

Let us look first at *Robin Hood and Guy of Gisborne*, which consists of fifty-eight stanzas, beginning with an ominous dream, which Robin tells to Little John. Together they set forth to seek the men who have threatened the outlaw in the dream. They come upon a yeoman clad outlandishly in a horsehide, and Robin is angry with Little John for asking the privilege of accosting the stranger. Up to this point there is nothing unusual in

---

[1] *The Popular Ballad*, p. 125, note 2.
[2] *Op. cit.*, pp. 114-15.   [3] *Op. cit.*, p. 115.

the presentation of the story, for even the description of the man in horsehide can be paralleled in plenty of ballads to which nobody would think of applying the epithet 'minstrel'. The scene then shifts. Robin and John part company on account of their ill-motivated quarrel, and we follow John back to Barnsdale. He finds the band routed by the Sheriff, takes a hand and kills an enemy by a chance shot, but is captured when his bow breaks. Again the scene shifts, this time with a down-right statement which is pure doggerel:

> Let vs leaue talking of Litle Iohn
> For hee is bound fast to a tree,
> And talke of Guy and Robin Hood,
> In the green woode where they bee.

Sir Guy, who has been unnamed hitherto, discloses his purpose of seeking the outlaw Robin Hood. There follows a friendly shooting match between them, the arrangements for which are made in dialogue; and after the contest they disclose their names to one another, which leads at once to sword-play and Guy's death. After mutilating the corpse, which he does with a characteristic ballad speech, Robin disguises himself in the horsehide and returns to Barnsdale. As Child pointed out,[1] no reason for this disguise appears in the ballad as we have it, since Robin cannot know that his men have been attacked by the Sheriff; but we need not conclude, as Child did, that there must 'have been a considerable derangement of the story'. Robin's action is unmotivated and absurd, but only as a hundred things in the finest ballads are unmotivated and absurd. How can the lord in *Fair Annie* (62), for example, after abducting the heroine and having seven children by her, possibly make the mistake of bringing her sister home as his bride? How came the sister's son to be at hand in *Johnie Cock* (114) to comment on the

[1] iii. 90.

struggle? At all events, Robin goes back to Barnsdale in his disguise and is received by the Sheriff as the slayer of Robin Hood. When he asks the privilege of dispatching John, he releases his comrade, and together they put their enemies to flight.

The narrative method in all this differs in no way from that of shorter ballads. Each little section is slightly more developed, that is all. If placed side by side with *Johnie Cock*, it will be seen to have all the same structural qualities, even to the shift of scene from place to place as the story proceeds. Although there is a double thread of action, moreover, in that Guy of Gisborne and the Sheriff of Nottingham are both on the track of the outlaws at the same time, the tale has the ordinary centralization on a single episode. It is all about the events of a single day. The fundamental structural characteristics are here, and there is no need whatever of placing it in a category apart.

The same thing is true of *The Hunting of the Cheviot* (162). The story is told in brief dramatic sequences, with little concern for any connective tissue. The Percy makes his boast; he comes out of Bamborough to hunt the deer, and the hunt is ended in four stanzas; suddenly Percy says that Douglas has promised to meet him, and the Scots come on the scene at once; the chieftains confront one another and agree to single combat, but are balked of that design by a squire of Northumberland; half a dozen stanzas give an impression of the battle; nine stanzas more tell how Percy slew Douglas, yet lamented his death; next we hear how Hugh of Montgomery avenged his master on the Percy and was himself killed; there is a glimpse of the carnage, which extended into the night, and a threnody for the noble dead; and finally we learn how the news was received at Edinburgh and at London, and how King Harry vowed reprisals. There is nothing epic in the manner of this stirring tale. Instead, it has the true ballad movement in swift and flashing scenes, each held only long enough to make the action clear, each connected only by the sequence of event with what precedes and follows it. Somewhat more than three times the length of the longest version of *Johnie Cock*, it possesses no structural peculiarity not found in the shorter ballad. This fact is not altered by the presence of stanza 24, oddly placed just before the opening of the fight, which appears to mark the poem as the work of some one conscious of a profession, if not an art:

> That day, that day, that dredfull day!
> the first fit here I fynde;
> And youe wyll here any mor a the hountynge a the Chyviat,
> yet ys ther mor behynde.

In point of fact, whatever may have been the role played in balladry by the minstrels who were so important in the eyes of Bishop Percy and Sir Walter Scott, and of so little account according to most nineteenth-century scholars, an examination of the material we possess, whether from manuscripts and old prints or directly from oral tradition, leads one irresistibly to the conclusion that professional singers did not follow one fashion in narrative and 'folk' singers another. Child recognized as proper ballads *The Boy and the Mantle* (29), *King Arthur and King Cornwall* (30), and *The Marriage of Sir Gawain* (31), and included them in his first volume, with this comment: 'They would come down by professional rather than by domestic tradition, through minstrels rather than knitters and weavers.'[1] This unproved and unprovable assumption is doubtless correct; for, as Professor Kittredge wrote somewhat later, 'they are indubitably ballads, composed in the popular style and perpetuated for a time by oral tradition'.[2] In other words, they have both the structural and the stylistic qualities common to the kind at large.

[1] i. 257.
[2] Sargent and Kittredge, *English and Scottish Popular Ballads*, p. xxvii.

The most convincing evidence that professional singers and reciters were not moving in one direction, and folksingers in another, comes, I believe, from *A Gest of Robyn Hode* (117), which has always been a rather troublesome phenomenon and still presents difficult problems. It is a poem of 456 stanzas, and 'may have been put together as early as 1400, or before',[1] by a compiler who was certainly not without skill. Professor Clawson's excellent study,[2] following out in greater detail the suggestions of earlier scholars, showed the probability that the *Gest* was made from something like a dozen ballads by a man of considerable ability, who shaped and welded the material into its present form. It is significant, as seems to have been too little remarked, that the constituent ballads could never have been disentangled with the degree of success that has been attained, unless they had preserved their original manner as well as their substance. In other words, the *Gest* remains a collection of ballads, though it is something else besides. The poet-compiler was at least so thoroughly in the temper of ballad-making that he cannot have altered greatly the songs he used in his attempt 'to give a complete and representative picture of the life and character of Robin Hood'.[3]

The poem was called by Child[4] 'a popular epic, composed from several ballads by a thoroughly congenial spirit'. Gummere went somewhat further, and wrote: '*The Gest of Robin Hood* is an epic poem in that it tells its connected story about a definite hero; and it is put together, smoothed, and completed into unity, out of sundry epic ballads which themselves make a single though not a coherent group.'[5] Yet Gummere, with his customary acumen, saw that this did not tell the whole truth, and added: 'Confined to humble tradition and the

---

[1] Child, iii. 40.   [2] W. H. Clawson, *The Gest of Robin Hood*, 1909.
[3] Clawson, *op. cit.*, p. 124.   [4] iii. 49.
[5] *The Popular Ballad*, p. 270.

interest of a class, it reached no advanced stage, and can be called full epic only by the courtesy of anticipation.'[1] The *Gest*, that is, is not an epic at all, despite valiant efforts to make it appear a link in a theoretical development from ballad to epic. It is not an epic because in general design it follows the pattern of medieval romances rather than of heroic stories, and in its parts keeps to ballad structure and ballad style. At the conclusion of his interesting and able monograph on this theme, Professor Hart, after working out the thesis that there is a consistent development from the simple ballad to the epic, by way of the *Gest*, makes the significant remark: 'Between the narrative art of *Beowulf* and that of all the other types just passed in review is a great gulf fixed.'[2] Although he modified this in the next sentence, his subsequent analysis of the structure and style of *Beowulf* shows the wisdom of the statement. The fact is, I think, that neither the *Gest* nor the Danish *Marsk Stig*, which is similarly compounded,[3] ought to be regarded as an unachieved epic. The ballad and the heroic epic have little in common save that each tells a story. On the other hand, it seems clear that at one time or another professional singers have had something to do with ballad-making. This is a matter to which we must return in another connexion.

By analysing ballads with various themes and only minor differences of structure, as we have been doing, we are able to see why they have their dramatic quality and their impersonal approach. Stories told, as these stories are, in terms of action could not well avoid having those characteristics. To the same structural cause must be attributed their common though by no means invariable

[1] *Op. cit.*, p. 271.
[2] W. M. Hart, *Ballad and Epic*, 1907, p. 295.
[3] See A. Heusler, *Lied und Epos*, 1905, pp. 41–6, for a valuable comparison of the two.

habit of bringing the events they relate close in apparent time to the moment of telling. *Thomas Rymer* (37), though a fairy story, begins as if it were a happening of the immediate past:

> True Thomas lay oer yond grassy bank,
> And he beheld a lady gay,
> A ladie that was brisk and bold,
> Come riding oer the farnie brae.

The action in *Dives and Lazarus* (56) is introduced quite as casually :

> As it fell out upon a day,
> Rich Dives made a feast,
> And he invited all his friends,
> And gentry of the best.

Instances like these are too frequent to need further illustration. Thus the hero of *The Bent sae Brown* (71) begins :

> There are sixteen lang miles, I'm sure,
> Between my love and me;
> There are eight o them in gude dry land,
> And other eight by sea.

Even when a particular event is to be celebrated, there is no effort to set it in its temporal relations. *Jock o the Side* (187) needs no introduction other than this :

> Peeter a Whifeild he hath slaine,
> And Iohn a Side, he is tane,
> And Iohn is bound both hand and foote,
> And to the New-castle he is gone.

As Gummere very justly said : 'Ballads still bear the mark of immediate relation to their theme, so that no particulars of time or place or person need to be given.'[1]

---

[1] *The Popular Ballad*, p. 81.

Only rarely does there appear such an introduction as that of *Musselburgh Field* (172):

> On the tenth day of December,
>> And the fourth yeere of King Edwards raigne,
> Att Musleboorrowe, as I remember,
>> Two goodly hosts there mett on a plaine.

Much commoner are opening stanzas like that of *The Battle of Otterburn*:

> Yt fell abowght the Lamasse tyde,
>> Whan husbondes wynnes ther haye,
> The dowghtye Dowglasse bowynd hym to ryde,
>> In Ynglond to take a praye.

2. BALLAD RHETORIC

I have already said[1] that I cannot regard the device for which Gummere coined the term 'incremental repetition' as essentially structural, and accordingly I think he erred in making it 'the touchstone and test of original ballad structure'. On the other hand, the interest and importance of such cumulative iteration cannot be denied. Gummere was not at fault in stressing it. We owe him a debt of gratitude, indeed, in this matter as in so many others, for seizing upon essentials and making them clear. His mistake lay in thinking incremental repetition a structural phenomenon rather than a rhetorical one. Miss Pound, in her attack on Gummere's position,[2] was justified by the facts when she wrote: 'Structural repetition is not a certain test of what is and what is not a ballad and it is not to be insisted upon in definition of the type, first because it is not always present in ballads, and second, because it is as characteristic of other folk-lyrics as it is of ballads.'[3] Both of

---

[1] See above, p. 98.
[2] Louise Pound, *Poetic Origins and the Ballad*, 1921, pp. 121–35.
[3] *Op. cit.*, p. 124.

these points are well taken, although the first is put in a way not quite fair to Gummere, who of course never said that all genuine ballads have such iteration, but only that the earliest ballads must have had it. His theory cannot be upheld, however, in view of the restricted use of incremental repetition in *Judas*, our ballad of earliest record,[1] and in plenty of other specimens that are by no means of modern coinage. Only a comparatively small number, indeed, employ it with even the appearance of structural intent. Equally destructive of the theory is the fact that cumulative iteration occurs quite as commonly in lyrical as in narrative poetry, and not only in folk-songs[2] but also in verse made with conscious artistry. In addition to the evidence assembled by Miss Pound from early English lyrics and non-popular carols, as well as from negro spirituals and popular songs, we should bear in mind the effective use of repetition in Latin hymns and other medieval verse. Iteration, both structural and incidental, is so frequently encountered in lyrics of many sorts that only the very strongest evidence should persuade one to belief in its basic importance in the formation of a narrative *genre*.

The real nature of incremental repetition in ballads can best be seen, however, by confining our attention to its appearance in the ballads themselves. Only very rarely does it serve, as in *Babylon* (14), or *The Maid Freed from the Gallows* (95), or *Lord Randal* (12), to mark the successive stages of the action. Where it is so used, the effect is very striking. Parallelism of this sort, holding us in suspense for the break that releases the ear while it resolves the situation, cannot fail to tighten the nerves a little—or make them very taut indeed, as *Edward* does,

---

[1] Miss Pound stated somewhat misleadingly (pp. 123, 136) that *Judas* has none of it. Stanzas 10–12, 15–16, show it plainly, though it is not organic.

[2] An admirable case of structural repetition in a lyric is *The One O*, Alfred Williams, *Folk-Songs of the Upper Thames*, 1923, pp. 286–8.

for instance. While the outlaw brother in *Babylon* makes his proposal to each sister in turn, receives from the first two the same despairing refusal, and kills them one after the other, we look forward to the climactic third with an instinctive expectation of something different to come. Yet there is no immediate change. The formula begins still again:

> He's taken the youngest ane by the hand,
> And he's turned her round and made her stand.

> Says, 'Will ye be a rank robber's wife,
> Or will ye die by my wee pen-knife?'

Her defiant reply, of course, snaps the thread:

> 'I'll not be a rank robber's wife,
> Nor will I die by your wee pen-knife.

> For I hae a brother in this wood,
> And gin ye kill me, it's he'll kill thee.'

The cumulative effect has been secured. There is nothing more to follow save the revelation of the brother's name and his remorseful death.

What seems not to have occurred to Gummere or to any of his critics is that this is nothing else than the systematic use throughout a poem of the always effective rhetorical device of parallelism in phrase and idea. That is to say, it is a kind of ornament, but ornament of the right sort, since it is woven into the stuff of the tale. It is of peculiar importance in balladry, not because in a comparatively few cases it is used to give form to the whole narrative, but because it is the commonest rhetorical figure employed to intensify some moment of the action, or repeatedly to give emotional colour to the story. Consider, for example, *Child Waters* (63), which, as Child wrote, 'has perhaps no superior in English, and if not in English perhaps nowhere'.[1] Certainly no more

---

[1] ii. 84.

moving tale of self-forgetful love has ever been told. All twelve of the variants known to me [1] show a free use of incremental repetition, which has much to do with the captivating quality of the ballad, yet in none of them is the parallelism more than incidental.

> 'If the child be mine, Faire Ellen,' he sayd,
>   'Be mine, as you tell mee,
> Take you Cheshire and Lancashire both,
>   Take them your owne to bee.
>
> If the child be mine, Ffaire Ellen,' he said,
>   'Be mine, as you doe sweare,
> Take you Cheshire and Lancashire both,
>   And make that child your heyre.'
>
> Shee saies, 'I had rather haue one kisse,
>   Child Waters, of thy mouth,
> Then I wold haue Cheshire and Lancashire both,
>   That lyes by north and south.
>
> And I had rather haue a twinkling,
>   Child Waters, of your eye,
> Then I wold haue Cheshire and Lancashire both,
>   To take them mine oune to bee.'

Furthermore, the passages of iteration in the different variants do not wholly correspond with one another. For instance, the fine version of the Percy Manuscript (A), from which I have just quoted, lacks the triplicate repetition at the crossing of the river, which is found in half a dozen copies, including the form (B) that came from Mrs. Brown of Falkland.

Examples of a similar kind could be multiplied almost indefinitely. Such cumulative iteration runs all the way from the haunting melancholy of *Sir Patrick Spens* (58) to the coarse humour of *The Wife Wrapt in Wether's Skin* (277):

---

[1] Eleven in Child, the twelfth in Greig, *Last Leaves*, pp. 51–2.

O lang, lang may their ladies sit,
   Wi thair fans into their hand,
Or eir they se Sir Patrick Spence
   Cum sailing to the land.

O lang, lang may the ladies stand
   Wi thair gold kems in their hair,
Waiting for thair ain deir lords,
   For they'll se thame na mair.

She wadna bake, she wadna brew,
For spoiling o her comely hue.

She wadna wash, she wadna wring,
For spoiling o her gay goud ring.

The contrast shows the usefulness of the device for varying ends. Often enough nothing but verbal emphasis is secured, as in *The Earl of Errol* (231):

He's taen his Peggy by the hand,
   And he led her thro the green,
And twenty times he kissd her there,
   Before his ain wife's een.

He's taen his Peggy by the hand,
   And he's led her thro the hall,
And twenty times he's kissd her there,
   Before his nobles all.

Sometimes a commonplace becomes curiously effective when repeated, as in *The Lass of Roch Royal* (76 A), where the same two stanzas are put into the mouth of the heroine when she goes to seek her love, and again into the mouth of Gregory when he learns that she has been turned away from his door:

'Gar sadle me the black,' she (he) sayes,
   'Gar sadle me the broun;
Gar sadle me the swiftest steed
   That ever rode the toun.

> 'Gar shoe him with the beat silver,
>   And grind him with the gold;
> Gar put two bells on every side,
>   Till I come to some hold.'

The sense of this may falter, but that it conveys the feeling of urgency no one can deny. In other words, it is pure rhetoric, just as is the cumulative iteration within a single stanza that may be illustrated from *Sir Hugh* (155 C) :

> Then out and cam the thick, thick blude,
>   Then out and cam the thin;
> Then out and cam the bonny heart's blude,
>   Where a' the life lay in.

Incremental repetition, however, though certainly the commonest, is by no means the only rhetorical phenomenon that distinguishes the ballad. Equally significant, because less often found in folk-songs that do not tell a story, is the not infrequent trick of repeating in action what has already been said in speech—a kind of parallelism quite different from the iteration we have been discussing. In *Bonnie Annie* (24 A), for example, the device is used three times. The ship's captain says to the frail heroine:

> 'Ye'll steal your father's gowd, and your mother's money,
> And I'll mak ye a lady in Ireland bonnie.'

And the following stanza runs:

> She's stown her father's gowd, and her mother's money,
> But she was never a lady in Ireland bonnie.

Because, of course, the ship refuses to sail with such a wicked creature aboard. (Oddly enough, the Irish captain's guilt is overlooked!) Annie says:

> 'Ye'll tak me in your arms twa, lo, lift me cannie,
> Throw me out owre board, your ain dear Annie.'

> He has tane her in his arms twa, lo, lifted her cannie,
> He has laid her on a bed of down, his ain dear Annie.

But when everything else has failed, and the sailors have admonished him again in the same sense and almost the same words, he throws his dear Annie into the sea. The device may be equally well illustrated from *Clerk Colvill* (42 A). The deceitful mermaid says to the hero:

> 'But out ye tak your little pen-knife,
> And frae my sark ye shear a gare;
> Row that about your lovely head,
> And the pain ye'll never feel nae mair.'

> Out he has taen his little pen-knife,
> And frae her sark he's shorn a gare,
> Rowed that about his lovely head,
> But the pain increased mair and mair.

And before his death he speaks to the family:

> 'Oh, mither, mither, mak my bed,
> And, gentle ladie, lay me down;
> Oh, brither, brither, unbend my bow,
> 'Twill never be bent by me again.'

> His mither she has made his bed,
> His gentle ladie laid him down,
> His brither he has unbent his bow,
> 'Twas never bent by him again.

Examples of this kind of parallelism can be found in great numbers, as every ballad-lover will recognize. Often the device has no other effect than to accentuate the broken, spasmodic movement of the story—what Gummere so happily termed[1] the 'leaping and lingering' of the ballad—which is occasioned by the dramatic structure. Often, again, the device is not even rhetorically effective, but descends into mere commonplace, quite as does incremental repetition at times. Occasionally, however, it gives a curious and very pleasing effect, which is like nothing so much as that produced by the statement preceding and explaining an action to come, familiar to all readers of early drama. Possibly there may be some

---

[1] *The Popular Ballad*, p. 91.

obscure connexion between the two, at least to the extent of a similar satisfaction in the kind of emphasis obtained by first proposing something in words and immediately getting it accomplished in deed. There can be no doubt that in cases like that of *Child Waters* (63 A), for example, this is very moving.

The ballad-makers, quite obviously, have always been fond of emphasis, however secured. Even such structural ellipses as we have already observed, though in themselves under-statements, tend to heighten emotional values, while the rhetorical devices employed are always frankly sensational. Both singers and listeners have liked their tales hot and strong, and have never objected to exaggerated statement any more than to violent action. We cannot suppose, for instance, that they have ever quite believed in the silver and gold with which Tam Lin's steed was shod, even though he was an 'elfin grey'. Yet they have used the stanza with slight variation in versions of *Lord Thomas and Fair Annet* (73), *Child Maurice* (83), *Fair Mary of Wallington* (91), and *Young Waters* (94), with no excuse save the excellent one of poetical hyperbole :

> The steed that my true-love rides on
> > Is lighter than the wind;
> Wi siller he is shod before,
> > Wi burning gowd behind.

Thus Janet of *Tam Lin* (39 A). Doubtless the same desire —to give a tale the touch of romance—accounts for the absurd but delightful extravagance recorded in *Brown Adam* (98), where the blacksmith hero is endowed with an anvil or hammer of gold. Similarly in *Thomas Rymer* (37 A) there is gross but magnificent extravagance about the journey to Fairyland :

> For forty days and forty nights
> > He wade thro red blude to the knee,
> And he saw neither sun nor moon,
> > But heard the roaring of the sea.

One finds the same tendency in statements about the mourning of women. May Margaret in *Clerk Saunders* (69) declares that:

> 'When seven years is come an gone,
>   Ther's nere a comb go in my hair ';

and the grotesque vow is repeated in *Bonny Bee Hom* (92), *Lord Livingston* (262), and *The Coble o Cargill* (242).

Some of the most striking of these heightened and hyperbolic passages are based on flashes of imaginative fire: they are memorable because something is visualized with the fine frenzy of true poetry. So in *Hind Etin* (41) the supernatural lover is gifted with a strength that dimly recalls barbaric hero-tales:

> The highest tree in Elmond's wood,
>   He 's pu'd it by the reet,
> And he has built for her a bower,
>   Near by a hallow seat.

Or, as another version (B) has it:

> He pu'd a tree out o the wud,
>   The biggest that was there,
> And he howkit a cave monie fathoms deep,
>   And put May Margret there.

There is a similar boldness of conception in what Johnie Cock (114) says of the wolf:

> 'The wildest wolf in aw this wood
>   Wad not ha done so by me;
> She'd ha wet her foot ith wan water,
>   And sprinkled it oer my brae,
> And if that wad not ha wakend me,
>   She wad ha gone and let me be.'

We remember the cry of the fated heroine in *Mary Hamilton* (173):

> 'But I'll put on my robes o white,
>   To shine through Edinbro town.'

This is no mere commonplace, though in one version of *Fair Janet* (64 A) we find the same image:

> But Janet put on the scarlet robes,
>   To shine foremost throw the town.

It is the same sort of poetic audacity that we find in *The Bitter Withy*:[1]

> Our Saviour built a bridge with the beams of the sun;

and in the Holy Child's simile in *The Cherry-Tree Carol* (54):

> 'O I shall be as dead, mother,
>   as the stones in the wall;
> O the stones in the street, mother,
>   shall mourn for me all.'

This is not to say that balladists have avoided commonplaces. It is notorious that cheek by jowl with the passages most pleasing to the sophisticated ear occur others quite indefensible by any canon of literary taste. They are inept, or clumsy, or so trite that only in folk-song would they appear at all. The texture of some of the finest narratives is marred—if one admits the validity of applying literary standards to such things—by cheap and worn-out doggerel. What can be said in defence of such a stanza as the following, from our noblest version of *Johnie Cock*?—

> His coat it was of light Lincoln,
>   And his breeches of the same,
> His shoes of the American leather,
>   And gold buckles tying them.

What can be said for the recurrent formula:

> When bells were rung, and mass begun (or sung),
>   And a' men bound to bed,

which means nothing and suggests nothing important?

[1] See F. Sidgwick, *N. and Q.*, 10th ser., iv. 83–4; reprinted *J. F.-S. S.*, ii. 300–2.

The outcry of the lover that he will kiss his dead mistress, cheek and chin, serves very well to indicate his passionate grief, but less well when the cheek is called 'rosy' or 'cherry' and the lips are termed 'ruby' or 'coral', as in different versions of *Lord Lovel* and *The Lass of Roch Royal*.

It has been common to attribute such infelicities to 'degeneration', but that explanation does not sufficiently take into account all the vagaries to which ballads are subject. Degenerate texts there are, certainly, ballads that have suffered through a good many generations of ungifted singers, ballads that have suffered through the meddling of urban rhymesters before drifting back into oral circulation. Yet the chances are that even under favourable conditions there have always been awkward and inept stanzas in most versions of most ballads. Although there is plenty of evidence, as we shall see later, for a guiding and shaping tradition in popular poetry, there is none whatever for a tradition of criticism. Passages that seem to us offensive or singularly weak would not trouble a folk-singer, any more than does the use of stock phrases.

Commonplaces, indeed, seem to have been used by balladists with as little hesitancy as their boldest and most striking phrases. They have never tried to avoid the obvious in order to be poetical, probably because they have never been conscious of making poetry, but only of telling a story in verse as effectively as possible. They have often, as a matter of fact, succeeded in producing by means of the set formula passages of admirable quality. Consider the recurring stanza, which runs with minor variations as follows:

> 'Go saddle to me the black, the black,
>   Go saddle to me the brown,
> Go saddle to me the swiftest steed
>   That ever rode from a town.'

Whenever this is used, we get the sense of haste and speed, and it serves as well in *Lord Lovel* as in *Lady Maisry* or *Little Musgrave and Lady Barnard*. The same feeling of urgency is communicated by the pages who run errands undeterred by broken bridges and the like. As Gummere wisely wrote, ballad commonplaces 'are mainly connected with the situation or the event, and so have a kind of permanence'.[1] Since these are tales of action, in which there is little effort to build up characters or settings in detail, we are satisfied with conventionalized descriptions like yellow hair and bodies 'as white as milk' or 'nut-brown', with heroines who are 'sewing a silken seam' and heroes who are 'stroking a milk-white steed'. Clothing is gaudy with silver and gold, or green and red, but there is no elaboration with respect to these things even in the longer ballads of outlaws and Border raiders. Description is stylized, as we say nowadays; and to a very considerable extent dialogue and event are stylized also. The phrasal commonplace is another illustration of the conventional rhetoric which, as we have already seen, permeates all the ballads. We who read them may not like some of the manifestations of this particular convention of the commonplace; we may find absurdity in it; but we ought to recognize it for what it is and to acknowledge the part it plays in some of the effects that please us best. *Mary Hamilton* (173) is stylized throughout, but it is not the less moving on that account:

> 'Oh little did my mother think,
>   The day she cradled me,
> What lands I was to travel through,
>   What death I was to dee.
>
> Oh little did my father think,
>   The day he held up me,
> What lands I was to travel through,
>   What death I was to dee.

[1] *The Popular Ballad*, p. 304.

Last night I washd the queen's feet,
  And gently laid her down;
And a' the thanks I've gotten the nicht
  To be hangd in Edinbro town.

Last nicht there was four Maries,
  The nicht there'l be but three;
There was Marie Seton, and Marie Beton,
  And Marie Carmichael, and me.'

3. THE BALLAD REFRAIN

Thus far I have made no mention of the refrains that are such a characteristic and interesting feature of ballads. It has seemed to me wiser to postpone the discussion of them until we should have completed our survey of the elements that have to do with the narrative itself. For the refrain, whatever its nature, does not advance the story, but is purely lyrical in function'. As Steenstrup remarked, it 'is essentially a subjective element', and through it 'the mood expresses itself'.[1] This statement needs modification in that, as we have seen, the mood appears adequately and even powerfully in the narrative part of the ballad; but without question the refrain echoes the dominant feeling of the verses to which it is joined. We can go as far as this without theory or conjecture, but farther than this we cannot go. Much as one would like to stick to plain fact and avoid speculation, one may as well acknowledge that we can reach no absolute conclusions about what the refrain has been in earlier centuries, and that we shall be compelled to form theories on rather insufficient data.

Before doing so, however, we had better look at the refrain as it appears in the English and Scottish ballads now extant. The situation is curious and somewhat baffling. 'Of the 305 ballads in Child's collection,' Gummere

[1] J. C. H. Steenstrup, *The Medieval Popular Ballad*, trans. E. G. Cox, 1914,

reckoned, '106 show in some version evidence of chorus or refrain. Of some 1,250 versions in all, about 300 have a refrain; but among the old ballads in couplets, out of 31 only 7 lack the refrain as they stand, and even these show traces of it.'[1] That is, about a third of the ballads have refrains in some version or other, but they appear by no means uniformly. These figures are almost certainly too low, however, as representing the actual state of things even in the later stages of ballad-singing. We must remember that a very large proportion of the specimens in Child's thesaurus are derived from broadsides or from recitation. Refrains would be sure to disappear to some extent in printing, and quite as easily when ballads were recited by an educated person interested chiefly in the stories they contained. Something like proof of this assertion can be found by looking at Gavin Greig's *Last Leaves of Traditional Ballads*,[2] which is perhaps the most valuable single volume of new texts collected since Child's day. Greig's most important contributor was Miss Bell Robertson, whose marvellous memory was stored with the words only. Like her mother before her, she recited but did not sing. Now, the proportion of ballads with refrains in Greig's collection is only a little higher than in Child's: out of 108 ballads there are 38 so provided. On the other hand, in the collections made within the past fifteen years that derive largely from singers, the proportion is significantly higher. Thus in Campbell and Sharp's *English Folk-Songs from the Southern Appalachians*,[3] 21 of the 37 specimens found also in Child have refrains; in Davis's *Traditional Ballads of Virginia*[4] 22 out of 51; in Cox's *Folk-Songs of the South*[5] 19 out of 34; and in *British Ballads from Maine*[6] 27 out of 56. In other words, half or more than half of the ballads represented in these volumes have refrains. The ratio is nearly the same with the speci-

[1] *The Popular Ballad*, p. 74, note 2. [2] Ed. A. Keith, 1925.
[3] 1917. [4] 1929. [5] 1925. [6] Barry, Eckstorm, and Smyth, 1929.

mens of English derivation collected by Sharp and the
other workers of the Folk-Song Society, and with those
in *Folk-Songs of the Upper Thames*[1] by Alfred Williams,
who got his material from singers though he recorded no
music. There are, moreover, eight ballads with refrains
in Greig's *Last Leaves* for which Child found no version
so arranged;[2] and in the American collections there are
several others in the same case. Yet by no computation
can it be estimated that many more than half of our
English and Scottish traditional ballads have been sung
with refrains since the period of collecting began.

The question arises whether this state of things shows
a departure from the original type or whether the refrain
need not be regarded as an absolutely essential feature of
the ballad at any stage in its history. To this question no
wholly satisfactory answer can be made, I fear. Gummere,
though acutely conscious of the difficulty,[3] was convinced
by his theory of choral origins that 'the refrain is an
organic part of the ballad'[4] and that at first ballads
'always had a refrain'.[5] Professor Kittredge has put it
'that there is abundant evidence for regarding the refrain
in general as a characteristic feature of ballad poetry
which gradually ceased to be essential'.[6] This statement
is slightly ambiguous, since the words 'in general' show
uncertainty; and it is in any case unsupported by argument. Miss Pound, in combating the opinions of Gummere, unfortunately contented herself with the dictum
that if the archetype of the ballad ever 'was a dance song,
the refrain formula ought to persist above all else, through
oral tradition and dance usage, as it does in the dance or

---

[1] 1923. [2] Child 105, 140, 218, 232, 251, 267, 269, 282.
[3] *The Popular Ballad*, pp. 77–8. [4] *Op. cit.*, p. 73.
[5] *Op. cit.*, p. 74. His argument is, however, not clear, since he says (p. 73):
'It establishes beyond all doubt the lyric and choral origins'; and (p. 78): 'We
can come to no conclusion until we get some proof of choral origins for the
texts themselves.'
[6] Sargent and Kittredge, *op. cit.*, p. xxi.

ring-game songs of which we are sure. It is what should identify the individual ballads.'[1] This does not help us to resolve our difficulties any more than does a theory of choral origins, since we have obviously no right to say that anything 'ought to persist' in one form or another. A sense of duty cannot be attributed to the wayward products of the human imagination.

Here is the situation as I make it out. Something like half of our ballads seem to have been sung with refrains, something like half have lacked them. The one unmistakable ballad, which we can trace beyond the fourteenth century—*Judas*, namely—has no recorded chorus. On the other hand, we have positive evidence from Elizabethan times that *The Fair Flower of Northumberland* was chanted by maidens, 'two of them singing the ditty and all the rest bearing the burden'.[2] We need not concern ourselves at present with the manner in which this ballad was sung, but only with the fact of the refrain. We know, furthermore, that of more recent days individuals have been singing some ballads with refrains and some without refrains, quite unconscious of making any trouble for scholars in so doing. They have been justified in their indifference, moreover, by the complete lack of distinguishing traits, whether in words or music, between the two. Neither in the structure and style of the ballad texts, nor in the quality of the melodies to which they are sung, can we find anything to make us suppose that we have to do with two classes of lyrical narrative. Whatever may have been the case with such songs in earlier centuries, we are manifestly dealing with what has become a single type. The ballad as we know it is an entity.

Before we embark on the troubled seas of theory, in

---

[1] *Poetic Origins and the Ballad*, 1921, pp. 76-7.

[2] See Deloney's *Pleasant Historie of John Winchcomb in his younger years called Jack of Newbury*, 1630, ed. R. Sievers, *Thomas Deloney*, 1904 (*Palaestra*, xxxvi), p. 195. The book was first issued in 1596 or 1597.

an attempt to explain the curious variation in the use of refrains, we should have in mind one further phenomenon, which concerns the ballads of countries adjacent to Great Britain. In Denmark, as the studies of Steenstrup most clearly showed, ballad refrains are almost invariably present. He found that only about a score of the specimens he investigated—some 520 altogether—lack a refrain,[1] and that in these cases there is good reason to suppose either that the refrain has been lost or that the ballads themselves have been imported from abroad within recent centuries.[2] As far as I know, no one has made a similar exhaustive investigation of French and German ballads; but it is safe to say, I believe, that they show the same variation that we find in our English and Scottish songs. Certainly one has only to turn the pages of collections to observe the lack of uniformity in treatment. Steenstrup came to the opinion that the refrain had never 'anywhere been felt to be so integral a part of the ballads as in the Scandinavian, and especially the Danish, ballads'.[3]

From all the facts before us, and without committing ourselves prematurely to any theory as to the origin of ballads, I believe we may reach certain tentative conclusions about the intermittent use of the refrain by British singers.

In the first place, it is certainly true that there existed a double tradition of ballad-singing down to the end of the sixteenth century at least: the one manner being that illustrated by Deloney's reference already quoted, which corresponded to the Scandinavian habit of having a leader or leaders chant the narrative verses, while a group followed with the chorus; the other attested by Sir Philip Sidney's famous statement in *The Defence of Poesie*, which says of some version of *The Hunting of the Cheviot* or *The Battle of Otterburn* that it was 'sung but by some blind crowder, with no rougher voice than

---

[1] *Op. cit.*, p. 96.   [2] *Op. cit.*, pp. 123–4.   [3] *Op. cit.*, p. 91.

rude style '.[1] The singing group and the singing individual seem to have been equally familiar to our
ancestors; and the only essential difference between
ballads like *The Fair Flower of Northumberland* and ballads
like *Chevy Chase* lies in the fact that the former have refrains and the latter have not. It is reasonable to infer, I
believe, that this difference is a very old one—that it runs
back many centuries, quite possibly to the twelfth or
thirteenth. *Judas* has no refrain, as we have noted, and
very likely never had one, although in any given case we
cannot be certain that a refrain has not been lost. The
habit of collecting ballads from recitation and the in-
creasing tendency to make ballad-singing exclusively a
matter of individual performance forbid any downright
statement that such-and-such a song never had a refrain.
Yet we do have warrant for saying that refrains are not
essential to the ballad as it has existed for several centuries.

A very interesting observation has been made by Professor Greene in a still unpublished monograph on the
English carol, to the effect that in certain instances,
though only rarely, our ballads have the kind of choral
element peculiar to the carol. As he says, ' the burden
characteristic of the carol-form is a line or group of lines,
most often a couplet, repeated after every stanza, often
linked to the stanza by rime, but essentially independent of and external to it '.[2] Ballads, on the other hand,
usually have refrain-lines alternating with narrative-lines.
The latter method may be illustrated by *Willie's Lyke-
Wake* (25 A) :

'Willie, Willie, I'll learn you a wile,'
    And the sun shines over the valleys and a'
'How this pretty fair maid ye may beguile.'
    Amang the blue flowrs and the yellow and a'.

[1] Ed. A. S. Cook, p. 29.
[2] R. L. Greene, *The English Carol before 1550*, Princeton dissertation, 1929
(on deposit in Princeton University Library), p. 78.

The carol-burden is shown to good advantage in *The Twa Magicians* (44) :

> The lady stands in her bower door,
> As straight as willow wand;
> The blacksmith a little forbye,
> Wi hammer in his hand.
>
> O bide, lady, bide,
> And aye he bade her bide;
> The rusty smith your leman shall be,
> For a' your muckle pride.

In what is apparently a combination with the ballad refrain, such a burden occurs in *The Elfin Knight* (2 A, B):

> My plaid awa, my plaid awa,
> And ore the hill and far awa,
> And far awa to Norrowa,
> My plaid shall not be blown awa.
>
> The elphin knight sits on yon hill,
> Ba, ba, ba, lilli ba
> He blaws his horn both lowd and shril.
> The wind hath blown my plaid awa.

Mr. Greene enumerates eleven instances of such external burdens in Child, and two others should be added. These thirteen ballads [1] show, we must believe, that there have existed 'two sharply differentiated forms of choral element, one of which was definitely associated with the ballad, while the other was as definitely associated with the carol (and the popular prototypes of the carol)'.[2] What this occasional use of the burden alongside the refrain implies as to the performance of ballads need not now be discussed. The present importance of the matter to us is the evidence it gives that ballads have sometimes

---

[1] 2A, 44, 82, 110A, K (not in Greene), 115, 178A, C, 200J (not in Greene; see versions A, C, G, *British Ballads from Maine*, pp. 269, 272, 276–7), 209 E, 222 D, 231, 290 E, 299 A.

[2] *Op. cit.*, p. 83.

taken over a metrical device more peculiarly associated with the carol, which was a lyrical and not a narrative form.[1] The same ballad, indeed, could be sung with either the one choral accompaniment or the other. The choral element, we may sum up the case, is a constant neither in use nor in form, though it is unquestionably an extremely important element in balladry.

4. THE METRE OF BALLADS

One final feature, intimately connected with the matters we have just been studying and with the music discussed in an earlier chapter, must be considered before we can pass on from description to theory and attack the difficult question of how ballads came to be what they are. We must look at the verse in which they are composed, and try to discover what contribution it makes to the total effect, which so obviously results from a composite of various elements. Our ballads have been composed for singing, whether or not to pre-existing melodies, and they are lyrics as truly as they are narratives— songs as well as stories.

Being lyrics, they follow the rhythmic forms of other folk-songs, recurrent patterns or stanzas that fit rounded melodies. Naturally enough, the structure of these stanzas cannot be clearly understood without observing the tunes to which they are set. Editors of ballads have often been at a loss as to the way a particular text should be printed, either because they have known no tune for it or have failed to observe the tune. Both the length of lines and the grouping of lines in stanzas are hard to determine without reference to melodies.

[1] Mr. Greene shows further (pp. 86–9) that the variants of *The Golden Vanity* and *The Farmer's Curst Wife* collected by Sharp give evidence for adaptation from one pattern to the other; and that the famous version of the *Corpus Christi Carol* in MS. Balliol 354 probably had the 'lullay' burden arranged for it.

This can best be illustrated by the commonest verse pattern of all, which has been known for a great while as the 'ballad stanza' and is usually written thus :

His footmen they did rin before,
His horsemen rade behind;
Ane mantel of the burning gowd
Did keip him frae the wind.
Young Waters (94 A).

This arrangement of the verse has passed over into literary tradition, I need not say, and perhaps is an accurate representation of what our poets have had in mind when using the pattern. Into that we need not inquire. It is not accurate, however, with reference to ballads, in which this common stanza is quite certainly a couplet with seven stresses to the line. Any one who will study the settings in such collections as those in the *Journal of the Folk-Song Society*, or Greig's *Last Leaves*, or Campbell and Sharp's *English Folk-Songs from the Southern Appalachians*, cannot fail to be convinced that this is the case. Let me show a specimen chosen almost at random, a variant of *Barbara Allan* (84) to a well-known melody,[1] as sung in Aberdeenshire twenty-five years ago:

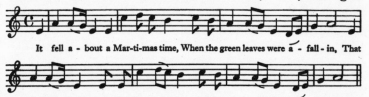

It fell a - bout a Mar-ti-mas time, When the green leaves were a - fall- in, That

Sir John Graeme from the West coun-try Fell in love wi Baw-bie Al-lan.

This is plainly an arrangement of two lines, not of four, as would be evident even without the music if our ancestors had not formed the habit of writing such patterns as quatrains. One has only to turn to the text of

[1] Greig, *Last Leaves*, p. 70. Quite as satisfactory for study would be the version of *The Baffled Knight* in Greig, p. 91.

St. Stephen and Herod (22), as set down in the fifteenth century, to see how natural the couplet is, how difficult a disposition of the words in quatrain-form would be.

As I have said, this couplet is the commonest metrical form of our ballads. One hundred and seventy-nine of the 305 specimens in Child follow it, although about a dozen of them have versions composed in other and different stanzas—a fact of significance for the history of ballads. At least four specimens,[1] furthermore, have stanzas of four seven-stressed lines, rhyming in couplets; and occasionally a ballad strays, as does *Dugall Quin* (294), from couplets to triads of the same seven-beat length.

Only less common than the line of seven stresses is the line of four. One hundred and eleven of the ballads in Child have this pattern, all but about a dozen of them following it consistently throughout all the versions I have observed. It has been assumed—without any proof whatever, I fear—that the ballads made up of couplets with lines of this length are the oldest of any preserved. With complete propriety, Child placed a group with this form at the beginning of his collection, all very interesting specimens of unquestionable antiquity, but with nothing about them to justify a belief that they are older as a class than many other ballads. The four-beat couplet, indeed, is found in certain songs like *The Bonny Earl of Murray* (181), *The Lads of Wamphray* (184), and *The Baron of Brackley* (203), which must have originated as late as the sixteenth or seventeenth century. According to my count, thirty-nine ballads appear in this couplet-form, while nine others[2] have stanzas of four lines rhyming in couplets. A majority of the ballads with four-stress lines, however—fifty-eight, to be more precise— is composed of quatrains in which the second line rhymes

---

[1] *Captain Wedderburn's Courtship* (46), *Captain Ward and the Rainbow* (287), *John of Hazelgreen* (293), and *Trooper and Maid* (299 A, B).

[2] 45, 104, 106, 170, 207, 234, 239, 272, 296.

with the fourth.[1] There is possibly a question whether this quatrain should be reckoned as being a couplet of eight-beat lines. An examination of both texts and melodies leads me to consider it a pattern of four lines; but the case is less clear than that of the so-called 'ballad stanza', already considered, which is certainly a couplet. One reason for my belief in the quatrain of four-stress lines is the existence of *Lord Randal* (12), which stands quite alone in its metrical structure. Each line of the stanza in this curious and beautiful song ends with a phrase of refrain, which is incorporated in the quatrain itself and obviates the use of rhyme in the ordinary sense :

'O where ha you been, Lord Randal, my son?
And where ha you been, my handsome young man?'
'I ha been at the greenwood; mother, mak my bed soon,
For I'm wearied wi hunting, and fain wad lie down.'

The numerous melodies that have been collected make the pattern of *Lord Randal* unquestionable, I think, as an interesting variation of the much-used quatrain that we have been discussing.

From what has gone before, the reader must have become aware that our ballads show a considerable variety of rhythmical structure. It is by no means correct to say of them, as Gummere did :[2] 'Ballad metres are almost uniform; the range is very slight; and they can all be reduced to variations of the immemorial verse of four accents.' On the contrary, the patterns are not of a dull uniformity, but as widely varied as could well be, considering both the narrative and the lyrical purposes for which they are employed.

Not only do we find lines of seven stresses and of four, in various stanzaic combinations, but we have four cases

[1] In a few cases, like 111 and 172, there is a fairly consistent attempt to make the first and third lines rhyme as well.
[2] *The Popular Ballad*, p. 325.

of what I take to be six-beat lines. The scheme of *Judas* (23) is difficult to make out; yet if it be set beside two versions of *The Laird of Wariston* (194 A, B), its form becomes at least a little less obscure and the verses are somewhat easier to read.[1] The six-stress couplet appears also, I believe, in a version of *The Baffled Knight* (112) from the west of England,[2] in *Lizie Lindsay* (226),[3] and in *The Crafty Farmer* (283).[4] One version of *The Baffled Knight*, I ought to note, presents a very odd phenomenon, which can be studied by comparing Child's D with Greig's Aberdeenshire variant.[5] It seems to me that this has to be taken as a couplet, of which the first line has six beats and the second seven.

As preserved, *The Hunting of the Cheviot* (162), *The Rising in the North* (175), and *King James and Brown* (180) are impossible to classify, since the stanzas—printed as quatrains—vary in the most confusing fashion with respect to the length of the lines of which they are composed. Lacking the guidance of melodies, one cannot be sure of what was intended. *The Beggar-Laddie* (280) is anomalous in another way, being composed of quatrains the first three lines of which have four stresses and rhyme together, while the fourth line has three stresses and is unrhymed.[6] Finally, I must note the case of that haunting ballad, *The False Knight upon the Road* (3), which should perhaps be set down as composed in four-beat couplets, but which presents such curious variations that I confess myself baffled by its rhythm.[7] It will serve to indicate

[1] Stanza 3 seems not to follow this pattern, but only stanza 3.

[2] Sharp, *J. F.-S. S.* ii. 19-20. Third version.

[3] See the melody in Greig, *Last Leaves*, p. 164.

[4] See the melody in Greig, *op. cit.*, pp. 236-7. The American versions printed by Combs and by Barry, Eckstorm, and Smyth are entirely different in form.

[5] Greig, *op. cit.*, pp. 90-1.

[6] The version in Greig, *op. cit.*, pp. 226-30, with two tunes, makes this pattern quite clear.

[7] See the melody in Davis, *Traditional Ballads of Virginia*, 1929, p. 549.

the need of more thorough-going studies of ballad metres than have as yet been made.

One characteristic of basic importance in the verse of ballads is nevertheless clear. Whatever the length of line and whatever the stanza form, the stresses fall with heavier and lighter weight in strict alternation. They are, as we say, primary and secondary. The effect of this alternation on the ear, when the verse is read, is subtly different from that of verse otherwise constituted, though I shall not try to say why it should be so. The explanation must be left to professed students of metrics and to physiological psychologists. For our purposes it is only necessary to observe some of the phenomena connected with rhythms thus produced. That the rhythms are captivating is shown not only by the popularity of ballads among readers unacquainted with the accompanying melodies, but by the extent to which modern poets have imitated them and thereby secured some of their most delightful metrical effects.

This alternation of primary and secondary stresses in the verse-scheme corresponds, of necessity, to a similar alternation of stress in the musical setting. The matter becomes far plainer, indeed, when the melodies are examined than when the verse is read. As far as my observation has gone, primary stresses almost invariably fall at the beginning of measures and thus correspond with the normal musical stresses.[1] Secondary stresses, on the other hand, ordinarily fall within the musical measures, though by no means always. When the music, for example, is in 3/4 time, the primary stress often comes at the beginning of one measure and the secondary stress at the beginning of the next measure, though this is not

[1] I have noted only two cases where the first stress in a stanza is not primary. In the variants, B, C, D, E of *Young Beichan*, recorded by Campbell and Sharp, pp. 40–42, the primary stresses coincide with the opening of musical measures, but in the two tunes for *The Beggar Laddie* to be found in Greig, pp. 228–30, this seems not to be true.

invariably the case. It must not be forgotten that singers have often varied the time within a melody, which greatly complicates the question of the relationship between the rhythms of the music and of the verse. The whole matter requires more study than has yet been given to it. I believe I am safe in saying, however, that the correspondence between verse stress and musical stress serves to unify the rhythmic patterns of the two and accentuates the qualities of each.

Another means by which the verse and melody of folk-songs are interlocked is the musical phrase. Sharp called attention[1] to this phenomenon, which is of great importance to an understanding of the verse. The phrase, it is perhaps needless to say, is not conterminous with a given number of measures, but corresponds to the line, or metrical unit, of poetry. Melodies are frequently built up in patterns that involve the repetition of one or more phrases. In other words, the parallelism so apparent in the texts of ballads finds a counterpart in the tunes. Whether this correspondence has been due to the music or to the verse, or whether they have influenced one another equally, can perhaps never be determined; but it should not be overlooked in an analysis of metrical structure. Further study of the matter might bring very useful results. This much is plain to see from the evidence in hand: to the correspondence between phrase and line is due something of the superior effectiveness that any ballad possesses when sung, as compared with even the best reading or recitation.

[1] *English Folk-Song: Some Conclusions*, pp. 73–8.

Chapter Six

BALLADS AS A RECORD OF THE PAST

THUS far we have been considering our British ballads with regard to their form and their content as stories. We have studied their relationship to the folk-songs of continental Europe, their poetical and musical qualities, their characteristics as narratives. We have looked at them almost wholly as a manifestation of popular art, which is on the whole their most important aspect, though not their only one. It has seemed to me wiser to describe them in this way, with some degree of completeness, before turning to another set of facts about them, as we must now do. Ballads are not simply narrative songs: they are folk-lore as well—a record of the past, in that they embody the experiences, the beliefs, and the imaginings of the people who have made and sung them. Their significance as a social phenomenon can thus not be appreciated without taking account of them as a record of the past, nor can a proper study be made of their origin unless we keep in mind how closely knit they are with the immemorial customs and instincts of the race.

To begin with, we must observe that people with an unlettered tradition, whether their culture has been primitive or relatively high, have never distinguished carefully between fact and fiction. They have regarded the tales they have memorized, whether in prose or in verse, as all on the same footing. They have found amusement in them, or some emotional release that has given them pleasure; and they have not weighed them as truth or fiction, because they have never learned to think in categories. In general, they have doubtless believed that the stories mirrored real happenings, just as they have accepted supernatural beings and events as a matter of course, but they have never worried about it. Whence they have made legends and clung to the memory of them with what seems to critical minds a certain frivolity; they have believed the incredible without attempting to test it by criticism; they have never even tried to discriminate between the plausible and the true.

Yet to condemn them as having no sense of truth or to scorn them as stupid would be altogether wrong, since these same credulous and inaccurate people may be able to recognize and report facts about most matters of ordinary life quite as well as more sophisticated folk. They merely do not differentiate categories with the same precision. This is well understood nowadays about the primitive races.[1] What is often overlooked is the fact that a state of mind similar to that of the primitive has remained among all peoples down to the present day, as one finds evidence on every hand when one looks. We who call ourselves civilized may perhaps think somewhat more clearly than do the natives of the Congo; we may keep things a little better in their proper categories; but we are notoriously incapable of dealing with evidence without making sad mistakes, and we are prone to believe what we wish to believe or what strikes our fancy.

It is not strange, therefore, that the makers and singers of European ballads—simple folk, though far removed from primitive culture—have not been reliable reporters of historical events. They have shown themselves to be interested in public affairs of various kinds, as the reader may observe for himself by reference to the analysis of themes in an earlier chapter,[2] but always in their sensational aspects and seldom with any understanding of their true significance. We should never turn to *The Rose of England* (166) for the light it throws on the triumph of

[1] See L. Lévy-Bruhl, *Les Fonctions mentales dans les sociétés inférieures*, 8e ed., 1928, pp. 76–102, 124–41.

[2] See Chapter III.

the Tudors, or to *The Rising in the North* (175) for an account of the rebellion of Northumberland and Westmorland in 1569. Although occasionally we learn details about some occurrence that seem to be veracious, as in *Northumberland Betrayed by Douglas* (176), which tells how the earl was delivered to the English, the history to be gleaned from ballads is fragmentary and fugitive, as far as actual events are concerned—random bits rather than coherent narratives.

Furthermore, despite the apparent objectivity of treatment to which I have called attention in an earlier chapter,[1] there is no doubt at all that happenings of the past are often sadly distorted in the ballads, and sometimes wholly falsified. *The Death of Queen Jane* (170) and *Queen Eleanor's Confession* (156), for example, rest on no basis of fact whatever, but at most on some kind of backstairs gossip that drifted away through the countryside. Similarly unsubstantiated and probably the fruit of malicious rumour is the hideous story in *The Fire of Frendraught* (196), which makes a Scotch laird burn two guests in his own house. Another very curious case is that of *The Baron of Brackley* (203), in which, as Child showed, the deaths of two men seventy-four years apart appear to have been confounded, to the manifest detriment of historical accuracy. In connexion with *Geordie* (209), the hero of which Kinloch and others 'believed might be George Gordon, fourth earl of Huntly', Child expressed the wise judgement : 'With regard to this hypothesis, it may at least be said that, if it should be accepted, the ballad would be quite as faithful to history as many others.'[2] We need not labour the point, I think. The ballads are unsafe guides both as to the facts and the perspective of history.

Yet it does not follow that they have no value as a record. Quite to the contrary, their worth is inestimable

[1] See pp. 8–10.　　　　　[2] iv. 124.

in more ways than one, because they reflect not only the
opinions and feelings of ordinary folk but their beliefs
and customs as well. The songs about Robin Hood give
us no assurance that such a hero ever existed in the flesh,
but they are a trustworthy index to the restiveness of the
common people under political, economic, and social
abuses, together with their ability to view even their
wrongs with tolerant humour—characteristics of at least
a considerable part of the English public through all the
centuries. Many of the events in the ballads of the
Border are doubtless set down without regard to what
actually occurred, but they represent faithfully the way
life went on in a wild region at a wild time. *The Battle
of Otterburn* and *The Hunting of the Cheviot* (161, 162)
are less important as chronicles of fact than of spirit.
Sir Andrew Barton (167) is a good case in point through
all its transformations—some of them so different from
the ballad as it appears in the Percy MS. and the early
broadsides that Child printed them under the separate
caption of *Henry Martyn* (250). There was a real Andrew
Barton, to begin with, whose exploits and manful death
were narrated by the English and Scottish chroniclers of
his time. Their accounts correspond roughly with the one
we find in the ballad as first recorded, though the latter
not only presents a highly imaginative picture of the sea-
fight but contains some obvious blunders of fact. The
versions collected in great numbers within the past fifty
years, however, show how very far tradition can deviate
from history; for not only is the hero's name often
changed, but his deeds and his fate have been altered
until no semblance of historical fact remains.[1] Yet despite the changes it has undergone, *Sir Andrew Barton* has
never ceased to exemplify the qualities that have made

[1] See Barry, Eckstorm, and Smyth, *British Ballads from Maine*, 1929, pp.
253–8, for an admirable analysis of the evidence that has appeared since Child
wrote his note.

the British, and their descendants along the eastern sea-board of America, sturdy maritime folk.

Nor should the sensationalism of ballad-themes deal-ing with domestic relationships blind us to the real value as social history of the pictures they give us. The virtues generally admired and the vices held in evil re-pute appear to be accurately represented. The emotional lives of ordinary people, their loves and hates, are mirrored with extreme simplicity and with no attempt whatever to make the worse appear the better. Even the scenes in which lords and ladies, or queens and kings, take part serve as well as those in which Jeanies and Williams are the actors to show the common conditions of life. There is a great deal of red gold in the halls of even quite modest gentlefolk, according to the ballads, and their dress on occasion is rich beyond compare; but the high-born do not differ from the people of low de-gree in anything save barbaric splendour. They have the same amusements, the same manners, the same habits of living, and the same ways of thought. In short, the ballads tell us a great deal of value about common folk and how they have pictured those above them in station, but very little that is trustworthy about the higher classes —unless we assume a social homogeneity in former days, despite consciousness of caste, that is extremely improb-able. What we learn from the ballads, I repeat, are the folk-ways of the past.

But not of any one century or period of the past. Nothing is more apparent or less disputed about the ballads than the curious way in which they mingle what is far off in time with what is less remote or actually con-temporary. It would not be true to say that folk memory never lapses, since certain habits of mind and behaviour, which must once have been very familiar for many cen-turies, appear to a very slight degree in the ballads. The best illustration of this is the paucity of references to the legends and ritualistic observances of the Church, as it existed in England previous to the reign of Henry VIII. In an earlier chapter[1] we have noticed the handful of ballads with themes drawn from stories of the medieval Church. This is indeed a scanty remnant, and the evidence they give of forgetfulness is borne out by the relatively sparse allusions to anything connected with the unreformed religion. The mass is recalled, but more often than not by oft-repeated commonplaces:

> When bells were rung, and mass was sung,
>   And a' men bound to bed.[2]

> The firstin kirk that they came till,
>   They gard the bells be rung,
> An the nextin kirk that they came till,
>   They gard the mess be sung.[3]

Occasionally a person makes the sign of the cross or makes use of holy water, like the heroine of *Tam Lin* (39), but in connexion with rites that are altogether pagan.

The Robin Hood ballads contain more reminiscences of the old faith than we find elsewhere—probably because most of our texts come from the seventeenth century, when the memory of such things had not grown dim with time. Robin Hood held the Virgin in great honour, it will be recalled (117); he compelled three bishops and an abbot to say masses at one time or another (143, 144, 145, 154); he dealt severely with monks, as well as bishops, who were recreant to their duty (117, 119); and he made a good death in religion after escaping from a wicked prioress (120 A). Palmers occur elsewhere, like the informer in *Johnie Cock* (114 A) and the unfortunate

---

[1] Chapter III.

[2] So in *Fair Annie* (62 A, 21). See Child's *Index* for a list of nearly thirty recurrences.

[3] So in *The Gay Goshawk* (96 A, 24). Child cites a dozen recurrences.

hero of *Old Robin of Portingale* (80), who by way of penance :

> shope the crosse in his right sholder,
> Of the white flesh and the redd,
> And he went him into the holy land,
> Whereas Christ was quicke and dead.

There are confused and faded recollections of Purgatory in *The Cruel Mother* (20) and *The Maid and the Palmer* (21), and equally vague is the reference to the Virgin in *Thomas Rymer* (37), where Thomas addresses the Queen of Elfland as ' thou mighty Queen of Heaven '.

It is only fair to say that no religious observances of any sort are very much stressed in the ballads as a whole. The people who sang them either lacked strong feelings about their faith or kept them separate from their amusements. When one recalls how little the popular drama of the Elizabethan period was affected by the religious controversies of the time, one is inclined to the notion that such matters went on over the heads of the ordinary folk—unless they became zealots, and neither went to the play nor continued to sing ballads. In any event, the comparatively insignificant part that religion plays in balladry should not be ignored in considering our songs as a record of the past. It is certainly a fact that customs and beliefs, which cannot be dated because they come from so remote a period, are more important as springs of action, more vividly present in consciousness, than is Christianity. Rooted deep in instinct, they have lived on to the threshold of our own day, though later customs and beliefs have been forgotten.

The ballads thus present what might be called a longitudinal view of the past, never adequate for any one period and completely careless of chronology, but immensely valuable to our knowledge all the same, because extending indeterminately into the centuries. We cannot hope to get from them a coherent picture of things as they stood at any one time, but simply the time-worn residue from many ages. Much has been lost from memory, but so much has persisted that any ballad may contain—no matter when it individually came into being —some reference to practices or conceptions that belonged in the first place to a very primitive state of culture. The mixture of the old with the relatively new is complete.

In *Johnie Cock*, for instance, and in a single version (114 A) we find an allusion to riding 'the fords of hell', which clearly implies a lurking notion that a barrier of water exists between this world and the next; we are told that the hero put on 'the Lincoln green' for his hunting, which recalls the industrial development of England in the later Middle Ages, but a few stanzas further on we discover that he wore shoes of 'American leather'; we see Johnnie drinking the hot blood of the deer he has slain, which is barbaric enough, even if it does not conceal a hint of sympathetic magic; we have a palmer entering the scene as an informer; we get a clear reference to a 'sister's son' as a man's next-of-kin; and in the hero's final speech we learn that for him, as for other primitive folk, there is no definite line of demarcation between the world of men and the community of beasts and trees.

> 'The wildest wolf in aw this wood
>   Wad not ha done so by me;
>   She'd ha wet her foot ith wan water,
>   And sprinkled it oer my brae,
>   And if that wad not ha wakend me,
>   She wad ha gone and let me be.'

Whereupon he addresses his 'bows of yew' as if they were alive and could stand by him as comrade supports comrade.

A systematic review of the survivals in balladry of

ideas that are ultimately pre-Christian reveals their
amazing persistence, despite all that has happened
since Columba and Augustine began their labours.
What we find is not scattered waifs and strays, but a
body of customary beliefs far more extensive than would
seem possible if the evidence were not so clear. This
evidence has recently been collected and arranged by
Professor Wimberly in an admirable book,[1] to which
all subsequent studies in this field must of necessity be
under heavy obligations. The reader who wishes a well-
nigh complete and excellently ordered account of the
folk-lore which is so important a part of ballad material,
should work through Mr. Wimberly's monograph.
A brief sketch is all that we shall have space for in the
present volume, and all that we need for our purpose.

We may as well begin with ghosts, since the way they
appear in the ballads reveals very plainly certain differences between the conceptions of the makers and our
own. In the first place, the ghost is neither a pale wraith
nor an emanation without substance, but simply a man
or woman who is dead. Accordingly, it can behave like
a mortal and often has to announce its status, since there
is nothing in its appearance to show that it has come
from the grave. So in one variant of *Sweet William's
Ghost* (77 A) the spirit ' tirled at the pin ' of Margaret's
door, and in others had to deny his sweetheart's request
for a kiss because of the danger to her, or say explicitly
' I'm nae a levin man ', before she recognized the nature
of her visitant. In *The Wife of Usher's Well* (79) the
mother appears not to understand that her sons have
not indeed come home to her ' in earthly flesh and
blood ', which more than anything else gives tragic
pathos to the story. She prepares a supper for them and
makes their bed, as she had been accustomed to do.

[1] L. C. Wimberly, *Folklore in the English and Scottish Ballads*, 1928.

Furthermore, the youngest brother warns the eldest :

> 'The cock doth craw, the day doth daw,
>   The channerin worm doth chide;
> Gin we be mist out o our place,
>   A sair pain we maun bide.'

They are dead, but they have the corporeal sensations of living men because, clearly, they have corporeal substance.

The ghost of *The Suffolk Miracle* (272) is equally material, though all our variants derive from a broadside which smells of ink, and could thus not be expected to reflect popular conceptions. *The Cruel Mother* (20) furnishes another good illustration. The murdered babies return in such unquestionable shape that the mother sees them playing ball and does not suspect that her crime has found her out. Elsewhere, as in *Sir Hugh* (155 A), the ghost is referred to as a corpse :

> And at the back o merry Lincoln
>   The dead corpse did her meet.

In one version of *Sweet William's Ghost* (77 F) the lover returns without arms because, as he explains :

> 'By worms they're eaten, in mools they're rotten,
>   Behold, Margaret, and see.'

In a word, the balladist does not distinguish clearly between body and spirit, or at least is unable to conceive of spirit without the body. A man who is dead, and who returns to familiar scenes, must appear as a dead man reanimated for the time, since death has changed his abode but not his substance.

It is characteristic of this conception that when ghosts disappear, they almost never vanish in a twinkling. Instead, they go back to the graves whence they have come, and they do so in a completely unsensational fashion. Different versions of *Sweet William's Ghost*, for instance, illustrate this. In one,[1] which certainly suffered from the

---

[1] Child A, from Ramsay's *Tea Table Miscellany*.

improving hand of an eighteenth-century editor, the lover 'with a grievous groan' is indeed said to have 'evanished in a cloud of mist'; but he was returning to his coffin and not to any world of spirits. In this version, as in three others,[1] Margaret wished to lie down in the grave with her lover, which emphasizes both his corporeal nature and the matter-of-fact way in which the living and dead meet one another. In three versions of *Proud Lady Margaret* (47 A, B, C) the heroine, repentant of her sin, offers in the same fashion to accompany her brother back to the grave, but is told that she is not ready for death :

> 'For ye've unwashen hands and ye've unwashen feet,
> To gae to clay wi me.'

Some of the reasons for the appearance of ghosts show the same materialistic conception that we have been observing, although others at least fail to enforce it. The dead lover of *The Unquiet Grave* (78), who is disturbed by the grief of a sweetheart, is obviously not pure spirit, but a being with sense perceptions like our own. So, too, are the lovers who are unable to rest in their graves until their 'troth-plight' is given back to them, as is the case in *Sweet William's Ghost* (77) and *The Brown Girl* (295). On the other hand, the dead who return to give good advice, like Willie in *Proud Lady Margaret*, or to take vengeance, like the terrible creature in *James Harris* (243), are not necessarily dead men set free from the grave, but may be ghosts in the more ordinary sense. In the latter instance, the returned lover counterfeits perfectly his living self, but he is in no way earth-bound like most of the dead men we have noticed, being a free rover and, in some versions, a demon with a cloven hoof rather than a proper ghost. The babies in *The Cruel Mother* appear like living children, as we have observed, but they speak like messengers from another world, in their announce-

[1] Child B, D, F.

ment of what their mother must suffer, rather than as self-appointed avengers. In *Sir Hugh* (155) the dead boy is chiefly concerned with getting proper burial, and in only one version (A) actually appears to his mother in visible form.

That the dead may be summoned from the grave is illustrated equally well by *Sir Hugh* and by *The Wife of Usher's Well*, for in each case it is the mother's longing grief that causes the return. Even more explicit, however, is the statement in one version of *The Twa Brothers* (49 B), which says of Lady Margaret :

> She put the small pipes to her mouth,
> And she harped both far and near,
> Till she harped the small birds off the briers,
> And her true love out of the grave.

No doubt this stanza came originally from *Sweet William's Ghost*, as Child thought ; but it shows the strength of the belief that the dead may be raised by one means or another—all the more, indeed, if it be a transferable commonplace. The means used in *Young Benjie* (86 A) to make a dead girl reveal the name of her murderer are not different in kind, even though in this case there has been no burial of the corpse. Marjorie's brothers leave the door ajar while they watch her body, which causes her to speak ' at the dead hour o the night ' : a magical rite still practised in Sir Walter Scott's day, as he testified, where murder was suspected.

But other supernatural beings than ghosts are taken for granted in ballads, and concern themselves with the affairs of mortals as a matter of course. Fairies, for example, though they are represented as a race apart with attributes of their own, are after all not very different from men and women. Professor Wimberly has pointed out[1] the rather striking fact that, except in the case of *The Wee Wee Man* (38) and a version of *The Queen of*

[1] *Op. cit.*, p. 168.

Elfan's Nourice (40),[1] ballad fairies are not diminutive creatures but quite ordinary in size. Except for their powers of making themselves invisible at will and of performing remarkable feats of other kinds, there is little to differentiate them from men. Fairy women are almost always beautiful, it is true, and gorgeously clad, but so too are most queens and fine ladies who appear in the ballads. Though immemorial in folk-belief, fairies are without question an embodiment of desire, just as are the knights and heiresses whose adventures in battle or love gave a vicarious experience of romance to rapt singers and audiences. Fairies are only a little more bespangled with jewels, a little better endowed with gold than the most fortunate mortals, because the freest rein could be given to fancy in describing them. They are what the country lad and country girl dreamed of being, untrammelled by the restrictions of a workaday world, uncontrolled by duty or loyalties of caste and code. The description of the Fairy Queen's court in *The Wee Wee Man* (38 B) is characteristic:

> Wi four and twentie at her back,
>   A' comely cled in glistering green;
> Thouch there the King of Scots had stude,
>   The warst micht weil hae been his queen.

The roof of the Queen's bonny hall was beaten gold, the floor of crystal: imagined opulence could go no further.

In the colour of their dress, the fairies just noticed are like most supernatural folk. Green is their colour, though it may glitter like gold. This is the garb of the Queen of Elfland in *Thomas Rymer* (37 A):

> Her skirt was of the grass-green silk,
>   Her mantel of the velvet fine,
> At ilka tett of her horse's mane
>   Hung fifty silver bells and nine.

---

[1] See C. H. Eldred, *J. A. F.-L.* xx. 155-6 (1907). This version, coming from Dumfries, is the second recovered, Child having but one.

The mermaid in *Clerk Colvill* (42 A) is likewise dressed in green, and there is a touch of the colour about mortals who stray into Fairyland. The hero of *Thomas Rymer* (A, C) has shoes of green velvet, and from *Tam Lin* (39 M) we learn that:

> There was four-and-twenty earthly maids,
>> Wha a' playd at the chess,
> Their colour rosy-red and white,
>> Their gowns were green as grass.

Only in three versions[1] of *Tam Lin* do we find a reference to an 'elfin grey', for in general fairy folk are resplendent, like True Thomas's enchantress, whom he takes to be Queen of Heaven.

Just as popular tradition did not distinguish any too clearly between mortals and fairies, so it drew no sharp line between fairies and other supernatural beings. We have noted that Janet in *Tam Lin* calls her lover 'an elfin grey'. The instance is a good one in point. Tam Lin turns out to be a bespelled knight, of course, who has been serving in the train of the Fairy Queen:

> Out then spak the Queen o Fairies,
>> And an angry woman was she:
> 'Shame betide her ill-far'd face,
>> And an ill death may she die,
> For she's taen awa the boniest knight
>> In a' my companie.'

Evidently elves and fairies were all the same to the singer from whom Burns got the words of this variant. Child called the elf in *The Elfin Knight* (2) 'an intruder in this particular ballad',[2] as he may well be, but his presence is another illustration of the vagueness about categories that is so marked throughout traditional lore. There can be no question that the malevolent lover in *Lady Isabel and the Elf-Knight* (4) was a supernatural being from the beginning; but his attributes are not those ordinarily attri-

---

[1] A, B, I.   [2] i. 13.

buted to elves. Whether represented as an elf or as a mortal, he appears to attempt the murder of the heroine merely for the sake of bloodshed. Neither in the British versions of the ballad nor in their Continental relatives is the nature of the creature made altogether clear—obviously because it has not been clear, for centuries at least, to those who have sung about it. The hero of *Hind Etin* (41) is another person of indeterminate status. In the four Scottish versions[1] he is scarcely more than an outlaw, though there are hints of his supernatural origin in his name, in the statement that he 'neer got christendome', and in the fact that on meeting Lady Margaret in the wood:

> The highest tree in Elmond's wood,
> He's pu'd it by the reet,
> And he has built for her a bower,
> Near by a hallow seat.

But 'the etin of the Scottish story is in Norse and German a dwarf-king, elf-king, hill-king, or even a merman'.[2] Here again there is evidence that categories of the supernatural are loosely held.

The same vagueness of idea about the difference between mortals and other creatures is shown by the stories based on the belief that a man or woman may exist in two quite different forms. The mournful and 'grumly guest' of *The Great Silkie of Sule Skerry* (113) was a man when on the land but a seal when in the sea, yet presumably always a merman. The jealous mistress who avenged herself on Clerk Colvill (42) was a lady as well as a mermaiden. A change of shape, moreover, is almost a commonplace of wizardry. In *The Earl of Mar's Daughter* (270) transformation is treated playfully, since Cow-me-doo can become bird or man at his own will, and at the proper time appeals to the more powerful witchcraft of his mother to turn a force of four-and-twenty men into

---

[1] Three in Child, a fourth in Greig, *Last Leaves*, pp. 29–31.
[2] Child, i. 361.

storks and his brothers into swans, in order to kidnap the willing bride. This is a mere flight of fancy, if you please, implying no real belief; and the same may be said of the loathly ladies in *The Marriage of Sir Gawain* (31) and *King Henry* (32). Such songs were intended for amusement, and should perhaps not be taken too seriously. Yet we must remember the matter-of-fact acceptance of the idea of transformation in all stories of this kind. A notion cannot be played with unless it is a commonplace. Of this *The Twa Magicians* (44) is the best possible example. There can be no question, in any event, that deep-seated conviction inspired grim tales like *The Laily Worm and the Machrel of the Sea* (36) and *Kemp Owyne* (34), in both of which wicked stepmothers lay spells on their husbands' children and transform them hideously. The incidental warning in *Leesome Brand* (15) not to shoot the white hind, 'for she is o the woman kind',[1] indicates equally a fixed belief in metamorphosis. *Allison Gross* (35) likewise shows something a good deal beyond a mere recollection of former faith in such transformations. The completely pagan quality of the ballad may be seen in the fact that the hero is saved from the power of the witch by the Queen of the Fairies, who happens by on Halloween and takes pity on him.

Not only is there confusion among categories of living creatures, and a well-marked tendency to describe the transference of individuals from one class to another, but a belief that inanimate things may at times show human attributes. Talismans, like the rings in *Hind Horn* (17) and *Bonny Bee Hom* (92) that by changing their appearance give information about a loved one—a commonplace of medieval romance—may probably be regarded as illustrating this. Much more clearly, however, the behaviour of certain ships gives evidence of the idea. The 'comely coug' of *Young Allan* (245) responds to his

[1] Found in Child A and Greig, *Last Leaves*, p. 16.

address; the vessels in *Bonnie Annie* (24) and *Brown Robyn's Confession* (57) are stern moralists, and will not suffer the presence of a guilty mortal. Most striking of all, as an illustration, is the scene in two versions of *Gil Brenton* (5 A, B). The hero demands of blankets, sheets, and pillows (or blankets, sheets, and 'sword that winna lie') whether his latest bride is a maid, and promptly receives the answer that she is not.

Witchcraft in our ballads cannot be wholly separated from the practices of such supernatural folk as we have recently been considering. The black magic, that is to say, consists to a remarkable extent in transformations like those performed by the stepmothers of *Kemp Owyne* and *The Laily Worm*, or by the witch of *Allison Gross*. Such malevolent spells are all of the same kind, whoever lays them. The interesting observation has been made by Professor Wimberly that the mortals who deal in magic, whether black or white, are not as a rule 'professional' practitioners of the art; 'that is, they are not pictured in folksong as "official" or public magicians, such as witch doctors or medicine men'.[1] Allison Gross is an exception: she was 'the ugliest witch in the north country'. For the most part, the person who works magic—and it is almost always a woman—simply has a knowledge of the necessary procedure and uses it on occasion to accomplish some desired end. As Professor Wimberly goes on to say, 'the ballads give no evidence of organized witch cults', which is a matter of some importance. Magic appears to be regarded as one form of traditional lore, to which any one from queen to peasant might have recourse in time of need. As Young Adler says in *King Estmere* (60):

> 'My mother was a westerne woman,
> And learned in gramarye,
> And when I learned at the schole,
> Something shee taught itt mee.'

[1] *Op. cit.*, p. 204.

Similarly, Mary Douglas in *Northumberland Betrayed by Douglas* (176) says that she has never loved witchcraft, but that she has learned 'part of it' from her mother, and thus is able to see future events 'through the weme of her ring'.

Magic in the ballads is thus rather homespun stuff, unless it is worked by beings of supernatural quality and powers. *Willie's Lady* (6), which in its British form unfortunately survives in only two versions, both from Aberdeenshire,[1] provides an admirable illustration of this, and at the same time the completest account of magical procedure to be found in the ballads. Willie's mother, though a 'vile rank witch of vilest kind', is nevertheless the mistress of a household like any other lady. We do not learn why she arrests the birth of her son's child—only the means by which she does it, and the means by which her wiles are countered. She resists the bribes and threats of the young couple, but is outwitted through an image in the form of a baby, a trick suggested by Belly (or Billy) Blind, who is a helpful household familiar of indeterminate nature, known to us also from his appearance in *Gil Brenton* (5 c), *Young Beichan* (53 c), and *The Knight and the Shepherd's Daughter* (110 f, g, m, n).[2] When the mother sees the supposed child, she reveals what she has done. In one version she has tied nine witch-knots and put 'combs of care' in her daughter-in-law's hair, hung a 'bush of woodbine' between their bowers, stabled a kid beneath the bed, and tightened the shoe on the wife's left foot. In the other version she has banded the young woman's arms, locked the frame of the bed on the side away from the wall, and placed a 'ted' under-

[1] Child's, from Mrs. Brown of Falkland, and the fragment in Greig, *Last Leaves*, pp. 4–5.

[2] Of indeterminate nature, because Burlow-Beanie, found in *King Arthur and King Cornwall* (30), appears as a seven-headed fiend with fiery breath, and yet may well be the same creature. Under command of the Green Knight, Burlow-Beanie proves a very useful assistant.

neath the bed. All these spells are of course easy to undo, once they are known. In their simplicity they are far from what one would expect of a professed sorceress, but precisely the kind of thing natural to the domestic practice of the black art.

White magic is of the same rather simple sort. In some of the versions of *Tam Lin* (39) the heroine removes the spell from her lover, according to his directions, not only by holding him fast while he is turned into a variety of strange shapes but by performing some kind of purificatory rite. In three versions[1] she takes holy water in her hand and marks a circle with it, presumably seizing the elfin knight as he passes through the ring. In another[2] she plunges him into well water at the end of his trials; and in two others[3] she dips him successively in a 'stand of milk' and a 'stand of water'. In several versions of *The Broomfield Hill* (43)[4] a maiden strews the broom-flower on her lover to make him sleep, adding to the effectiveness of the spell in one text by enclosing him in a magic circle, while in other variants[5] only the circle is used. Here again there is nothing but uncomplicated lore of the countryside. The same thing is true of the means used in *King Estmere* (60), despite the romantic background of that story, to change the complexion of the adventurous brothers and make them invulnerable. 'An hearbe within this field' does it all.

Benevolent magic, but much less homespun in quality, is the test of chastity found in *Gil Brenton* (5) and in one version of *Leesome Brand* (15)[6], which consists of seeing

---

[1] Child, D, G, Greig, *op. cit.*, pp. 26–9.

[2] Child A.   [3] Child B, 1.

[4] Child A, B, C, also J. H. Combs, *Folk-Songs du Midi*, 1925, p. 128, and *The Pearl Songster*, 1846, quoted in Barry, Eckstorm, and Smyth, *op. cit.*, p. 440.

[5] The four English variants printed in *J. F.-S. S.* iv. 110–16, all take this form, although one of them has the rite preceded by the administration of a sleeping-draught.

[6] See Greig, *op. cit.*, p. 16.

whether a young woman is able to sit in a golden chair. We remember, too, the famous cloak at King Arthur's court in *The Boy and the Mantle* (29), and the horn in the same ballad, from which no cuckold could drink. In *Leesome Brand*, again, the hero restores his lady to life by three drops of blood—Saint Paul's in one version—which he takes from a horn at his mother's bed-head. Such cases as these do not reveal magic as practised, it is obvious, but that much more wonderful art which existed solely in the fancy of believers. Supernatural beings, of whatever nature, could do extraordinary things as a matter of course; but except for the spells, which we have already noted, mere mortals are generally confined to feats that involve little beyond the wisdom of experience, whether real or imagined. A witch in *The Gay Goshawk* (96), for example, advises the use of drops of burning lead in order to see whether the heroine is really dead, which is not magic at all but a cruel ordeal hardly borne by the girl for her lover's sake.

To fairy folk or other supernatural beings amazing powers are attributed without stint. A stanza in *Hind Etin* (41 A) is typical :

> He's built a bower, made it secure
>   Wi carbuncle and stane;
> Tho travellers were never sae nigh,
>   Appearance it had nane.

Fairies can thus dwell invisible, and they can change their shape at will, as we have seen. They can also transform other persons with equal ease. It is dangerous to touch them, as is shown by the kiss with which True Thomas seals his doom in *Thomas Rymer* (37); it is dangerous to listen to their music, as we learn from *The Elfin Knight* (2) and *Lady Isabel and the Elf-Knight* (4); it is dangerous to meet them unawares unless one be very clever, as we are informed by such riddling ballads as *The False Knight upon the Road* (3) and *Riddles Wisely Expounded* (1). Any sort of wonderful thing may take place, in fact, once the boundaries of ordinary experience are passed. It occasions no surprise when the musical instrument made of various parts of the drowned girl's body in *The Twa Sisters* (10) reveals the guilt of the murderess. Nothing could be more significant of the general inclination to accept as a matter of course the amazing event of whatever sort than the final stanzas of two versions of *James Harris* (243 E, F), which recount the destruction of the ship in which the Demon Lover has carried away his unfortunate early love. In the one ' he sunk the ship in a flash of fire ', and in the other:

> He strack the tap-mast wi his hand,
>   The fore-mast wi his knee,
> And he brake that gallant ship in twain,
>   And sank her in the sea.

The point is that this ballad has been almost completely rationalized, even in these two versions, becoming the story of a sailor's vengeance on a ship-carpenter's wife. Only as she spies her lover's 'cloven foot' is she prepared, or are we, for the sensational endings I have quoted. To the balladist, however, the day of miracles is never past.

The evidence we have been looking at with reference to dead persons, to supernatural beings of various sorts, and to magic and miracle, all points to the survival, in somewhat vague and disordered reminiscence, of very primitive beliefs and customs. We cannot safely reconstruct from it a picture of the way our ancestors thought, felt, and acted at any one period of the past; but we can appreciate the conservatism which has led them never to let go utterly anything that has once become rooted in their instinctive life. If it appears that the people who made and preserved the ballads had minds that were rag-bags, in which oddments from various stages of cultural development might any day appear, we need not be shocked or surprised. He who looks for a well-arranged set of concepts, and for behaviour based reasonably thereon, is doomed to disappointment, whatever the group he is observing. Even professed philosophers sometimes act, one has noted, in accordance with their inheritance from the neolithic age rather than in the light of pure reason. Simple folk, living uncritically, may therefore be forgiven for holding fast to quite inconsistent ideas and observances. Our ballad-singers of the past few centuries have not been a primitive people, in the anthropological sense, or even pagans ; but they have kept a residue of very ancient lore.

The fact, for example, that two of the ballads show clear evidence of a belief in transmigration of souls does not prove that their history as songs goes back to a time when this belief was generally held, but it does show a lingering survival of notions about metempsychosis. In both *The Maid and the Palmer* (21) and *The Cruel Mother* (20) the idea is associated with retribution for sin, and in both the transformations end in hell. It is interesting that the stages through which the wicked woman of the latter ballad is doomed to pass vary somewhat in different versions, indicating that the idea has not been so alien to popular thought as to make changes impossible. Similarly, versions of no less than nine different ballads [1] end with the commonplace that out of the graves of unhappy lovers spring a rose and a briar, or a briar and a birch. This mirrors—even if vaguely—the notion that the dead may be transformed into trees, which is current among primitive folk throughout the world.

So, too, some of the talking birds and beasts reflect a belief that the human soul may inhabit the body of a creature lower than man in the scale of being. We have

---

[1] See Wimberly, *op. cit.*, pp. 38–40, for a careful analysis of this matter.

already seen [1] that this may be due to vagueness of categories or to magical spells; but we must recognize the probability that sometimes, as is true in several versions of *Young Hunting* (68), there is an identification of a dead man with animal or bird. The parrot, the pyet, the popinjay, or—more simply—the 'bonny bird' is none other than Young Hunting himself, slain by his jealous mistress but able to denounce her because his soul has merely changed its dwelling-place. Thus in *Leesome Brand*, as has been made clear by the publication of Greig's Aberdeenshire version,[2] the young heroine becomes a 'white hind' as soon as she dies; and the 'fallow doe' of *The Three Ravens* (26) is certainly the mistress of the dead knight:

> She buried him before the prime,
> She was dead herselfe ere even-song time.
>
> God send every gentleman,
> Such haukes, such hounds, and such a leman.

The secret powers residing in names furnish another illustration of vestigial beliefs that are well worthy of note. Although common in the folk-lore of most countries, this notion has been almost obliterated from British memory. The clearest case of it is in *Riddles Wisely Expounded* (1 c), where the devil is to put to flight when the young girl he is tempting utters his name. The name and the person are so completely identified that Clootie's disguise is stripped from him:

> As sune as she the fiend did name,
> He flew awa in a blazing flame.

In such instances, no doubt, ballad-singers have been wholly unconscious of continuing a way of thought that can be traced back, at least conjecturally, to the dim past when a mysterious power of personality first came to recognition—what anthropologists, borrowing a

[1] See *ante*, pp. 145-6.   [2] See *Last Leaves*, pp. 16-17.

convenient term from the South Seas, have come to know as *mana*. The effective force of traditional memory, which can preserve unrelated ideas through uncounted generations, could not be better illustrated than from such waifs and strays.

Of the same sort, but much better preserved, are notions connected with the blood. It was felt, for example, that blood, as the principle of life, had some occult virtue and might be preserved with advantage by the enemy who had killed a person.[1] We find this illustrated not only by certain versions of *Sir Hugh* (155 F, H, J), which is a story of ritual murder, but quite clearly in *Lamkin* (93) and intrusively in *Little Musgrave and Lady Barnard* (81 G). In *Sir Hugh* the Jew's daughter planned to use the blood of the murdered boy in the evil practices so curiously and persistently attributed to the Hebrew race ; and the vengeful Lamkin—who must originally have been a far more sinister figure than the disappointed mason he seems in extant versions of the ballad—cannot but have had in mind a similar disposition of the blood which he and the nurse collected in a basin:

> 'O scour the bason, nourice,
>   and mak it fair and clean,
> For to keep this lady's heart's blood,
>   for she's come o noble kin.'[2]

Professor Wimberly, following Child,[3] thinks that the reference to catching blood in ' basin of pure silver ', which appears in *Little Musgave*, was borrowed from Lamkin. This may well be true, but that does not make the allusion less interesting, since the trait would scarcely have strayed into another ballad unless some singer felt it to be natural that Lord Barnard should wish to save the blood of the man he had slain.

[1] This seems to me a more probable explanation than that advanced by Wimberly, *op. cit.*, pp. 76–8.

[2] 93 A.   [3] ii. 243.

A curious passage occurring in several versions of *Barbara Allan* (84), though not in those printed by Child, has been classified by Professor Wimberly[1] with those just considered; but I believe that it has a somewhat different significance. The dying lover, who has been scorned by Barbara, says to her :

> 'Look down, look down, at my bed-side,
> You'll see a bowl o'er flowing;
> And in that bowl there's my heart's blood,
> That's shed for Barbara Ellen.'

There is no question here of preserving the blood for any sinister purpose: it is bequeathed by the man simply because it is somehow regarded as a symbol of his personality. The same idea, that the soul is the blood or intimately connected with the blood, may be further illustrated by the 'penknife' in *The Cruel Mother* (20 Q) that cannot be wiped clean, and by the way blood gushes from the wounds of a corpse when the murderess comes near, as in *Young Hunting* (68 B, C). So, too, the widowed lady in *The Braes o Yarrow* (214 E, F, G, M) drinks the blood of her husband when she finds him slain.

Interesting because they are based on this same primitive conception, and equally because they reflect a social custom of earlier centuries, are the traces of blood-brotherhood that appear in the ballads. In *Adam Bell* (116) three friends go to the forest together as outlaws and 'swear them brethren', and in *Bewick and Graham* (211) a tragic story turns on the fact of a similar relationship, which is taken for granted just as it is in medieval romances.[2] In neither instance is the blood

---

[1] *Op. cit.*, pp. 78–9. He cites the Virginian variant printed above, for which see Tolman, *J. A. F.-L.* xxix. 160–1, as well as C. Burne, *Shropshire Folk-Lore*, 1883–6, p. 543, Greig, *Last Leaves*, pp. 68, 257, and Merrick, *J. F.-S. S.* i. 111 (from Sussex). To be added are two variants, one from Louisiana and one from Cape Breton Island, in Davis, *Traditional Ballads of Virginia*, 1929, pp. 304, 333.

[2] See, for some account of the rite and its survival, my article, *Englische Studien*, xxxvi. 193–201 (1906).

rite mentioned, any more than it is in connexion with Chaucer's Palamon and Arcite ; but the sacred character of the oath is clear, at least in *Bewick and Graham*. It is one instance, among many, of how custom may survive belief.

Indeed, the evidence in ballads of folk-ways that have lost the significance they must once have held is very considerable, as it must always be among people who are conservative in behaviour. Some of the cases of magical practice at which we have been looking cannot be supposed to have been anything more than mere superstitions—using the word in its proper sense—within the period when they have been incorporated in ballads ; and many of them cannot be fully understood without reference to the lore of folk who have never emerged from a primitive stage of culture. What lies behind the notion that candles will gleam more brightly when they pass above a dead man in the water is extremely difficult to say, yet we doubtless have a reference to a real practice in *Young Hunting* (68):

> Thay left off their ducking o the day,
> And ducked upon the night,
> And where that sakeless knight lay slain,
> The candles shone full bright.

Four versions of the ballad preserve this trait.

Similarly, ordeals by fire and by battle were not unknown customs within the period of balladry, though a deal of complicated explanation is required to show how they came to be regarded as valid tests of guilt or innocence. The ordeal of fire appears in *Young Hunting*, which has just been cited in another connexion. Half a dozen versions end with a scene that represents a fire as failing to injure a bower-woman, who has been merely an accessory after the fact, and consuming the guilty lady who has killed her lover. So in *Sir Aldingar* (59) the guiltless queen was thrown into a 'tun of fire' just before a child champion 'came ryding forth of the east' (as the English version has it) or a knight appeared to prove her innocence by arms (as the Scottish form says). In *James Hatley* (244) a youth does battle with the man who has accused him of stealing the king's jewels, and of course triumphs.

Burial rites, as one would expect, are extremely well illustrated in the ballads, some of them clearly associated with definite beliefs and some of them harder to explain, though quite as customary. Bells ring for the passing soul, for the wake, for the interment. As we read in *Clerk Saunders* (69 A):

> The bells gaed clinking throw the towne,
> To carry the dead corps to the clay.

The mingled laments and merry-making of those who watch the dead are amply shown. The honours paid by way of clothing and adorning the corpse are extravagantly pictured—wishes, no doubt, fathering the thought. In *The Gay Goshawk* (96 B) the supposedly dead girl's smock is made:

> The one side of the bonny beaten gold,
> And the other of the needle-work.

The coffins and the biers of the same ceremony glitter with silver and gold. All the pitiful circumstance of death is paraded for us in the songs, for their makers have been inclined to dwell on these things. Although death is bravely met, even by those who die on account of their misdeeds, all fey folk have a customary tendency to concern themselves with the place and manner of their burial. A curious case of the sort is the injunction of the heroines in *Leesome Brand* (15 B) and *Sheath and Knife* (16 A), which is echoed in *Willie and Earl Richard's Daughter* (102), that their graves shall be made where a shot arrow falls. Testamentary instructions of a more normal kind are a commonplace.[1]

---

[1] For a detailed analysis of these matters see L. C. Wimberly, *Death and*

Although marriages are recorded in great numbers, the ritual of them is much more incidentally treated than that of death, which should occasion no surprise. Save for untoward accident, weddings do not provide dramatic incident of the sort that would be elaborated in a ballad, whereas death has the fascination of a great mystery and often serves as a grand climax. We get bridal feasts when they are interrupted, as is the one in *Katharine Jaffray* (221), by a preferred wooer, or when they are made the scene of some such tragic event as occurs in *Fair Janet* (64), but for the most part the balladists are content with the bare mention of bells and merry-making.

Birth, as the twin mystery of death, is recorded with considerable detail about customs. For example, the well-known tabu on the presence of a man during child-birth is found in at least seven different ballads,[1] invariably in the form of an admonition from the woman to keep at a distance. The knots in the heroine's hair in *Willie's Lady* (6) recall at least the custom of unloosening knots to aid parturition. Presumably the 'roddins' demanded by the heroine of *Willie o Douglas Dale* (101) were to serve the same end, for the princess asks also for 'Marywell water'; and her travail was soon at an end. If the 'roddins' refer to the berries of mountain ash, there is homely magic at work here, since the rowan shares with the birch a reputation for uncanny powers. The pangs of labour, which Sweet Willie endures in one version of *Fair Janet* (64 F) can scarcely be said to point to an established custom, but they do emphasize the primitive character of the lore about childbirth, since sympathetic affliction of this sort has been reported from peoples of low culture in many parts of the world.

Burial Lore in the English and Scottish Popular Ballads, 1927 (University of Nebraska Studies, no. 8).

[1] 15 A, 24 A. B, 63 J, 64 C, D, H, 101 D, 102 B, 103 A, B (also Greig, *Last Leaves*, pp. 79–81).

Dreams, though sufficiently common in ballads, are neither so extraordinary in kind nor so frequent as one would expect from the folk-lore of other sorts that appears. It has been said of the dreams with truth that they 'point almost invariably to death and misfortune';[1] and it may be added that their range is limited. If one considers the importance of visions of every sort in our older narrative literature, one cannot fail to be surprised at the small part they play in the motivation of ballads. They are, moreover, exclusively ominous, and almost always portents of evil. Most common is a dream of swine— usually red—and a bower—or a bride-bed—full of blood, which occurs in no less than four songs,[2] while a variant of it turns the swine into swans, as in *Lord Livingston* (262). The fact that this was so frequently used, and so easily changed, leads one to suspect that it may have been taken rather as a proper adornment for a ballad than a serious presage of misfortune. Yet it is known from other sources that dreaming of swine is unlucky. *The Braes o Yarrow* (214) furnishes somewhat more interesting information about the lore of such omens, since in different versions the heroine is warned by a dream of pulling green heather, the heather bell, the birch, and apples green, all of which are objects plausibly connected with ideas of the supernatural. Two versions of *Clerk Saunders* (69 D, E) have a woman dream that she is cutting (or combing) her yellow hair and dipping it in blood. One of the most curious of all the visions is that of Douglas in *The Battle of Otterburn* (161 C):

> I saw a dead man won the fight,
> And I think that man was I.

There are dreams, too, of the death of others, as we should expect, though only a few. Usually the interpretation is

[1] Wimberly, *op. cit.*, p. 62.

[2] *Clerk Saunders*, 69 E, *Young Johnstone*, 88 D, *Fair Margaret and Sweet William*, 74 A, B, C, *Lord Thomas Stuart*, 259.

quite simple, as when Robin Hood, after his dream of being bound and beaten by two yeomen, deduces[1] that he is in danger. More like the elaborately symbolical dreams of medieval chronicle and romance is the one in *Sir Aldingar* (59 A), which by exception is a portent of good fortune rather than bad. The meaning of anything like this could not have been found without the intervention of a seer, but it stands quite alone. The dreams for the most part are homely stuff, like the practice of magic and much else in ballad lore.

The same thing is true of the omens that come to people while awake. They are more numerous than dreams, and unquestionably representative of popular belief, though less rich a collection than could have been made by a little inquiry in any county, English or American, a couple of generations ago. Such portents occur in the ballads quite casually, of course, because it was natural for singers to think that misfortune was likely to be preceded by a warning. In four versions of *Lord Derwentwater* (208 E, F, H, I), for example, the hero's gold ring burst from his finger and his nose began to bleed as he mounted his steed to answer the summons of the king, while in three of them his horse stumbled soon after he set out. Such a combination of events certainly justified what follows:

'These are tokens enough', said my Lord Derwentwater,
    'That I shall never return.'

Ordinarily a single omen suffices. Some one stumbles on a stone, or rings break asunder, or a nose bleeds, or a heel comes off a shoe, as happens in *Mary Hamilton* when the heroine goes to her trial. It is unlucky to catch sight of a mermaid, to look over the left shoulder, or to see the new moon clasping the pale circle of the old. All these are familiar portents, and do not need much comment.[2]

---

[1] *Robin Hood and Guy of Gisborne*, 118.
[2] For a more elaborate analysis see Wimberly, *op. cit.*, pp. 69–77.

They are interesting to us chiefly by way of showing still another field of folk-lore, which is adequately illustrated in our ballads, though not so amply that one could gain a notion—failing other sources of knowledge—of the extent to which life used to be coloured by such superstitions.

What is true of one aspect of the past in the ballads is true of all. They furnish us a great deal of interesting and valuable information about what has been thought and felt and done as a matter of custom, but they present no coherent record of either historical event or of popular belief and custom at any one particular period. We are quite as likely to encounter in them some habit of life characteristic of the sixth century as of the sixteenth. In other words, they incorporate, though in a fragmentary way, the imaginative history of a mixed race, which—like some other European stocks—has been at once wonderfully conservative as to the past and not a little careless. The record as a whole is very precious, not because it is well ordered and coherent, which it is not, but because it is genuine. In these songs emotional attitudes have not been misrepresented for fashion's sake or because of a literary tradition. If we grant that some of them came from the uninspired brains of vagabond minstrels or obscure bards of the countryside, we can at least be sure that their verses were keyed to the popular ear. We cannot trust their report of what occurred on this occasion or that, but we have every reason to trust the record they present of habit and belief.

Ballads are not the poetry of really primitive folk, and they are far from primitive in the art they show. The reason why they contain so many things that lead us back to the feelings and thoughts of a very distant past is that folk-songs have been less influenced by the schools than any other artistic product. Their makers have not been troubled by new wine and old bottles. They have clung to their inheritance of old ideas and old ways, and have accepted the new without mental disturbance. The resulting confusion has probably never even been apparent to them. We must beware of thinking that the ballads themselves go back to the beginning of things, simply because they illustrate so well the persistence of racial memory. On the other hand, we do well to cherish every available variant of them, since it is for the most part by fleeting and fugitive glimpses that they present their record of the past.

Chapter Seven

THE NATURE OF BALLAD VARIATION

W E have seen that neither the words nor the tunes of ballads are constants. They could not possibly remain unaltered, considering the fallibility of human memory, which plays as many tricks with the unlettered singers of folk-songs as it does with the rest of us. The testimony of collectors is everywhere the same: that singers of ballads are quite unconscious of changing them and yet never sing them, line by line and musical phrase by musical phrase, quite like their neighbours. There is plenty of evidence, indeed, that many singers—usually, it appears, those most accomplished in the art—have introduced variants of their own making. Sometimes, as has been shown, they have been incapable of reproducing exactly what they themselves have sung.

This is consistent with feats of memory that strike with amazement those of us who depend on books for our knowledge, and keep no great store of verbally organized material in our heads. Interesting testimony to the number of songs an individual may have in his repertory is given by Mr. Alfred Williams in *Folk-Songs of the Upper Thames*,[1] who says that he has 'frequently come into contact with those who have assured me that such and such a one knew from two hundred to three hundred pieces'. He goes on to tell of the singing matches that used to take place in the region he worked through, when one man would 'sing continuously for twelve hours—from morning till night—and have a fresh piece each time.' Such a contest would not have been confined to narrative songs, of course, but it implied the knowledge of a very large number of ballads for all that. More definite if less

[1] 1923, pp. 14-15.

astounding evidence comes from numerous collectors. Sharp tells us[1] that Mrs. Jane Gentry of Hot Springs, Virginia, supplied him with sixty-four songs; and Miss Bell Robertson of Aberdeenshire—who could not sing, but recited verses she had memorized seventy years earlier in some cases—gave Greig variants of no less than seventy-six ballads or ballad fragments.[2] The anonymous 'Old Lady', who furnished Skene and Scott with material, knew more than forty ballads, while cases of individuals who have been able to sing from twenty-five to thirty-five are not uncommonly recorded.

Yet even Miss Bell Robertson, whose memory seems to have been singularly accurate,[3] probably made some minor changes in her texts without being conscious of it, and unlettered singers have constantly varied both words and music. Any effort to recover an 'original' or 'authentic' version is thus quite fruitless, for all renditions have equal standing as long as the ballad remains in free circulation, unaffected by alien influences of one sort or another. Though one may be inane, and destined to perish at birth, while another is vigorous and attractive, each is truly the ballad while it is being sung. Indeed, if we could recover the text of a ballad as it was composed in the first place—an impossible task, as a very slight study of variants will show—we should still have to admit the equal value of the later forms. The paramount interest of the ballad lies, that is to say, in its existence as a malleable creation, subjected at every remove to the probability of change in both words and melody. To know a ballad thoroughly one ought in theory to know all the variants of it that have ever been sung. Since this is just as impossible as it would be for a botanist to study every individual of a given genus, we have to make shift with

[1] Campbell and Sharp, *English Folk-Songs from the Southern Appalachians*, 1917, p. xi.
[2] See *Last Leaves*, 1925. My own count.   [3] *Op. cit.*, p. xxxiii.

such specimens as come to hand, a less representative selection than the biologist works with, no doubt, but fortunately adequate in many instances to our needs—thanks to the zealous collectors of the past century and a half. We can be as judicial and unimpassioned, at least, in our study of variants as are our colleagues to whom a field of primroses is a laboratory rather than a wash of colour or a manifestation of Divine grace.

To put the matter otherwise, the interest of the ballad as a form lies even more in the constant remaking which the individual specimen undergoes than in its original making. Perhaps we shall never know quite certainly how ballads came to have the peculiarities that are theirs, though we can speculate about the matter to great profit, and we cannot be at all sure how this specimen or that came into being; but the divergent versions furnish us with material that can be closely studied and judicially weighed. More satisfactory knowledge about the nature of folk-songs, formally considered, can be attained by this means, I believe, than in any other way. The processes by which both words and melodies keep continually changing, yet only very slowly become transformed into something quite unrecognizable as the same, present without doubt the central problem in connexion with popular poetry and music. Only by understanding those processes can we find out why ballads and other folk-songs have qualities of their own that are the result neither of blind chance working upon degenerate strays from an ordinary garden of song, nor of a mysterious power somehow resident in the ignorant folk when emotionally stimulated.

There is nothing at all new, of course, in the idea that the words and tunes of songs are subject to constant variation when orally transmitted. Students of the ballad have been aware of this for a long time past. The brothers Grimm understood well enough that tradition played an important part in the history of folk-song, though they were too much interested in the question of origin to pay heed to the possibility that in the kaleidoscopic shift of texts might be found the key to what they regarded as a mystery. It was Jacob Grimm's fate, indeed, to darken counsel, since scholars have wrangled over his words from his own day to this. There is no point in our reviewing here the course that criticism has taken in dealing with the matter of variants in transmission. Every writer on ballads has accepted the fact of it, but has almost always cited the fact merely to support one or another theory about the beginnings of balladry: sometimes to show that the folk which has made song may do what it will with its own, sometimes to argue that the illiterate have mangled good literature and music by their ignorant mouthings.

Some twenty-five years ago John Meier[1] seemed at moments to comprehend that there was more than this in the ceaseless variation of words and melodies by those who have sung them. There was wisdom in his statement: 'Only by observing the alterations which have occurred in individual songs taken over by the folk can we come to really well-founded and clear ideas about the formal style of their music and texts.'[2] Sensible, too, as far as it went, was his remark that the development of a song in oral circulation determines its character as a folk-song; but unfortunately he made no effort to distinguish between the casual malformation of current songs by people without a homogeneous tradition, and ballads or other genuine folk-songs as moulded by a traditional art. His purpose was wholly destructive, indeed—to show that popular poetry and melody were but warmed-over

---

[1] In a series of papers collected under the title *Kunstlieder im Volksmunde*, 1906, a book which scarcely deserved, I believe, the gibes of Gummere (*Beginnings of Poetry*, p. 164; *The Popular Ballad*, p. 27), though the author failed to see the point of some of his accurate observations.

[2] *Op. cit.*, p. 5.

dishes from the table of aristocracy, which blinded him to the real significance of the variants he studied with so much zeal.

What Grundtvig and Child had in mind, as they patiently collected and classified their texts, it is impossible to be quite sure. One cannot accuse them of undervaluing the evidence of transformation, since they presented it so carefully; but I have never found an explicit statement from either of them to the effect that ballad variety might explain the qualities they treasured. Neither the scholars who followed immediately in the footsteps of Child, nor those who carried on the work of Grundtvig, gave much attention to the phenomenon of variation as a possibly important element in the development of folk-song. Although, as I have said elsewhere,[1] Gummere gave the impression in talk of not underrating the value of studying variants, he allowed in what he wrote a very restricted part to oral tradition. This is what he said of it: 'It accounts for the many variants, the versions more or less diverging in stuff and style, of a given ballad, and for all the peculiarities which that sort of transmission must bring about; but it will not account for the original ballads or for most of those specific qualities which set them off from poetry of art.'[2]

To the best of my knowledge, three scholars, working independently in different countries, and with different materials, at about the same time, share the honour of first recognizing the crucial importance to folk-song as an art of what has happened in oral transmission. The first of them to reach this conclusion was apparently Cecil Sharp, who as early as 1907 wrote: 'The method of oral transmission is not merely one by which the folk-song lives; it is a process by which it grows and by which it is created.'[3] Sharp was primarily interested in

[1] *Modern Philology*, xxi. 20. [2] *The Popular Ballad*, pp. 64–5.
[3] *English Folk-Song: Some Conclusions*, p. 10.

music, and thus built up his argument with closest attention to the variations of melody which he observed and
studied to such good purpose; but he was convinced that
what happened to the music happened also to the words
of songs. According to his view, the principles of 'continuity, variation, and selection'[1] explain the nature of
both text and tune in all traditional songs. In a sort of
creed which he formulated in 1919, repeating certain
phrases that he had used earlier, he stated his belief 'that
the most typical qualities of the folk-song have been
laboriously acquired during its journey down the ages,
in the course of which its individual angles and irregularities have been rubbed and smoothed away, just as the
pebble on the seashore has been rounded by the action
of the waves; that the suggestions, unconsciously made
by individual singers, have at every stage of the evolution
of the folk-song been weighed and tested by the community, and accepted or rejected by their verdict; and
that the life-history of the folk-song has been one of continuous growth and development, always tending to ap-
proximate to a form which should be at once congenial
to the taste of the community, and expressive of its
feelings, aspirations, and ideals.'[2]

Something like this must have been in the mind of
Mr. Phillips Barry when he wrote, in 1910, that even an
'ephemeral popular' melody, 'given time enough and
folk-singers enough, may remain in tradition so long, that
its form and melodic structure will be more or less
markedly changed'.[3] This might seem to be merely a
re-statement of John Meier's position, if it had not been
followed up on more than one occasion by other brief
pronouncements, which make Mr. Barry's belief somewhat clearer, though he has never, as far as I am aware,

[1] *Op. cit.*, p. 16.
[2] *English Folk-Songs, Selected Edition*, i, p. viii.
[3] *J. A. F.-L.*, xxiii. 440–1 (1910).

developed his theories at length. I take it he would not be unwilling to have his phrase 'individual invention, plus communal re-creation',[1] quoted as embodying the opinion he has held for a long time past. In the paper containing this phrase he amplified his statement to this effect: 'We have to do with a dynamic phenomenon. The process is one by which a simple event in human experience, of subjective interest, narrated in simple language, set to a simple melody, is progressively objectivated.'[2] This, though cryptically said, must mean that through individual variations a ballad comes to have the qualities peculiar to itself; and the process indicated is apparently not to be distinguished from that described by Cecil Sharp.

In 1914, the distinguished Spanish scholar, Don Ramon Menéndez Pidal, whose work in many fields of literary study has been so important, began the publication of a series of works on popular poetry that are of the highest significance.[3] Although he did not use music to help solve the mystery of variant texts, and thus lacked one resource of Sharp and Mr. Barry, he developed within the next decade what is perhaps the most comprehensive and satisfactory account of the effect of oral transmission on verse that any one has given us. His insistence that 'variants are not accidents' but are essential to the process of communal poetizing, and that at any point beauty may come in,[4] has done much to combat the view that changes of text are either mere corruptions or else haphazard alterations without much significance for the poem's destiny. Especially impressive is his study of

---

[1] *Modern Language Notes*, xxviii. 4 (1913).

[2] *Op. cit.*, p. 5.

[3] I wish to acknowledge my obligations to Professor S. Griswold Morley of the University of California for first calling my attention to these studies, which I did not know until I had formed my own views.

[4] *Poesía popular y Poesía tradicional en la Literatura Española*, 1922, p. 22. Reprinted in *El Romancero, Teorías e investigaciones*, p. 37.

the geographical distribution of the variants of *Gerineldo*,[1] in which he shows not only that the 164 known copies of the ballad may be grouped with quite remarkable accuracy, but that the orally transmitted versions have been affected to only a very slight degree by the printed texts that have been in circulation since the sixteenth century. Inasmuch as he has shown more clearly than any one else the differences that exist between the Spanish *romances* and the traditional verse narratives of other lands,[2] it is doubly interesting that his conclusions as to the way oral transmission has affected them should square so closely with those of Sharp, which were reached by quite another road.

In a paper that appeared in 1923,[3] I endeavoured to clarify the problem of ballad-making by calling attention to the indisputable fact that among the variants of texts a very considerable proportion have qualities that warrant the enthusiasm with which ballads have been regarded by poetry lovers, as distinguished from students of folk-lore, ever since Percy issued the *Reliques*. Not only do we find a constant shift of phrase and event, a constant re-creation of the song, as Sharp and Barry have shown so well, but also—a point made by Menéndez Pidal— the occurrence, not infrequently, of variants of the same event and the same passage, each of which has striking effectiveness and beauty. My approach to the problem was by way of these scattered but very remarkable manifestations, which close the door once for all on the notion that nothing can happen in oral tradition save progressive degeneracy and corruption. I was thus emphasizing a phase of the question that not even the three scholars I have just mentioned made of primary importance.[4] I

---

[1] *Revista de filología española*, vii. 229–338 (1920).

[2] See 'Romances y Baladas', *Modern Humanities Research Association*, i. 1–17.

[3] 'The Making of Ballads', *Modern Philology*, xxi. 15–28.

[4] In a brief article in *Publications of the Modern Language Association*, xliv. 622–30 (1929), Miss Louise Pound takes me to task for assuming that I had

did this because I believed it to provide the most satisfactory clue to the nature of the art by which folk-song
has come to be something more than a social phenomenon
without aesthetic value. Further study has convinced
me even more strongly that I was right in my belief.
There may be several ways by which the matter could
be clearly presented; but I know of none so profitable
as attention to textual and musical variants that have
'merit', according to the ordinary standards of sophisticated taste. At least, I can demonstrate better by
focusing the inquiry thus, than by any other means
what appears to me to be the nature of ballad variation.

Consider the rather simple case of *The Unquiet Grave*
(78), which Child printed in nine forms, some fragmentary, while a dozen more copies have since come to light.[1]
Among all these variants the differences are slight, but
significant. The story is of a lover who disturbs the repose
of a sweetheart by mourning overmuch. At the beginning
we get a vow of extravagant grief, and at the end of a year
and a day a dialogue in which the ghost makes its com-
plaint. The only change of substance that appears is in
the sex of the lover who has died. We may guess that
originally he was a young man, as most of the variants
have it; but we cannot be sure that such was the case,
for the situation is accommodated sufficiently well to the
other possibility. Very interesting is the opening stanza,
the first two lines of which illustrate how various, and
yet how happy, may be the changes of phrase in a text:

> The wind doth blow today, my love,
>   And a few small drops of rain.[2]

anything new to say in the paper, but she altogether misses the point of my
argument.

[1] See Sharp, *J. F.-S. S.* ii. 6–8, *English Folk-Songs*, ii. 18–19; Broadwood,
English Traditional Songs and Carols, pp. 50–55; A. G. Gilchrist, *J. F.-S. S.* v.
137–8; E. M. Leather, *Folk-Lore of Herefordshire*, 1912, pp. 202–3; A. Williams,
Folk-Songs of the Upper Thames, 1923, p. 76.

[2] Child A, from Sussex.

How cold the wind do blow, dear love,
  And see the drops of rain.[1]

Cold blows the wind oer my true-love,
  Cold blow the drops of rain.[2]

Cold blows the wind today, sweetheart,
  Cold are the drops of rain.[3]

Cold blows the wind tonight, sweet-heart,
  Cold are the drops of rain.[4]

Cauld, cauld blaws the winter night,
  Sair beats the heavy rain.[5]

How cold the winds do blow, dear love!
  And a few small drops of rain.[6]

Cold blows the winter's wind, true love,
  Cold blow the drops of rain.[7]

Among these eight ways of saying the same thing there is little or nothing to choose. Not only is it impossible to reconstruct the original wording, but it is equally impossible to select the variant that best embodies the idea. All are evocative, after the manner of good lyrical verse, all follow the verse pattern with what would be regarded as subtle variation if they were the work of known poets. Later stanzas confirm the evidence from the first. Quite evidently the singers who have at one time or another changed the texture of the poem have not been mere blunderers. The variants cannot be dismissed as freaks of memory simply. Without the guidance of critical theory, artistry of a sort has been at work.

[1] Child B, from Suffolk.

[2] Child C, from Suffolk, E, Gipsy version, F, from Shropshire, L.E. Broadwood, *op. cit.*, pp. 54–5, from North Devonshire.

[3] Child G, from Cornwall.   [4] Child H, from Devonshire.

[5] See Child v. 475, *Charles Graeme.*

[6] Broadwood, *op. cit.*, pp. 50–3, two versions from Surrey.

[7] Williams, *op. cit.*, p. 76, from Gloucestershire and Oxfordshire.

Very different in the variations it shows is *Sir Lionel* (18), yet none the less instructive. In this case we have a version from the seventeenth century[1] with which to compare the texts taken down in the nineteenth and twentieth centuries. The transformation here is in substance quite as much as phrase, yet it is a striking fact that the variants of later record tell a much more coherent tale than the earlier one—except those that are mere fragments. It so happens that the version of the Percy MS. has been mutilated, but one may doubt whether in its complete state it was altogether clear: probably because the transcriber failed to remember or to copy down the whole poem. What we have tells how Sir Lionel, while hunting, finds a knight slain and a lady sitting in a tree, who informs him that a wild boar has killed Sir Broning. He turns to fight the boar. At the end of a break, we find him wounded, but disdaining to accept humiliating terms from a giant—whose appearance is not accounted for—though he does accept a respite of forty days and leaves the lady as a hostage. When the forty days are up and he is healed, he blows his bugle and is met by the lady, who gives him the enigmatic message from the giant that the three of them will sup together that night. Just as he is warning the lady to flee, in case he should be worsted, the copy fails us. A Scottish version[2] tells how Graeme adventured the woods of Tore in spite of the menace of a wild boar and a giant, and killed the two successively. The action is perfectly clear. In two versions from Worcestershire[3] Sir Ryalas, or an unnamed hunter, encountered a lady on a tree-top and learned that she was there because of a wild boar. After he killed the boar, a wild woman, its owner, flew out at him to take vengeance for the death of her 'pretty spotted pig', and was killed in turn. Again, we have a coherent story.

---

[1] Child A, from the Percy Folio MS.
[2] Child B. [3] Child C, D.

Recently a version from North Wiltshire has been printed,[1] which simplifies the tale by making Sir Rylas find the wild woman in the tree, thus making one character serve for two. She threatens him with the boar:

> 'There is a wild boar all in this wood,
> He'll eat thy flesh and drink thy blood,
>   As thee beest a jovial hunter.'

After the boar has been killed, she demands of him 'thy horse, thy hounds, and thy fair lady',—and has her head split open for her pains. The simplification has done no injury to the brisk narrative. More closely related to this Wiltshire version than are any of those printed by Child is an American one found in many variants from Virginia, North Carolina, Kentucky, and Missouri,[2] where it is known as *Old Bangum* or *Bangum and the Boar*. In all the copies reported, save one, the story is reduced to a warning about the wild boar and the subsequent battle, but it remains vigorous and satisfying as an episodic narrative. In the single variant that goes into more detail,[3] Bangum meets a fair maid, who gives him warning about the boar. The interesting point about all these versions, it seems to me, is the evidence they give that changes and even abbreviations do not necessarily imply any structural degeneracy. *Sir Lionel* has become a better ballad, rather than a worse one, since the middle of the seventeenth century when the scribe of the Percy MS. copied it down.

That even the central elements in a ballad story may be changed as it circulates orally is very well illustrated

[1] Williams, *op. cit.*, pp. 118–19.

[2] See A. K. Davis, *Traditional Ballads of Virginia*, 1929, pp. 125–32; Campbell and Sharp, *English Folk-Songs from the Southern Appalachians*, 1917, p. 28 (No. Carolina and Davis G); J. McGill, *Folk-Songs of the Kentucky Mountains*, 1917, pp. 78–81; D. Scarborough, *On the Trail of Negro Folk-Songs*, 1925, pp. 51–2 (Davis F); Belden, *J.A.F.-L.* xix. 235 (1906); Moore, *Modern Language Review*, xi. 397 (1916). The two last named are fragments from Missouri.

[3] Davis A.

by the case of *Jellon Grame* (90). Two forms of the ballads have been found, both in Scotland. In one[1] Lily Flower is murdered by her lover because he fears her father's anger if their child should be born. In the other[2] May Margerie is killed by Hind Henry because she has preferred Brown Robin to him. In both forms the boy who is born at the time of the murder grows up to avenge the slayer, having been reared by his father Jellon in the first version and by an aunt in the second. The motive for the murder thus differs altogether in the two, and with it the nature of the vengeance which the young man takes. Presumably one form of the story is earlier than the other, yet so satisfactorily is each developed that neither has any valid claim to priority. Oral tradition within a limited geographical area has managed to make two good narratives out of one.

Changes of another sort appear in such a ballad as *The Two Sisters* (10), of which Child printed twenty-seven versions and variants, while at least forty-one other variants have since been recorded or published. In this case the central fact in the story—that a girl was drowned by her jealous sister—remains constant throughout a bewildering set of alterations. With this theme the imaginations of British singers, not to mention their Scandinavian cousins, have played at will. Sometimes the sisters are the daughters of a king and sometimes of low birth; the pleas of the drowning girl for mercy vary widely, and are sometimes omitted altogether; sometimes her body, when found by a miller or a member of his family, is bedecked with splendid clothing; in many instances some part of her body is used in making a musical instrument, while in many others there is no mention of this feature; in a whole group of variants the miller is as wicked a villain as the wicked sister, and either completes the

---

[1] Represented by Child A and the Aberdeenshire fragment in Greig, *Last Leaves*, pp. 70–1.   [2] Child B, C, D.

process of drowning or strips the body before throwing it back into the water, though in other instances he is altogether humane. No analysis—even Child's admirable discussion—could possibly reduce to order, I believe, the mass of inconsistent detail that appears about the central theme, or disentangle what is accretion from what belongs to the original story. Yet the fact remains that a large number of the versions are excellent, each in its way, and impress us almost equally by the pathos with which they invest the tale. In other words, a single ballad—since we must assume that it had somewhere and sometime a beginning—has become diversified by the processes of variation into a considerable number of virtually independent ballads, which treat the same theme in different ways but with approximately equal success. For convenience we may continue to refer to the ballad of *The Two Sisters*, but we ought to remember that the different versions really constitute a group of related poems.

The same tendency to what cannot be called anything else than re-creation, with the same happy results, is shown by many another ballad in isolated stanzas, even when the narrative as a whole has been little changed in tradition or has become less good. So in *The Wife of Usher's Well* (79) the words and actions of the mother, when her missing sons return, are reported quite differently, yet with almost equal power:

> 'Blow up the fire, my maidens,
>   Bring water from the well;
> For a' my house shall feast this night,
>   Since my three sons are well.'

> And she has made to them a bed,
>   She's made it large and wide,
> And she's taen her mantle her about,
>   Sat down at the bed-side.[1]

· · · ·

[1] Child A, from West Lothian.

'O eat an drink, my merry men a',
  The better shall ye fare,
For my twa sons the are come hame
  To me for evermair.'

O she has gaen an made their bed,
  An she's made it saft an fine,
An she's happit them wi her gay mantel
  Because they were her ain.[1]

.   .   .   .   .

She spread her table wide and long,
  Put on it bread and wine.
'Come eat, come drink, my sweet little babes,
  Come eat, come drink of mine.'

'No, mother, we don't want your bread,
  Nor either want your wine,
For yonder stands our Saviour dear,
  To him we are resigned.'

She fixed her bed in a narrow back room,
  Put on it white, white sheets,
And on the top a golden spread,
  That they might better sleep.[2]

The irony of the situation has been realized almost equally in these three versions, the differences among which extend deeper than phrasing to the imaginative conception of the scene. Unquestionably the song has been created anew, as it has been transmitted from singer to singer and has travelled from Scotland to Virginia.

The case of *Mary Hamilton* (173) is valuable for our purpose in a slightly different way. Among the twenty-eight versions listed by Child and the eleven or more variants since recorded,[3] there is a rather wide discrep-

---

[1] Child B, from Peeblesshire. [2] Davis, *op. cit.*, p. 281.
[3] Greig, *Last Leaves*, pp. 107–9; Barry, Eckstorm, and Smyth, *British Ballads from Maine*, 1929, pp. 258–64; J. H. Combs, *Folk-Songs du Midi*, 1925, pp. 141–3; Davis, *op. cit.*, pp. 421–2.

ancy of handling; and they fall into two groups,[1] only one of which gives the reason for Mary's execution— namely, her seduction and the murder of her baby. Almost all the variants repeat with little change the immortal stanza :

> Last nicht there was four Maries,
>   The nicht there'l be but three;
> There was Marie Seton, and Marie Beton,
>   And Marie Carmichael, and me.[2]

Many of them, too, have in one form or another Mary's appeal to the past, as she goes to her death :

> Last night I washd the queen's feet,
>   And gently laid her down;
> And a' the thanks I've gotten the nicht
>   To be hangd in Edinbro town![3]

The expression of this idea, unlike that of the stanza about the four Maries, varies greatly, yet almost never fails to strike the right note of pathos.

> Yestreen I wush Queen Mary's feet,
>   And bore her till her bed;
> This day she's given me my reward,
>   This gallows-tree to tread.[4]

> Yestreen I made Queen Mary's bed,
>   Kembed doun her yellow hair;
> Is this the reward I am to get,
>   To tread this gallows-stair![5]

> Oh aften hae I dressed my queen,
>   An saft saft made her bed;
> And now I've got for my reward
>   The gallows-tree to tread.[6]

---

[1] See the admirable analysis in Barry, Eckstorm, and Smyth, *op. cit.*, pp. 259–60.

[2] Child A.   [3] Child A.   [4] Child B.

[5] Child C.   [6] Child G.

> Seven years an I made Queen Mary's bed,
>   Seven years an I combed her hair,
> An a hansome reward noo she's gien to me,
>   Gien me the gallows-tows to wear! [1]

> O wha will comb Queen Mary's heed?
>   Or wha will brade her hair?
> And wha will lace her middle sae jimp,
>   Whan I am nae langer there? [2]

> Last nicht I dressed Queen Mary,
>   An' pit on her braw silken goon,
> An' a' the thanks I've gat this nicht
>   Is tae be hangd in Edinbro toon. [3]

Evidently these lines have been re-composed at least six times by persons with some gift for imaginative and rhythmic expression.

Very effective as an illustration of what has happened in such cases is a stanza of *Bonnie James Campbell* (210), that poignant lament which manages to compress into a few lines a whole story of grief. One version [4] ends with words supposed to be uttered by the man as he meets death :

> My house is unbigged,
>   my barn's unbeen,
> My corn's unshorn,
>   my meadow grows green.

Nothing could better express the feeling of one to whom the end has come too soon. Yet in other versions [5] his bride, with equal propriety, is made to say:

> The meadow lies green,
>   the corn is unshorn,
> But bonnie George Campbell
>   will never return.

[1] Child N.   [2] Child W.
[3] Barry, Eckstorm, and Smyth, *op. cit.*, pp. 258-9.   [4] Child A.
[5] Child C; and Barry, Eckstorm, and Smyth, *op. cit.*, p 280.

Still another [1] turns the bride's lament into this :

> My meadow lies green, and my corn is unshorn,
> My barn is to build, and my baby's unborn.

Finally, there is a most interesting variant from West Virginia, [2] which shows an adaptation to local conditions without loss of emotional effectiveness, though rhyme has not been preserved :

> My house is not shingled,
>   my barn is not raised,
> My crops are not gathered
>   and my babe has not come.

Examples such as I have been giving, which show variation in poetic phrase, in formal handling of the story, or in the plot itself, yet no deterioration, might be multiplied indefinitely. In the paper already cited, which I published in 1923, I made the estimate that of the ballads in Child's collection we should be the poorer for the lack of variant texts ' in no less than sixty-five cases '. I now recognize that this estimate was far too small. Although one cannot make anything like an exact census of ' good ' versions, since what may awaken enthusiasm in one lover of poetry may leave another cold, it still remains true that there exist a great number of texts that are independently and absolutely attractive on their own merits. In the process of oral transmission variations have occurred that are not enfeebled distortions of a vague original, but genuine refashionings so ably made that we should not hesitate, if the matter concerned literature rather than popular lore, to attribute them to different poets of notable gifts. Out of the vast welter of the commonplace, which we should not for a moment forget in our survey, shine these poems, which have the magic that has been felt by persons sensitive to beauty ever since the days of Philip Sidney.

[1] *Op. cit.*, p. 282.   [2] Combs, *op. cit.*, p. 144.

They are necessarily re-creations rather than haphazard reminiscences of a common original, since so many of them are mutually incompatible. Stanzas, among which we can with difficulty choose the best, parallel one another; this way of telling a story has certain advantages over that, and that over this, yet the two are inconsistent with each other. No mosaic can be pieced together that will include all the admirable things from a group of versions. Out of all the good versions you cannot make something better, because you cannot possibly include all the good elements in a composite. The ballads have been constantly changed as they have been sung, and often, it is evident, to their advantage, though there is no reason to suppose that deterioration has not been at work to some extent in every region and in every period. One cannot believe that good taste has at any time been possessed by all the members of a community.

A parallel to such oral re-creation, which may make the process clearer, is to be found in the circulation of popular kinds of literature. Menéndez Pidal has argued forcibly that there may be a written tradition, analogous to an oral tradition, by which a poem will be refashioned to suit the varying taste of different times and different audiences. In both cases the work is regarded as common property, something impersonal that may be treated with absolute freedom. I cannot do better than quote Menéndez Pidal's summary of the matter: ' When the various manuscripts of a poem differ constantly from one another in such a way as to be not more or less inexact copies, but anonymous recensions of the work, we have a phenomenon of written literary tradition wholly analogous to oral tradition, which always reproduces works in variant form. The oral variant represents what an individual singer makes of the popular poem, thus becoming co-author or joint-owner in it; similarly, the written recension represents the action by which a new author appropriates to himself a work that he considers common property. Finally, every work reproduced in variants or in recensions is a work in which various authors collaborate, a collective product; and a work traditionally refashioned by various authors, whether orally or by writing, acquires fundamental qualities of anonymity and popularity, which make us place it in a realm of literature different from that of works made by a purely individual art.'[1]

What has happened to texts has happened also to tunes, as I have tried to show in an earlier chapter.[2] A statement of Sharp's concerning this deserves to be kept in view. 'A melody is not suddenly born in the composer's mind ready made, complete in every detail. On the contrary, it assumes many shapes, and suffers innumerable changes before it reaches the form which satisfies him and which he ultimately uses. . . . Now, the successive forms, through which a melody passes in the mind of a composer during the process of composition, correspond to the variants of a folk-song.'[3] The analogy is of course not complete, since the processes by which the composer perfects his tune are self-directed and his work tends to approach some ideal he has more or less consciously set for himself, whereas the variants of a folk-song are the products of many minds. Each variant pleases the singer of it, no doubt; but we can scarcely suppose that he has made changes because of any conscious dissatisfaction with the melody as he has heard it sung by others, or that he will experiment with possibilities as the schooled composer does. If he makes successive changes in a tune, it is because at a given moment a new turn comes to him that

---

[1] R. Menéndez Pidal, *Poesía Juglaresca y Juglares*, 1924, pp. 449–50. For an illuminating sketch of the conditions under which popular literature in the Middle Ages was preserved or varied, see K. Sisam, *Fourteenth Century Verse and Prose*, 1921, pp. xxx–xxxviii.

[2] See Chapter IV.

[3] *English Folk-Song: Some Conclusions*, p. 13.

seems the right and inevitable one. Apparently he is unaware of the novelty, for the tune as he sings it is the tune as he knows it. Yet among the shifting variants of folk-melodies there occur a great number with such beauty of phrase in the same passage that they deserve remembrance. It is seldom possible to select the absolute best, just as we cannot often say that this or that ballad text is more appealing than every other one. Not only have all the same authenticity, but many have qualities so excellent that they forbid the belief in folk-tunes as mere waifs and strays.

In this connexion, the phenomenon of form in the variants of melodies must be taken into account. What is true of the texts, which may change the substance of a story very materially yet make a good narrative of it all the same, is true of the music of ballads and other folk-songs. A tune continues to have a pattern—to be, in other words, a true melody—no matter what changes it undergoes. It may be varied almost or quite out of existence, but it remains a tune. Even more clearly than the sets of words, which sometimes become mere fragments, the music remains structurally sound until it is forgotten altogether.

Such evidence as I have been presenting leads inevitably, I believe, to certain important conclusions about the nature of variation in folk-song. The existence of so many variants, both melodic and textual, which are manifestly not due to haphazard, undirected substitution for what has been forgotten, shows a widespread power of musical and poetic expression completely justifying Grimm's 'Das Volk dichtet'. There is nothing in the evidence to show that all the members of a regional or social group have possessed this power, but more than enough to establish its reality on the part of a large number of persons in times not remote from our own. Indeed, with regard to music it appears that the latter generations of singers have continued to be able to adapt tunes according to their own taste with considerable success, while such a stanza as the one quoted above from a West Virginian variant of *Bonnie James Campbell*, as well as the good narrative structure of a great many ballads of American record that have preserved no magic of phrase, shows that the gift and taste for refashioning the verse did not disappear with the eighteenth century or the nineteenth. In the sense of re-creation, ballad-making has continued to be a living art down to our own times, if indeed it has wholly perished even now.

To put the matter otherwise, variation cannot possibly be due to lapses of memory only, else good versions would not be multiplied. A singer without skill in his craft could not substitute something just as good for the passage he failed to remember. The poetaster may occasionally deviate into sense, but neither he nor his musical equivalent ever stumbled into making something beautiful through sheer forgetfulness. Inadvertence will explain patched and ignoble specimens of balladry, but not the great number of cases in which we find mutually exclusive variants of about the same merit.

How, then, are we to account for the phenomenon? It seems to me that we are forced to accept belief in a tradition of artistry current at least in certain groups or families and in certain regions, and probably continuing from century to century, which has guided the re-making of folk-songs. Without the existence of such a tradition, the changes inevitable when words and music are transmitted orally would have resulted in the swift destruction of any beauty, and *a fortiori* could not have produced the parallel versions of considerable merit such as I have pointed out above. About the origins of ballads we can only speculate, but about the effect of tradition upon them we have clear evidence. Let us postpone until later the question as to how ballads came into being and as to how the artistry established itself that has moulded them. For the moment we shall do better to abstain from all theorizing and stick to the fact that folk-songs have somehow been shaped by tradition into variant forms, which not infrequently possess undeniable beauty of structure, of rhythm, of phrase.

We need not be troubled, when we say that art has gone to the making of variants, by feeble versions recorded long ago or by the fact of modern deterioration. It is impossible to suppose that every one, even in a region with an excellent tradition of music and verse, would develop good taste or be gifted with the ability to repair the defects of his memory with anything above mere commonplace. Nature supplies bunglers, no matter how high a general level be reached in any art or any craft. I cannot believe that an age of balladry has ever existed in which all the versions sung kept to a lofty plane of musical and poetic attainment. Degeneration of noble themes and captivating tunes must have been going on ever since ballads became current, though there is every reason to conclude that conditions grew worse for them by the end of the sixteenth century.[1]

On the other hand, we are forced by the multiplicity of admirable versions that have come down to us to believe that there was a time when a large number of individuals were so affected by a sound tradition of music and verse that they could compose or adapt ballads in such a way as to make what was worthy of remembrance. We shall see later that some of them may have been middle-class folk rather than peasants, and that some of them were certainly ' minstrels '—professionals of a sort. The art they practised, however, was beyond all doubt distinguishable from that by which the

[1] See Chapter IX.

higher classes were beguiled, a popular if not a rustic art. In the old days there was surely a diffusion of knowledge and good taste about such matters that could not be paralleled anywhere in our modern world of specialized activities.

There has been too much stress on the illiteracy of folk-singers, with the implication that they are and have been ignorant. It cannot be too strongly urged that they have been, first and last, well trained in the music and poetry they have loved and perpetuated. The question of reading and writing is beside the point, since they have needed neither letters nor musical symbols. The habit, recorded by Sharp,[1] of changing a melody from one mode to another, to which many singers have been addicted, is of itself quite enough to show the soundness of their heritage in music. As Sharp says, 'change of mode is of the nature of free translation rather than of exact transposition'. Such singers have therefore been able to fashion true patterned melodies to their own liking, which is a feat seldom attempted nowadays by any one not a trained musician. In a sense, the persons who have made these varying forms that we admire must always have been trained musicians, just as they have been far from unskilled in verse; but they have acquired their knowledge with so little effort, being in the tradition of it, as to be almost unconscious of artistry. Without theory, they have yet possessed the craft in so sound a way that they have usually been able to supply the gaps in a tune or a story when memory has failed them, and now and then to make notable improvements in the songs thereby.

What I have been setting down about the nature of ballad variation seems to me proved by the clear evidence of the case. Beyond this, we may draw certain conclusions that must remain conjectures, though they are sufficiently

[1] *Op. cit.,* p. 26.

justifiable. We may permit ourselves to guess, for example, that variants have been introduced in two ways. Often, as has been suggested, singers must have forgotten musical or verbal phrases, and have repaired the gaps as best they could—sometimes admirably and sometimes to the detriment of the ballad. There is reason to believe, however, that other singers have been unable to resist the impulse to make alterations even though their memories have been extremely accurate. An old man in Somerset, whom Sharp knew, reproduced words with extraordinary fidelity but varied 'every phrase of his tune in the course of a ballad'.[1] It was Sharp's judgement that such musical changes as those made by this man were 'nothing less than inspired invention'.[2] They were obviously introduced because his imagination set him to playing with his themes precisely as the imagination of the schooled composer develops his material, turning it this way and that until he has secured an effect satisfying to his taste. The essential difference between the two processes lies in the unconsciousness of the folk-musician, whose experiments are not directed towards a desired end but are the random efforts of a moment. Is it too much to suppose that what some individuals have not been able to refrain from doing with melodies, other individuals have done with the words of the ballads? I see no reason why we may not believe that some of the verbal variants, which we regard as worthy of admiration, may not be the work of persons with an instinct for playing with rhythmic patterns in words, of Miltons who though inglorious have not been content to remain mute. Such an individual would make changes unconsciously because he could not resist the impulse to experiment. Only we must not let ourselves be deluded into the notion that any poet-singer, whether urged by a failure of memory

---

[1] *Op. cit.*, pp. 17, 21.

[2] *Op. cit.*, p. 24.

or by his own fancy, has ever been able to produce a beautiful variant unless grounded firmly in his traditional art.

As to the origins of the art we have to fall back, again, on conjecture. The evidence for its existence— prolonged after a fashion even to our day—seems to me irresistible, but the evidence about its beginnings is less satisfactory than one could wish. Quite possibly it was influenced to some extent by precepts and practices learned from musicians and poets who would have regarded themselves as sophisticated. Into such matters we must inquire when we come to consider the origin of the ballad as a formal type. There is nothing in balladry as we know it to compel the opinion that the art of it was a wholly isolated growth, in no way derivative from the earlier traditions of the European stock. Such a phenomenon would be perhaps unique in the history of culture, since everything human appears to emerge from something that went before. The differencing elements in the art of folk-song, however, and its long-continued independent existence permit the belief that it developed in practice to what it is—or was until evil days befell it. That is to say, if the individual ballad has acquired its quality by successive stages in oral tradition, as seems to me clearly the case, we may properly conjecture that the art of which it is a product grew up likewise in the hands of those who practised it. That they had no theories about it, no laws of criticism, matters not at all, since the development of the arts has in all time tended to outrun the analysis of them. Ballads, like all folk-song, have come to be what they are because, generation after generation, men and women have loved to sing and have learned from one another how to sing.

Chapter Eight

THE ORIGIN AND DEVELOPMENT OF THE BALLAD AS A MUSICAL AND POETICAL FORM

IN considering the origin of ballads as a *genre* we must perforce leave the firm ground of observable phenomena and venture into a doubtful region of inference. We can no longer limit our inquiry to what exists, and is therefore susceptible of analytical description. The beginnings of any form in art can seldom be determined very precisely, even when the product is one cultivated in urban centres and by restricted groups; and the difficulties are enormously increased when we have to deal with something not confined to the people of a single race and cultivated for the most part, as far as we can learn its history, by the humbler social groups, which is the case with the ballads. We have to form our theories on the basis of evidence that is scantier than we could wish and in some respects of doubtful worth. Caution is necessary, yet without a certain boldness of conjecture the problem cannot be attacked at all.

Scholars have been curious about the origin of ballads for a long time, and have disagreed rather violently in the conclusions they have reached. It is not because of any disrespect for what they have done, but because the whole matter has been somewhat clouded with prepossessions and prejudices, that I shall avoid a set review of the positions that have been defended. We shall not profit, I feel sure, by continuing the intermittent warfare that has been carried on for more than a century by communalists and individualists. Could the truth be reached along those lines, there would have been peace between the combatants ere this; but peace has not come.

Rather there has developed increasingly a sense of bewilderment among fair-minded men, together with a lassitude that has retarded progress towards the solution of what is, after all, one of the most fascinating problems in the history of the arts.

I do not flatter myself that I can guide the reader to a sure knowledge of how the ballad came into being as the particular sort of verse narrative with musical accompaniment that it is. I am only too well aware that about certain important matters I cannot offer even a tentative explanation. I believe, however, that a fresh statement of the problem can be made, which will clarify it and perhaps suggest profitable studies for the future. A clear understanding of what we do not know about a question is much more useful than an attempt to draw definite conclusions from insufficient evidence. Only with an aim thus restricted should I dare write about the origin of ballads at all, for I realize clearly the difficulties that confront the explorer in this field.

First of all, we must bear in mind that, when we are discussing the origin of the ballad form, we are not primarily concerned with the way this or that particular melody and poem came into existence. There are two distinct problems, quite evidently, both very interesting and important, but not to be confused. We should like to discover, on the one hand, what gave rise to the mould or pattern of ballads, and we should be glad to know, on the other hand, how and when the individual ballads of our traditional store were made in accordance with that pattern. Since many of them are comparatively modern, as is witnessed by the stories they relate, though others may well be of very considerable antiquity —ageless, if not exceedingly old—we can be certain that at least a great number were composed long after the mould was fully formed and set. This is stating the case with the utmost moderation. As a matter of fact, it is highly improbable that a majority of them have an individual history that goes back to the Middle Ages, though we have convincing evidence that the type they represent was known in the thirteenth century. In so far as we can be sure that the tradition of making has not altered with the centuries, we have the right to use ballads composed in the sixteenth century in discussing the formal characteristics of the medieval type ; but we must be careful not to attribute a later fashion to an earlier day if by any possibility we can avoid it, and we must continually remember that nearly all the extant versions of our ballads stand at the end of a long chain of tradition. The marvel is that *Judas* should exhibit the same qualities as *The Bitter Withy*, and *Johnie Cock* as *Johnie Armstrong*. The question we have to put to ourselves, when we speak of origins, is this : how and when was the pattern formed that has given rise, as a tradition in music and narrative verse, to the noble but somewhat tattered array that collectors and editors have gathered?

In the second place, we ought never to forget that the ballads of different countries, although they have such marked similarities of narrative structure as to belong unmistakably to the same *genre*, differ widely among themselves in metrical form and poetic style. The implications of this well-known fact have never been stated, so far as I know, by students of ballad origins ; but they appear to be of fundamental importance, once they are clearly grasped. The song we call *Lady Isabel and the Elf-Knight* (4), for example, is found in the oral tradition of at least ten countries, with versions so intricately interwoven that they have baffled all attempts hitherto made to trace the wanderings of the theme with anything like certitude, yet quite clearly they compose a group by themselves. They are more intimately connected than are the scattered versions of the same folk-tale, in that they have structural qualities in common. At the same time the metrical form of the narrative song in Hungary is not, I make out—and could not be expected to be— at all like the form prevailing in Scotland. Differences in language, differences in historic tradition, and in some cases a varying musical habit make it inevitable that a ballad like *Lady Isabel and the Elf-Knight* would have to be recast—not simply translated—as it moved from land to land.

In looking at the question of ballad origins, in trying to see how the pattern of them came into existence, we are thus faced again with two problems instead of one ; and we shall have more chance of eventually solving them if we keep the two distinct. We wish to know how it happens that people all over Europe sing their stories with a marked tendency to focus them on a single episode, to present the action dramatically, and to treat the material impersonally. We wish to know, in the second place, when it was that ballads with these characteristics began to be made in Great Britain, how they were made, and why they have the formal qualities that they share with similar narrative lyrics of certain other countries, though not of all countries. In other words, there is the question as to why the stories are told in the way they are, which is a constant throughout Europe, and there is the question of their poetical and musical dress, which is a variable.

I take pains to make these distinctions clear, because I am convinced that only by observing them have we much hope, now or in the future, of emerging from the fog that has enveloped the problem since it first aroused the interest of scholars. I do not say that we shall find easy and simple answers to our questions because we are able to put them plainly, but I believe that it is well worth our while to clarify our ideas about the goal we have in mind. At the risk of appearing over-precise and pedantic, I shall sum up the matter by saying that we must try to answer three separate but interrelated questions: (1) What was the origin of the narrative form peculiar to ballads—to use the English term for something very differently designated in other languages? (2) What was the origin of the melodic and poetical form found in the British ballads, as well as in some of their continental relations? (3) What was the origin of the individual ballads that make up our collections?

In trying to answer all of these questions, we are hampered at the outset by the lack of any fixed dates. Just as we cannot hope to discover for most individual ballads a *terminum a quo*, we are equally unable to fix upon the century when such narrative songs as a class were first composed. Since the *genre* developed and has been perpetuated by oral tradition, we have no right to take as the period of its genesis the time when writers first mention it or some one records a set of words. *Judas* is found in a manuscript of the late thirteenth century, which proves only that by that time there were ballads in England with the form we know so well, but gives us no real clue as to how long before that date they existed, since only by the merest chance have we this scrap of evidence.[1] Without it, we should not know with certainty that anything of the sort existed before the fifteenth century. An oral tradition could thrive for a long while, naturally, without receiving the slightest attention from men of letters or compilers of commonplace books. There is, in short, no direct evidence whatever as to the period when the ballad as a narrative form, or the ballad as a melodic and poetical form came into existence. Any opinion at which we may arrive must be a matter of inference.

Yet it seems wholly improbable that the centred, dramatic, and impersonal story-song of medieval and

[1] Almost the same thing is true of Danish ballads. See Steenstrup, *The Medieval Popular Ballad*, trans. Cox, 1914, pp. 254-6.

modern times goes back to a very remote century. The little we can discover about the singing habits of the people of northern Europe before and after the Great Migrations does not warrant the belief that they composed and chanted anything like our ballads. The poetry that survives in pre-Conquest English is, to be sure, altogether literary—the work of men who had read and to some extent assimilated the legacy of Rome. Yet it is so unlike anything of antiquity, both in form and spirit, that we have every reason to suppose that the differencing elements are characteristic of whatever tradition of poetry the Germanic peoples had when they encountered Christianity and the culture of southern Europe. In so far as *Beowulf* and *Waldere* are dissimilar from anything in Latin poetry, they may safely be taken as showing to some degree the manner and form of northern narrative verse of the old time; but in no respect have they the slightest resemblance to the ballads of a later age.

We know from Bede's testimony[1] that singing took place on festal occasions in Anglo-Saxon England to the accompaniment of the harp; and we might be tempted to believe that such lays as Cædmon's fellows sang in turn were the precursors of ballads, save that we get some notion of their quality from the songs reported in *Beowulf*. The narratives chanted at Hrothgar's feast suggest in no way whatever the ballads of later tradition. What the *carmina* were that Aldhelm made and King Alfred esteemed so highly[2] we are unlikely ever to discover: we know only from his works in Latin that the elegant Bishop of Sherburne was not the man to write without conscious artifice. Even if his songs were narratives, of which there is no evidence, there is no reason to suppose that they had the characteristics of ballads. William

---

[1] *Historia Ecclesiastica*, iv. 22, ed. Plummer, i. 259.

[2] See William of Malmesbury, *De Gestis Pontificum Anglorum*, ed. Hamilton, 1870 (Rolls Ser. 52), p. 336.

of Malmesbury, who used Alfred's now lost *Manual* as his authority, says that one of them was still 'popularly sung' in his own time, but regrettably gives no hint as to its nature. That stories in verse from the pre-Norman period circulated orally up to the twelfth century would be clear enough from another statement by William of Malmesbury, who rounds off an account of King Athelstan's authentic history with some stories, for the truth of which—careful man!—he does not vouch. He says that the tales came 'rather from songs worn down by the process of time than from books composed for the instruction of posterity'.[1] Traditional songs these; but the detailed circumstances that William reports— relating to the birth of Athelstan and the death of his brother Edwin—are not what one would expect to find in ballads. Again we must regretfully conclude that the evidence proves nothing except the oral transmission of narrative verse. It helps us in no way towards establishing the early existence of the ballad form.

Much has been made, and rightly—since they are very curious—of the two couplets that a twelfth-century chronicler of Ely inserted in his account of the foundation.[2] He says that King Cnut, while passing the monastery, heard the monks sing, and composed a *cantilenam*, or song, of which the opening ran as follows:

> Merie sungen the muneches binnen Ely
> Tha Cnut ching reu ther by.
> Roweth cnites noer the land
> And here we thes muneches sæng.

[1] 'Magis cantilenis per successiones temporum detritis, quam libris ad instructiones posterorum.' *De Gestis Regum Anglorum*, ed. Stubbs, 1887–9 (Rolls Ser. 90), i. 155.

[2] See Thomas Gale, *Historiae Britannicae, Saxonicae, Anglo-Danicae*, 1691, in the *Historia Eliensis*, ii. 27. This work was compiled by Thomas not long after 1174, while the second book seems to be based on a chronicle begun by Richard of Ely between 1108 and 1131. Gale printed from the MS. now Trin. Coll., Cambridge, O.2.1, which is the only one containing the chapter in question,

There follows a Latin translation of the verses, with the statement that they, and what followed them, 'are even to-day sung publicly in choruses and remembered in proverbs'.[1] Just what the later verses of the song could have contained, and what the chronicler meant by saying that they were 'remembered in proverbs', is hard to see. Certainly we have no right to conclude from his words that the song was a narrative;[2] but the English verses furnish evidence that the four-beat couplet with the ballad lilt was used as early as the twelfth century at least, and presumably in the eleventh. That is all, however. There is not even a hint in all this of a narrative with the structural characteristics that appear after 1200.

There is no point, furthermore, in attempting to prove the earlier existence of ballads with these characteristics by reference to the poetry of primitive races. When evidence is lacking for a period relatively more recent, it is idle to hope to find something more positive for remoter times by studying conditions among backward peoples. At best we should be dealing with analogies merely, and with analogies of a very dangerous sort. If we could discover in Melanesia, or any other remote region of the world, a set of story-songs that conformed closely to the European traditional ballad, which no one has done, we should still be unable to argue with propriety that the kind of lyrical narrative we are studying goes back to the distant past, 'for we should still lack proof of its existence in the cultures from which medieval civilization emerged.' Neither the Roman world nor the races beyond the borders of the Empire furnish any evidence, and without such evidence we cannot push back the probable date for the genesis of the type beyond the Middle Ages.

as Professor A. Elsasser informs me. A later edition is that of D. J. Stewart, *Liber Eliensis*, Anglia Christiana Society, 1848.

[1] 'Quae usque hodie in choris publice cantantur et in proverbiis memorantur.'

[2] A point made by Miss L. Pound, *Modern Language Notes*, xxxiv. 162-5 (1919).

In three ways, and in three ways only, it seems to me, can the study of primitive custom be of any use to us in this matter. We can learn from such observation : (1) that the power or the habit of verse-making and music-making, though not universal, is more widely diffused among folk with a simple culture than among people whom we call civilized ; (2) that songs are ordinarily made as the result of some immediate and definite stimulus, which is more often than not concerned with tribal matters and sometimes results in improvisation; and (3) that song is intimately related to the dance. The importance of these conclusions lies not in any evidence to be drawn from them that the history of ballads has been continuous since an early stage of our racial history, or even that ballads are primitive in quality. Attractive though the notion is, reason forbids our agreement with Gummere when he writes : 'Ballads still hold their own as the nearest approach to primitive poetry preserved among civilized nations, scanty as the records are.'[1] No, all the arguments in this sense confuse valuable analogy with proof of identity. As we shall see, the poetry of primitive races differs essentially from the ballads and other folk-songs of Europe. Furthermore, the plain fact is that we cannot trace the ballad beyond the later Middle Ages. We have no right to take a great leap in the dark from that point to an undesignated century when the European races were still primitive, and to say that the poetry of those times was probably like that of modern European folk-singers.

We learn something of value, indeed, from observing the songs and the way of making them among peoples of lower culture; but it is neither the continuity of a particular form of lyrical narrative through uncounted generations nor the essential organic identity of ballads with primitive verse, but rather the remarkable similarity

[1] F. B. Gummere, *The Beginnings of Poetry*, 1901, p. 180.

between the habits of verse-making among uncivilized races and among those large majorities of civilized folk who have not fallen until of late under the immediate influence of schools and the traditions of conscious artistry. If composing verse and music of a sort can be shown to be not a specialized function of a few persons, but a diffused habit, if making songs under stress of some immediate stimulus has been a common phenomenon, and if dancing has been associated with such songs among widely scattered races with no cultural connexions, we are safe in assuming these things to be constants in the development of any popular *genre* at any time. They cannot serve as criteria by which to define the ballad or any other form, but they may well serve to help explain the development of some of the qualities that ballads actually possess.

As to the first point, the diffused rather than specialized habit of musical and poetic expression, the evidence seems to me conclusive. This does not mean communal composition in the sense of immediate participation by all the members of a group in the making of individual songs (or even communal proprietorship in every case), but simply a very widespread tendency to make songs of a rudimentary sort. We are dealing now with fact, not conjecture. Howitt reports of the Australian aborigines that their ' songs are very numerous, and of varied character, and are connected with almost every part of the social life, for there is little of Australian savage life, either in peace or war, which is not in some measure connected with song'. He goes on to say that some of the songs 'are descriptive of events which have struck the composer', and that the makers 'are the poets, or bards, of the tribe, and are held in great esteem. Their names are known in the neighbouring tribes, and their songs are carried from tribe to tribe.'[1] It must be remembered

[1] A. W. Howitt, *The Native Tribes of South-East Australia*, 1904, pp. 413–14.

that Australian tribes are small, and their poets therefore relatively numerous. Similarly, we read of the Melanesians : 'A poet or poetess more or less distinguished is probably found in every considerable village throughout the islands; when some remarkable event occurs, the launching of a canoe, a visit of strangers, or a feast, song-makers are engaged to celebrate it.'[1] Song-making is a function of tribal life, indeed, among all such peoples. The matter is thus bluntly stated with regard to the Melanesians of New Guinea: 'Any one will compose a topical song; in fact, a man will begin singing one in the club-house, making it up as he goes on, and the others will join.'[2] Even more striking is this evidence from the Andaman Islands: 'Every man composes his own songs. No one would ever sing (at a dance) a song composed by any other person. There are no traditional songs.'[3] This is an extreme case, no doubt, for most tribes keep songs in remembrance, but it is worthy of consideration. Although these Andamanese have the habit of composition, they could not be expected to develop songs with special and typical characteristics—such as our ballads have, for instance.

There is evidence from various parts of Africa that a professional class of singers has existed among the Negro and Bantu peoples, but not to the extent of monopolizing the craft. Miss Kingsley reported[4] from West Africa that she had met five such singers in various regions during her travels, and had heard of others: all provided with ' song-nets ', in which were tied objects like pythons' vertebrae, bits of hide, and the like. A story which the minstrel would sing for a fee was connected with each object. Slightly earlier such men had been found

[1] R. H. Codrington, *The Melanesians*, 1891, p. 334.
[2] R. W. Williamson, *The Ways of the South Sea Savage*, 1914, p. 237.
[3] A. R. Brown, *The Andaman Islanders*, 1922, p. 132.
[4] M. H. Kingsley, *West African Studies*, 1899, pp. 149–50.

wandering about in North-East Africa, improvising their songs;[1] and within the present century similar nomads have been encountered among the Bantus.[2]

In general, however, the African tribesmen sing their songs for themselves, and sing them on many occasions and in many ways, either in choruses or individually. The songs are for the most part not narratives, which is the way of songs the world over; but a good many of them tell stories after a somewhat elementary fashion. The evidence for Africa is like that for other regions: there is singing almost everywhere and for all sorts of reasons. Some of the songs are improvised, some so old that the meaning has been forgotten. If we grant the name of poetry to these products, we cannot deny that the folk who sing them, like the natives of Melanesia, regard song-making as a part of ordinary life, and not a specialized gift to be practised by a class of persons set apart for the purpose.

The evidence for this state of things is exceptionally well marshalled for the Indians of North America, whose music and poetry have been studied by the most devoted and painstaking observers. Matthews[3] says of the Navajos, for example, that they are adept in improvising songs, which is more remarkable because of the highly conventionalized quality of the poetry thus made. In other words, among these folk, who have developed a more than respectable culture of their own, we find a close analogy to conditions that appear to have prevailed in Europe before the spread of popular prints and education. Given a tradition of music and poetry in which a whole people shares, there will appear plenty of composers and verse-makers capable of observing even

---

[1] Paulitschke, *Ethnographie Nordost-Afrikas*, 1896, p. 164.
[2] See H. A. Junod, *The Life of a South African Tribe*, 1912–13, ii. 167–9; C. W. Hobley, *Bantu Beliefs and Magic*, 1922, p. 273.
[3] W. Matthews, *Navaho Legends*, 1897, pp. 23–4.

difficult conventions.[1] It matters not at all that the Navajo songs, to which I am referring, are not narratives, but—like most Indian songs—merely suggest a story when the composer has one in mind. What concerns us now is the fact that a great many of the people make songs as a matter of course, and are capable of making them according to a set fashion.

We have just seen that improvisation occurs among the Navajos. There is evidence from the time of the Jesuit missionaries [2] that other Indian tribes have made songs in this way, as is the case in many other parts of the world.[3] This is not to say that primitive poetry and music, as they have been observed, have generally been extemporized, for tradition is peculiarly strong in the lower ranges of culture as a rule, and preserves with tenacity anything that has been made. From all con-tinents we hear of peoples who have kept in their songs words and phrases of which the meaning has been totally lost. Nor because we find improvisation with considerable frequency need we conclude, with Gummere, that 'short improvisations are the earliest form of individual poetic art'.[4] It may, or may not be true; certainly it has never been proved, and probably never can be. The question, furthermore, has little importance in connexion with the matters we are considering—the savage analogies of European traditional poetry. What should interest us is a general condition, of which improvising is merely

---

[1] For interesting evidence of this see F. Boas, *The Central Eskimo*, 1888, pp. 649–52 (Bureau of American Ethnology, Ann. Report VI).

[2] See Lafitau, *La vie et les moeurs des sauvages Ameriquains*, 1732, ii. 217. For recent evidence see F. Densmore, *Chippewa Music*, 1910, pp. 1–2 (Bulletin of Bur. Amer. Eth., 45).

[3] See, for example, W. Radloff, *Proben der Volkslitteratur der türkischen Stämme Süd-Siberiens*, 1866–8, iii. 34 n., 41; P. Ehrenreich, *Zeitschrift für Ethnologie*, xix. 32 (1887); R. W. Williamson, *op. cit.*, p. 237; T. Whiffen, *The North-West Amazons*, 1915, pp. 196–7, 199–201, 208–10; A. R. Brown, *op. cit.*, pp. 131–2.

[4] *The Beginnings of Poetry*, 1901, p. 394.

one of the manifestations: namely, that poetry among primitive races seems to be made to a quite remarkable extent as a result of some immediate connexion with the object, the feeling, or the event which is the subject of the song.

Any work of the imagination, to be sure, whether simple or extremely complex, must be the result of one sort of stimulus or other. Even a poem so deliberate in design and execution as *Paradise Lost* had its inciting cause, while there may be a very direct relationship between a lyric and the impulse out of which it has sprung in the mind of the poet. Yet in the literature made by sophisticated persons, especially if they are men of genius, there is the greatest difficulty in establishing the connexion between the completed poem and the initial impulse. If we may judge by what great men have written and said about the inception of their various works, the relationship between cause and effect is often exceedingly tenuous, and hard to come at even by the individual who has had the experience.

This is far from the case with the songs of primitive races. Each is associated with some particular event, or rite, or experience, and has little or no significance by itself. As a student of the music of the American Indians phrases the matter : ' no Ojibway song is complete in itself. For entire comprehension it depends upon something external, a story, or a ceremony.' [1] Howitt reports the common belief among the Australian aborigines that their songs came ' from the spirits of the deceased, usually of their kindred, during sleep in dreams '.[2] He cites the interesting case of a man of the Wurunjerri tribe, who composed a lament for a brother supposedly slain by magic. This man believed himself

[1] F. R. Burton, *American Primitive Music*, 1909, p. 163. See also A. C. Fletcher, *Indian Story and Song*, 1900, p. 115.

[2] A. W. Howitt, *op. cit.*, p. 416.

'inspired by something more than mortal'.[1] In such instances, obviously, improvising takes place, though the immediacy of the stimulus is the most important factor. We should note, moreover, that even when there is no question of supernatural aid, a very direct connexion exists between the occasion for the song and the making of it. For example, Howitt quotes a song that came to a fisherman 'not in sleep as to some men, but when tossing about on the waves in his boat with the waters jumping up round him'.[2] Umbara composed his song while the experience was going on, and the words embody his fear of upsetting in the tumult of the waves.

Such examples might be multiplied if there were any need to do so. There would be little point, however, in presenting with great detail the evidence for a condition which seems to be world-wide among primitive folk. Wherever we can get at their experience, we find the same phenomenon : unpremeditated composition about matters of immediate concern to them, whether events or feelings. In other words, we never come upon a race which has not some development of the twin arts of poetry and song, and the possibility of an immediate recourse to them under due emotional stimulus. We must remember, it is true, that the simple peoples of latter generations have cultural histories as long, if perhaps not so interesting, as our own, and that observation of their habits cannot show in any direct way how music and verse began, since we never get beyond a stage where art exits. We do, however, find in actual existence a state of affairs wherein the vocal arts are inchoate and undifferentiated. As one observer has put it, in describing the Ojibway Indian : he 'has no word for poetry. Whatever departs from plain prose is *nogamon*, song, which means that his poetry is not only inseparable but

---

[1] *Op. cit.*, pp. 418, 422.   [2] *Op. cit.*, pp. 422–3.

indistinguishable from music.'[1] Under such conditions, and indeed wherever a close union between music and poetry of simple kinds has been maintained, spontaneous utterance under direct stimulus, but according to a traditional art, can be found.

In the third place, dancing is habitually, though not invariably, associated with song among the peoples whose habits we have been considering. How close the connexion is may be illustrated from a tribe in North-East Africa, which uses the same word for both song and dance,[2] as we have just seen that some Amerindians fail to distinguish verbally between melody and verse. The ceremonial dances of the Indians themselves have been so often described that it is necessary to do no more than refer to them. Not all of them are accompanied by song, though in default of it the rhythm is maintained either by the beating of drums or the clapping of hands. I myself remember the harvest dance of the Pueblo Indians at Acoma, the movements of which are curiously syncopated and timed to the thudding of drums, while what appears to be unrelated song goes on at a distance. More frequently, however, song and dance are united in Indian festivities, as they are among other races generally throughout the world. The exceptions[3] do not, I believe, invalidate the idea of a fairly constant relationship, which is all one could expect. I am not urging, please note, that song gave rise to dance, or dance to song, nor do I wish to argue that in the beginning of things the two invariably went together.[4] All we need to bear in mind is the simple fact, which no one is likely to dispute, that songs are not uncommonly

[1] F. R. Burton, *op. cit.*, p. 106. See also A. C. Fletcher, *op. cit.*, p. 121.

[2] See R. Paulitschke, *op. cit.*, p. 217.

[3] See, for example, E. S. Craighill Handy, *The Native Culture in the Marquesas*, 1923, p. 316.

[4] Though some observers believe that they did. See A. R. Brown, *op. cit.*, p. 247.

danced among the peoples whom we classify roughly—
and inaccurately enough—as primitive.

I have made sufficiently clear, I hope, my opinion
that we cannot hope to solve the problem of the origin
of ballads by direct reference to the conditions of
musical production obtaining among such races. In the
long debate between advocates of the theory that ballads
took their rise in choric dances and the determined opponents of that theory, evidence from this source has
been used more or less frequently, but not with the
effect of clarifying the difficulties of either party. Gummere,[1] who stated the former view with a greater
wealth of learning and a more brilliant scholarly ingenu-
ity than any one else has shown in discussing the origin
of British ballads, never distinguished quite sufficiently,
it seems to me, between the question as to how poetry
came into being and the wholly different question of the
development of the ballad form in medieval Europe. He
was thus led into presenting, as evidence for the development of the ballad type from communal festivities,
phenomena that could at best be no more than analogues.
Confusion immediately resulted. With stout common
sense—as his critics have seldom done him the justice
of noting—he recognized and more than once asserted
that ' the actual traditional ballad of Europe is not to
be carried back into prehistoric conditions';[2] yet on the
same page with a statement of this kind he could write
of the ' survival of primitive and communal poetry as it
can be detected in the ballads and the popular rimes of
Europe '. The difficulty is clear, I believe : having been
impressed by the similarity that exists between the singing and dancing habits of savage tribes and certain

[1] Introduction to *Old English Ballads*, 1894, *The Beginnings of Poetry*, 1901,
'Primitive Poetry and the Ballad', *Modern Philology*, i. 193–202, 217–34, 373–90
(1904), *The Popular Ballad*, 1907, *Cambridge History of Literature*, 1908, ii.
449–74.

[2] *The Beginnings of Poetry*, p. 163.

features of balladry, he concluded too hastily that the latter must somehow be the product of the former. At the same time, as we have seen, he never forgot that the ballad form we know emerged out of darkness in the thirteenth century.

Those of his critics who have marshalled anthropological evidence have not been in better case, however. Miss Pound, for example, though she attacked Gummere with quite unnecessary asperity,[1] failed altogether to detect the essential fallacy in his argument and gathered a good deal of material, valuable in itself, to show that many of the songs of the so-called primitive races are individualistic in composition and performance, and that they are not invariably connected with any dance. She vehemently denied the possibility that ballads could have developed in medieval Europe through the practice of singing and dancing in chorus at festivals; and she tried to confute this view chiefly by reference to conditions of poetic production among uncivilized races, while at the same time she asserted that they had nothing whatever to do with the matter. She thus involved herself in a series of logical errors that destroyed the value of her book as a constructive argument, although the evidence she presented served to point out some of the difficulties of the communal theory of origins as it had been stated by Gummere.

If we may accept as three constants of popular poetry and music the phenomena discussed above, we shall not be surprised to find analogous conditions present in medieval Europe. That they were there, indeed, some centuries before we have any evidence about the ballad as such, we have every reason to believe. The famous passage from Bede, which we have already noted, is important in this connexion. Legend may well have romanticized the story of how Cædmon began his work

---

[1] L. Pound, *Poetic Origins and the Ballad*, 1921.

as a poet; but the account of the way his fellows sang in turn, when the harp went round, is treated so completely as a matter of ordinary custom that we have no reason to suspect its veracity. We need not suppose that these dependants of the Abbess Hilde at Whitby always, or even generally, improvised, any more than Indian braves used to do when each sang his special song at a feast, but we have every right to believe that some of them at least were not content to reproduce what they had learned from others. The miracle was not that a cow-herd should sing, but that this dumb Cædmon should quite suddenly become vocal in praise of God the Creator. That he sang anything like a ballad, or even sang to a melody, I am not, of course, suggesting.

As for the dance, the practice is so abundantly attested in Europe [1] that we need not rehearse the evidence here except for the one instance of early medieval dancing which bears directly on the question in hand. This is the story of the cursed dancers of the German village of Kölbigk in the Duchy of Anhalt, which gained wide currency soon after the occurrence it pretends to describe.[2] In brief, the legend runs that one Christmas morning, early in the eleventh century, a group of young men and women were dancing in the churchyard, to the annoyance of the priest, who was saying mass. As a result of his curse, the youths and maidens continued to dance for an entire year, after which some of them died and others became vagabonds, afflicted with what we call St. Vitus' dance. This fantastic legend was elaborated in different ways as it spread

[1] For abundant illustration see E. K. Chambers, *The Medieval Stage*, 1903, i. 160-71, and E. Faral, *Les Jongleurs en France au moyen âge*, 1910, pp. 90-2. For the sixteenth century see C. R. Baskervill, *The Elizabethan Jig*, 1929, pp. 9-10.

[2] The best account of the ramifications of this legend is by E. Schröder, 'Die Tänzer von Kölbigk', *Zeitschrift für Kirchengeschichte*, xvii. 94-164 (1897). To be supplemented by G. Paris, *Journal des Savants*, 1899, pp. 733-46.

throughout northern Europe. One version, connected with Wilton Abbey, and clearly from an English source, says that a pilgrim named Theodoric, who at least pretended to be one of the unhappy dancers, came thither and was eventually healed at the shrine of St. Editha. His story of what happened to himself and his companions included the song by which they accompanied their dance in the churchyard:

> Equitabat Bovo per silvam frondosam,
> Ducebat sibi Merswinden formosam.
> Quid stamus? cur non imus?

Bovo was the name of the oldest of the young men, according to this account, and Merswinde that of one of the female dancers.

In all the circumstances, it would be rash for us to assert that this scrap of verse was actually sung in the churchyard of Kölbigk. Schröder thought that the original version of the legend contained it,[1] since some form of the name Merswinde appears in all three of the groups into which the variants are divisible, and Bovo in two of them. Gaston Paris suggested[2] that the stanza might have been taken from a song current at the time when Theodoric's account was put together. Although the document, as we have it, is pretty clearly English, the song may well have appeared in an earlier version on the Continent. Paris inclined to the belief that Lorraine was its place of origin. At all events, we have manuscript evidence for the names from the eleventh century, and for the verses from the twelfth. It does not matter greatly, so far as we are concerned at present, just where the stanza was made. Whether it came from Germany, or Lorraine, or England, it attests equally well two things: first, that the couplet with a lilting movement, so familiar to us in ballads of northern

[1] *Op. cit.*, p. 140. [2] *Op. cit.*, p. 745.

Europe, was a commonplace of the twelfth century, and was used with a refrain; and, secondly, that dancing to a song with verse of this sort was also a matter of course. It suggests, furthermore, that the practice of improvising variations on old songs had become an established custom by that time, for though Bovo may have been leading the beauteous Merswinde by the hand, he was not actually riding through the leafy wood while he sang. The adaptation of the verses to the sacrilege of the dancers was far from perfect. The dancers are shown as singing about some lover and his lady, who have nothing whatever to do with village-folk like themselves. The names may have been changed, as so often happens, or a coincidence of names—together with the appropriate refrain—may have been responsible for the insertion of an earlier song in legendary account.[1]

We do not certainly know, of course, that this scrap, translated from some vernacular tongue or other, was the opening stanza of a narrative song, because we have no means of guessing how it went on. We can only say that it presents a situation in precisely the way of a ballad. Why were the prototypes of Bovo and Merswinde riding through the leafy wood at all unless to some adventure? The approach to the subject is not that of pure lyric, but of such narratives as we have been studying. We shall not go far wrong, therefore, in regarding the couplet and refrain as the earliest record of the existence of such ballads in Europe. As I have remarked previously, the fact that an example of the type dates from a given century does not prove that other specimens may not have been composed long before that time. If, however, *Equitabat Bovo* be a fragmentary

---

[1] Suggested by Paris. An English account based on Theodoric's by Robert Mannyng of Brunne (*Handlyng Synne*, vv. 9041, 9052) says that Gerlew, one of the dancers, 'endited' or 'wrought' the song, but in the Latin Gerlew 'fatale carmen orditur'.

ballad, we can at least push back the date of origin for the species by one century, and possibly by two, since *Judas* was not written down till close upon 1300. The song is thus of the utmost importance in the history of balladry.

To its metrical form we must later return. For the time being, however, we had perhaps best direct our attention to the problem of how the ballad—or whatever other name one chooses to give it—originated as a narrative type, drawing what conclusions we can from the rather thin evidence at our command. About this matter, it is proper to say frankly, we can at best do no more than make conjectural inferences from all too scanty material.

In the opening chapter of this volume I drew attention to the fact that European ballads in general possess at least three characteristics in common. I said that ' a compressed and centralized episode is the ordinary narrative unit, that dramatic presentation of action is the ordinary narrative method, and that impersonality of approach to the theme is the ordinary narrative attitude '.[1] What explanation can one give, we must now ask, for the appearance of songs with these qualities among European peoples from the twelfth century on ? It will not help us to postulate a dancing throng that had been composing and modifying ballads since primitive times ; and it will be even less helpful to shut our eyes fast against the clear evidence of things, and deny that ballads are anything more than the cast-off brats of literature and music. We must scrutinize carefully such data as we can find, and attempt to weigh the probabilities of the case with all of them in view.

First of all, we may postulate that the habit of singing, both individually and in chorus, was as prevalent in the tenth and eleventh centuries as it has been in most other

[1] See pp. 10–11.

times and regions. Without this premise, we should not be able to proceed with an explanation of any sort. What people sang would of course depend in large measure on traditional custom, though innovations are always possible in any society. That narratives of some sort were sung even before the period we have in mind is beyond question. We know, furthermore, that dancing in village centres, often in and about the churches, had before this time been sufficiently common to disturb some at least of the clergy. As to the nature of the dances, we get no information more precise than that about Kölbigk, where the young folk joined hands, according to all accounts, and must therefore have engaged in some kind of round.[1]

Remembering these habits of the people, we may conjecture reasonably that stories would be sung to tunes like those used in the dance, whether the stories were made for the dance or not. Although Bovo and his friends appear to have danced to a melody which was the accompaniment of a narrative song, the matter of primary importance is not so much the association of story with dance as of story with dance tune. In other words, as I have intimated earlier in this volume,[2] it seems to me that the singing of a narrative to a melody is the kernel of the whole matter. Wherever and whenever that adaptation was made, the ballad as we know it came into being. By the twelfth century it was accomplished, and it may perhaps have occurred at least as early as the eleventh century.

To put the case another way, the peculiarities of ballad structure, as they appear throughout most parts of Europe, are explicable if we remember that the

[1] Paris, *op. cit.*, p. 735, n. 7, suggests that the dance cannot have been a closed ring, because the arm of the priest's daughter is pulled in an attempt to remove her. But the dancers join hands, and 'girando' is used to describe their movements.

[2] See p. 73.

stories are moulded to fit a recurrent melody. Their compression, their centralization, with the impersonality that results from the dramatic treatment of a theme, and, above all, the swiftly moving action, are precisely the qualities that would arise, almost inevitably, from the practice of singing stories to brief tunes. To each repetition of the melody would fall some little scene, some bit of dialogue, or perhaps some longer speech. There would frequently be iteration, as a matter of course, though such iteration seems never to have become an essential structural feature. A story composed to fit a recurrent melody, or composed simultaneously with such a melody, could not well fail to have a dramatic quality. It would be forced into such form by the circumstances of its performance. Quite possibly, too, the habit—age-old, if we may trust in this particular to the analogy of savage verse—of making songs under direct stimulus of the event or feeling that is celebrated in them may have something to do with the vivid suggestiveness of the verse thus produced. The presence or immediate recollection of whatever happened to be the subject would certainly tend to develop the practice of reproducing it mimetically. Thus the story would be told not as something remote in time, but almost as if it were being re-enacted, step by step, with repetition of the melody.

I see no reason to doubt, furthermore, that the dance played its part in the formation of the ballad type, though I cannot believe it to have been the dominant factor. It is unnecessary to suppose that songs were invariably danced, while the tradition of ballad-making was establishing itself, or that dances were invariably accompanied by song; but whenever the two were joined, the rhythms of movement would surely accentuate the tendencies already discussed. The dance lends itself to pantomimic gesture, which in turn would emphasize the

dramatic presentation of a story. We have seen how
Bovo and his companions both danced and sang. It is
easy to understand that in such a case there would be a
direct effect of the repeated rhythm of the melody,
beaten out in physical movement. Such a group, singing and dancing, could not well avoid—if some event
were in their minds—expressing it in the dramatic way
of the ballad. Each repetition of the melody would
necessarily correspond to a stage of the dance, and so of
the story. The action, moreover, would be sharpened
and focused for the participants. Bovo would feel himself riding away through the leafy wood as he circled
about, clasping the hand of Merswinde. Not taking it
too seriously, to be sure, for this was a Christmas frolic,
he would none the less dramatize the situation because
momentarily feeling himself an actor in it.

This does not imply, however, the customary participation of all the members of a group in making
a song, for neither a melody nor the outline of an
imagined story can well emerge from more than a single
mind. Even though a self-constituted leader set the
tune and chanted a first stanza, his companions—dealing,
let us suppose, with well-known events—could scarcely
contribute their share, unless the manner and method of
such songs had become established in traditional use.
One cannot believe that 'communal composition' in
this sense took place while the ballad type was becoming
fixed, though instances of it have been known in modern
times. With or without the accompaniment of dancing,
individuals, we must suppose, fashioned the earliest
ballads—those that ultimately set the form. Some of
them, it is natural to surmise, were professional entertainers, minstrels or other members of that amorphous
tribe whose activities are so difficult to arrange in
orderly sequence, though they have left their traces on
the history of every century. Since it was their business

to amuse, they may have had their part in establishing the fashion of story-telling in song that grew up, it appears, in the eleventh or twelfth century. Yet it would be unwise of us to believe, for reasons already given, that to minstrels of any sort should be attributed a dominating influence in the process.

What I have said above about the evolution of a new lyrical narrative, centralized, dramatic, and impersonal, popular of appeal and practice, born of the habit of melodic song and probably fostered by the habit of the dance, does not imply, in the second place, that the earliest ballads had great virtues of form and texture. There has been an unfortunate tendency on the part of scholars to take it for granted that earlier ballads are likely to be better than later ones, and to lament as the loss of a great treasure the total disappearance of at least a very large proportion of those that can have been originally composed as early as the fifteenth century. It should be pointed out that we have no means of knowing whether they were indeed of a superior quality. Our sole specimen of thirteenth-century record certainly gives no evidence that such was the case. *Judas* is a good ballad, but it has no transcendent excellence. One has to admit the possibility that the earliest compositions may have been much less attractive as narratives and as songs than later ones became.

The suggestion has been made that a form of story-telling akin to the *cante-fable* of medieval literature was perhaps the root whence ballads grew : that the habit of relating a tale with bursts of song interposed led in time to the elimination of the prose framework and the consequent development of the narrative in verse.[1]

---

[1] First proposed as a theory, so far as I know, by J. Jacobs, *English Fairy Tales*, 1898, p. 247, and developed with both tact and abundant learning by Miss M. W. Beckwith, *Publications of the Modern Language Association*, xxxix. 455-83 (1924).

This theory is in many ways very interesting, and as stated by Miss Beckwith deserves a most respectful consideration. It is true that among folk-tales from various regions of the world we find examples of the practice described.[1] There can be no doubt whatever that it has been common and widespread, particularly in Africa and America, though the evidence for it in Europe is less satisfactory than in other quarters. So far, so good. The theory, furthermore, is the only one thus far advanced, except for my own as presented above, that takes into account the double nature of the problem of ballad origins. It attempts, as I have been attempting, to show how the structural form of the ballad came into existence, leaving the problem of metrical form for other explanation.

One weakness of the hypothesis lies in the assumption it shares with that defended so ably by Gummere, an assumption which has been adopted by some of his most ardent opponents. To accept it, we should be compelled to believe in a process of gradual development from the songs of primitive times to those of the later Middle Ages, when ballads come to light. For this, as we have seen, there is no evidence. If we grant, as we may, that something like the *cante-fable* was to be found among European folk-tales at an early date, we still have to account for the differentiation by which the elements of song sloughed off the narrative prose and became unified in a new form. Why, after telling *Märchen* with interlarded songs for countless generations, did men fall into the habit of singing their stories altogether—when they sang them at all—and employ to this end only those

[1] In addition to those cited by Miss Beckwith, her own *Jamaica Anansi Stories*, 1924, should be consulted. See also, E. Torday, *Camp and Tramp in African Wilds*, 1913, pp. 138–41, for the Congo; J. R. Swanton, *Haida Texts and Myths*, 1905, pp. 94–9; F. Densmore, *Teton Sioux Music*, 1918, pp. 495–7; and *Pawnee Music*, 1929, pp. 100–10 (Bulletins of the Bureau of American Ethnology, 29, 61, 93), for Amerindian specimens.

portions that had been lyrical? Miss Beckwith supposes that this was done when the events of a tale became 'familiar to the folk',[1] but she can suggest no impelling cause. This is the second weakness of the hypothesis. Ingenious though it be, the theory seems to me much less well based than the one outlined above. The interesting versions of *Little Musgrave and Lady Barnard* (81) and *The Maid Freed from the Gallows* (95), which Miss Beckwith found among the Jamaican negroes, can be easily explained by their old habit of making and reciting folk-tales in the mixed form of verse and prose. These people have transformed the ballads into a kind of narrative familiar to their race long before their forced migration, and not forgotten in the West Indies, as their stories about Anansi[2] clearly show. The beast-tales are African in origin, and have retained in the New World their structural characteristics as well as their humour and pathos.

Thus far we have concerned ourselves with possible answers to the first of the three questions propounded at the beginning of this chapter: What was the origin of the narrative form peculiar to European ballads in general? It would be foolish to pretend that a wholly satisfactory solution of this difficult problem has been found. There should be some profit, however, in having envisaged it clearly, as I hope we have done. Let us see whether an examination of the second problem stated may not throw some further light upon the development of the *genre* in both its phases. The second question is this: What was the origin of the melodic and poetical form found in British ballads, as well as in some of their Continental relations?

First, let us see what facts are at our command. We know that the ballads of Great Britain and its closer neighbours have been made according to various metrical

---

[1] *Op. cit.* p. 467.   [2] See p. 215, n.

patterns, though almost invariably with an unmistakable rhythm that is shared with other folk-songs. This rhythm, we can be sure, results from a close correspondence between verbal and musical phrase. We may safely estimate that something like half of our British ballads have been sung with refrains since the period of collecting began, but we have no clear evidence as to the proportion of them that were so provided in earlier centuries. Those first written down appear without refrains, but may nevertheless have been accompanied by them as actually sung. Of primary importance, as in the matter of the development of the narrative structure—and possibly to an even greater degree—is the relationship between verse and melody. The dependence of the one upon the other cannot be too strongly stressed. There can be no doubt whatever that they have been mutually important throughout their common history.

All too little, unfortunately, is known about popular music in the Middle Ages. It is deplorable, but not strange, that the musicians of those times did not record what they must have heard in various forms. Their interest was naturally either in ecclesiastical music or in that of the courts, both of which were much more sophisticated and complicated than the tunes for dancing and singing can possibly have been. That courtly music can have had any marked influence on the melodies sung and danced by the people is in every way unlikely, for the simplification of elaborate music of this sort could scarcely have been achieved except by conscious effort, to which there would have been no incentive. The case would have been different with ecclesiastical music, which was restricted by the decorum of the Gregorian system to simpler forms. Yet it has to be remembered that two of the tones of this system, one of which corresponds to our major mode, were forbidden to church composers because so often used for unworshipful songs of the people.[1] All in all, it is safest to conjecture that an art of simple melody grew up alongside the musical art of the Church, based on the same conceptions and probably to some extent influenced by it.

In avoiding the romantic view, sometimes expressed, that in the Middle Ages all classes shared the same amusements and the same arts, we need not fall into the opposite error of supposing that folk-music and folk-poetry grew up in a vacuum. It would be extremely odd if what was heard in church did not somehow affect what was sung on the green and by the fireside. If balladry, as well as other folk-song, was a cultural phenomenon rather than a heritage of primitive ages, which we must in reason believe, there can be no question that it was subject to influences from without; and with respect to music the influences must have been chiefly from ecclesiastical sources.

Why should not the same thing be true of the metrical forms that ballad verse had assumed by the twelfth and thirteenth centuries? Valiant attempts have been made to show that rhythms of the sort antedated the Norman Conquest and were a purely native product.[2] There can be no doubt that alliterative verse had changed its character somewhat before the end of the Old English period, or was in process of change. Some of the poetical insertions in the *Anglo-Saxon Chronicle* show this markedly. The general tendency, however, appears to have been towards breaking up the older tradition of verse rather than adopting a new one. Only in occasional passages, which may be illustrated by the conclusion of one of the *Charms*, do I find anything that markedly suggests the lilt of such verse as became

[1] C. J. Sharp, *English Folk-Song: Some Conclusions*, p. 43.

[2] Notably by J. W. Rankin, *Publications of the Modern Language Association* xxxvi. 401–28 (1921), in a very learned and interesting though inconclusive article, which has scarcely received the attention it deserves.

common enough after the time when we know that folk-
song had established itself.

> Sitte ge, sigewif, sigaþ to eorþan!
> Næfre ge wilde to wudu fleogan!
> Bec ge swa gemindige mines godes,
> Swa biþ manna gehwilc metes and eþeles.[1]

These verses conform to the alliterative pattern, but
they have as well something of the movement of the
four-beat ballad couplet ; largely because each half-line
has the same arrangement of stressed and unstressed
syllables. A charm like this is, of course, completely un-
literary, and might be taken as important evidence for the
existence of native verse of the ballad sort, if only it could
be shown to be an early product. Unfortunately we cannot
date any of the charms, and therefore cannot argue that
this is older than the eleventh century, which is when it
was written down.[2] Whatever its age, the form in which
it appears may well be one it assumed at a relatively late
date, quite as the charms collected in our own day have
assumed a modern dress, though some of them are
undoubtedly of ancient origin. These considerations,
together with the fact that the verses conform, after all,
to the alliterative pattern, should warn us against regarding it seriously as evidence for a tradition of native
verse in rhymed couplets with alternating strong and
weak stresses.

The *Hymns of St. Godric*, which must have been composed before 1170 if they are genuine productions of
the hermit of Finchale, as seems to be the case, have
interest in connexion with this matter. Godric was an
unlearned person, and the three scraps of verse attributed
to him have no merit as literature. They do show, how-

---

[1] Grein-Wülker, *Bibliothek der angelsächischen Poesie*, i. 320.
[2] MS. Corp. Christi Coll., Cambridge, 41. For the date see M. R. James, *Catalogue of the Manuscripts in the Library of Corpus Christi College*, 1912.

ever, that the long line of the older verse, with its four sharply defined stresses, could become without much difficulty a line suitable for use in the four-beat couplet of folk-song. In this case the alteration goes further than in the *Charm* quoted above, but it does not conceal what I believe to have been the dual origin of the verse form. The first of the so-called hymns runs as follows :[1]

> Sainte Marie virgine,
> moder Iesu Cristes Nazarene,
> onfo, scild, help thin Godric,
> onfang, bring hehlic with the in godes ric.

> Sainte Marie, Cristes bur,
> maidenes clenhad, moderes flur,
> dilie mine sinne, rixe in min mod,
> bring me to winne with self god.

These verses show clearly, it seems to me, what an in-expert—though truly devout—poet, whose ear was attuned to the rhythms of the traditional alliterative verse, was likely to accomplish when he tried to make in the vernacular something that sounded like a Latin hymn. I venture the explanation, because I can see no other that fits the case. Godric's rough-hewn couplets do not tend to prove the existence of any kind of stanzaic verse in pre-Conquest times ; on the contrary, they make that possibility more remote. What they do show, if not altogether conclusively, is how the older poetry merged into the new when affected by hymns of the Church.

Miss Pound was not far from the truth, though she reached the conclusion by the wrong path, I think, and drew some unjustifiable inferences from it, when she

---

[1] I quote the conflated text by Zupitza, *Englische Studien*, xi. 423 (1888). The texts, which occur in various Latin MSS., are individually very faulty, nor is it possible to make them smooth except by conjectural emendation.

wrote: 'Medieval ballad literature emerged under the influence of clericals.'[1] I can see no reason for believing that clerks themselves had any considerable part in originating either the structural or the poetic form of the ballad; but I am convinced that too little attention has been paid, except by Miss Pound, to a more than probable ecclesiastical influence upon the nascent *genre*. It is only fair to say that, in advancing her hypothesis of clerical influence, Miss Pound was careful to suggest that 'in something like it, may perhaps be found the explanation best satisfying all the conditions'. If I combat her theory that 'ballads began with clericals', I do so because it offers a wholly inadequate explanation of the very special characteristics that ballads from many parts of Europe possess, and no suggestion, moreover, of a motive for the composition of such songs.

With regard to the metrical form of British ballads, however, and of verse in similar rhythms from the Continent, it seems to me justifiable to believe in some sort of influence from the Latin hymns of the Church. As soon as accentual rhythms began to replace the earlier quantitative metres, there appeared in the hymns a tendency to alternate primary or heavy stresses with lighter ones: a tendency that must certainly have been due to the musical accompaniment. This tendency became so marked by the eleventh and twelfth centuries that no one who looks through a collection of hymns with attention can fail to distinguish it. It is evident in the following Ambrosian stanza quoted by Bede:[2]

> Apparebit repentina
> Dies magna Domini,
> Fur obscura velut nocte
> Improvisos occupans.

[1] *Poetic Origins and the Ballad*, p. 190.
[2] *Opera quae supersunt*, ed. J. A. Giles, 1843–4, vi. 77.

It is still clearer in this rhymed hymn by Peter of Cluny, who died in 1156:[1]

> Salve, virgo benedicta,
> Quae fugasti maledicta,
>   Salve, mater altissimi,
>   Agni sponsa mitissimi.

We may account for this similarity of movement in the verse of hymns and of popular songs in three different ways. We may conjecture that the popular verse was imitated from the ecclesiastical; we may suppose that the hymns changed from quantitative to accentual verse because there was already in existence popular poetry with such rhythms; or we may guess that both developed as they did because sung to the strongly marked rhythms of not very dissimilar music, with a considerable influence exerted first and last by the ecclesiastical upon the secular verse. Fortunately the difficult question as to the rise of accentual verse in Latin does not immediately concern us. What we need to consider is only the probable course of things in northern countries like Great Britain. I submit the following conjectural statement as an explanation that at least does no violence to the little evidence we possess.

The old alliterative verse, as we have seen in the *Charm for Swarming Bees*, might easily take on the semblance of four-stressed lines whenever the same type of half-line was used throughout a passage. The characteristic quality of the verse disappears at once when it is so treated, for the variety of the position of stressed in relation to unstressed syllables is what gives alliterative poetry its peculiar effect. Yet almost by inattention, one would think, verses like the *Charm* I have quoted might come into being. If, then, a people whose ears were

---

[1] See Dreves and Blume, *Ein Jahrtausend Lateinischer Hymnendichtung*, 1909, i. 242.

attuned to such poetry began to make secular songs, as St. Godric appears to have made his feeble religious ones, to fit rounded melodies, they would achieve something not too remote from the older verse, yet similar in cadence to the Latin hymns. How close they might be to one another in rhythm is shown by the song attributed to the dancers of Kölbigk, quoted above, which is a translation from the vernacular into Latin, yet perfectly reproduces the rhythmic effect of later folk-song.

I am conjecturing, of course, that the people who made stories for singing under these conditions were responsive to the same impulses which were operative throughout the larger part of Europe at about the same time. In all cases, musical form would have been the determining factor in the development of both the structure and the poetic dress of the narrative *genre* thus created. To the extent that the musical form varied from land to land, the verse form would vary. Once a regional tradition had developed, moreover, there would begin an interchange of products : the baffling migration of ballads that has so clearly taken place, century after century, though by devious ways.

As to the part that dancing had in all this, I do not see how it can be viewed as a constant constructive factor, though it must have been an auxiliary of great importance. Under the excitation of it, a rudimentary ballad might be composed, sometimes by adaptation of an older song, sometimes *de novo* when a sensational event was uppermost in the minds of the group. The habit of dancing, certainly as common as the habit of singing, must furthermore have tended to emphasize the rhythms of song until they became instinctive and unconscious. In this way, as I conceive the matter, the dance may well have been an enforcing element in the development of popular music and poetry. If it was secondary to melody, it yielded only to melody in importance, and without its operation the tradition of folk-song could scarcely have taken the course it did.

As to the refrain, the evidence is far less satisfactory than one could wish. We have seen in an earlier chapter[1] that a good case can be made out for the constant appearance of it in Scandinavian balladry, but that in Great Britain, Germany, and France the use of it has been intermittent. In these circumstances I do not see how we can reasonably take it as a formative element of primary importance in the development of the ballad type. Quite possibly there may have been from the beginning a double tradition: a set of ballads, presumably danced, which had refrains, and another set without them. In both cases the melody, to which the verse was intimately accommodated, would be the controlling element, while the subconscious effect of the dance as a training in rhythm would be felt even when stories were sung for the stories' sake only. This would account for the absence of the refrain in such an early piece as *Judas* and its presence in the song of the dancers of Kölbigk. It would help to explain, too, the curious phenomenon of *Twelfth Day*,[2] which seems to me to be clear evidence that the traditional ballad was so firmly established by the thirteenth century that it could be imitated by a pious versifier, quite as it was imitated in the nineteenth century by eminent poets.

At this point we may properly turn to the last of the three questions which were asked at the beginning of this chapter: What was the origin of the individual ballads that make up our collections?

The answer we give to this question will depend to a great extent on whether we accept the validity of the idea that ballads, as well as other folk-songs, were composed and varied in accordance with a traditional habit of accomplishment and taste established in some such way as I

[1] See pp. 117–24.   [2] See *ante*, p. 34.

have sketched above. Even though my conjectural re-construction of the processes by which the tradition grew up should not be so accurate as I hope, it would still be possible to accept the notion of a controlling and moulding tradition. Indeed, it seems to me that we emerge from the shadows and come into a much clearer region when we turn from the origin of the form to the way the pattern has been used by successive generations. Unless one is blind to the demonstrable fact that there is art of a special and attractive sort in the music and verse of folk-song, and art in the narrative form of ballads, one cannot possibly look at them as mere waifs and strays. The essential fallacy in the reasoning of those who accept the view that they are nothing more is this: they make no attempt to explain how and why songs launched on the tide of popular tradition acquire the characteristics by virtue of which they are a *genre* apart. In other words, they ignore the question of how the pattern was formed, though they recognize that ballads conform to a certain pattern. In this, though they deride as mystery-mongers those who have seen the real problem and tried to solve it, and though they pose as men of stout common sense, they credit a mystery darker than the faith of the extremest 'communalist'.

If the existence of the traditional pattern be granted, there can be no difficulty about reconciling the various notions that have been held about the composition of individual ballads, for each of which there is a certain amount of evidence. There is no reason why such min-strels as were not hangers-on of great houses, but enter-tained the squire, the townsman, and the lower orders of country folk,[1] should not have made ballads according to the popular mode, and have added them to their reper-tories. Even though what the minstrel composed might

[1] For a classification of such professional entertainers see E. Faral, *op. cit.*, pp. 66-86.

in its first state be somewhat more conscious than ballads otherwise fashioned, and might lack certain qualities that we regard as characteristic, it would soon be reformed in popular transmission. Such professional vagabonds as I have in mind, moreover, would themselves have been so little differentiated from the people to whom they sang that they must often have been completely in the current of the tradition. For them, making a ballad would not have been imitating a ballad. The early and frequent use of the form by minstrels may perhaps explain the development of the cycle of tales about Robin Hood, to which we get reference in the fourteenth century. By the time of *Piers Plowman*[1] Robin's exploits were evidently well known, though some of the extant ballads are certainly of later origin.

We may reasonably suspect, too, that some of the ballads based on popularization of ecclesiastical lore, like *Judas*, *St. Stephen and Herod*, or *Dives and Lazarus* were first composed by singers who had use on occasion for pieces with a religious tinge. The fact that the ballad first copied in a manuscript happened to be of this sort does not mean that such songs were the earliest ones in circulation,[2] for any religious and moralizing verse had a better chance than secular poetry of being written down; but it may well indicate an interest in ballads on the part of persons or groups that minstrels would have been anxious to satisfy. At least, this seems to me a more probable explanation than that clerks composed them, though it is not impossible to believe that a clerk who was of the people might have made ballads, like any other man, once the tradition of them was established.

---

[1] Sloth says:

But I can rymes of Robyn Hood and Randolf erle of Chestre.

(B. Passus v. 402, C. Passus viii. 11. Ed. Skeat, i. 166–7.)

[2] As Miss Pound would have us believe, *op. cit.*, p. 187.

Of a quite different origin, no doubt, was the ballad to which John Barbour referred about 1375 in *The Bruce*,[1] when writing of the victory won by Sir Andrew Hercla over Sir John de Soulis, governor of Eskdale.

> I will nocht reherss all the maner;
> For quha sa likis, thai may heir
> Young women quhen thai will play,
> Syng it emang thame ilke day.

Evidently Barbour had in mind songs made in the countryside, as ballads of the Border, according to Leslie, were made. In the sixteenth-century translation of Leslie's Latin we read this about the Borderers: 'They delyt mekle in thair awne musick and Harmonie in singing, quhilke of the actes of thair foirbeares thay haue leired, or quhat thame selfes haue inuented of ane ingenious policie to dryue a pray and say thair prayeris.'[2] It is impossible to say whether the song that the Scots made after Bannockburn, of which Robert Fabyan tells us,[3] was professional or non-professional in its composition. We can hardly doubt, however, that the stanza quoted by Fabyan is the beginning of a ballad. 'Than the Scottis enflamyd with pryde, in derysyon of Englysshe men, made this ryme as foloweth.

> 'Maydens of Englonde, sore maye ye morne,
> For your lemmans ye haue loste at Bannockisborne,
>   With heue a lowe.
> What wenyth the kynge of Englonde,
> So soone to haue wonne Scotlande
>   With rumbylowe.

'This songe was after many dayes sungyn, in daunces,

---

[1] xvi. 519–22. Ed. Skeat, Scottish Text Society, 1894, ii. 69.

[2] Leslie, *Historie of Scotland*, trans. J. Dalrymple, 1596. Ed. E. G. Cody, Scottish Text Society, 1888, i. 101–2.

[3] *Chronicles*, ed. H. Ellis, 1811, p. 420. The first edition of Fabyan appeared in 1516.

in carolis of the maydens and mynstrellys of Scotlande.'

If the content as well as the authorship of the Bannockburn song is not wholly clear, we have evidence of not much later date from Scotland that ballads, of which copies survive, were being sung. *The Complainte of Scotlande*,[1] published in 1549, lists eight 'sueit sangis' heard among some shepherds, including *The Battle of Harlaw*, *The Hunting of the Cheviot*, and what appear to have been *The Battle of Otterburn* and *Broomfield Hill*. There is mentioned, besides, a ballad not in Child's collection, *The Wedding of the Frog and Mouse*, which was registered for printing in 1580 and has been sung of late in America.[2] It is very puzzling that another list in the *Complainte*,[3] which enumerates a group of 'dances', should include *Tam Lin*, *Johnie Armstrong*, and *Robin Hood*. Since two of these bear the names of identifiable ballads, we must conclude that the list refers to the dancing as well as singing of lyrical narratives. Quite possibly the dances had become dissociated from the words, in the case of these particular specimens; but they could scarcely have been entitled as they are unless ballads had been danced as well as sung. Indirectly, therefore, the references in the *Complainte* have a value beyond their interest as showing that certain ballads were known in the sixteenth century.

A more specific allusion to the performance of ballads, though it tells us nothing about their composition, is the passage in Thomas Deloney's *The Pleasant History of John Winchcomb . . . called Jack of Newbery*, which describes how the hero entertained King Henry. Among other

[1] Ed. J. A. H. Murray, 1872, pp. 64–5 (E. E. T. S., Extra Series 17, 18). See also pp. lxxxiii–lxxxix.

[2] See Kittredge, *J. A. F.-L.* xxxv. 394; D. Scarborough, *On the Trail of Negro Folk-Songs*, 1925, pp. 46–50, and L. W. Payne, *Publications of the Texas Folk-Lore Society*, no. v, 1926.

[3] *Op. cit.*, p. 66.

amusements provided, 'the maidens in dulced manner chanted out this song, two of them singing the ditty, and all the rest bearing the burden'.[1] The song follows, a version of the *Fair Flower of Northumberland* (9). However much Deloney may have tampered with the ballad in printing it, he is not likely to have described a method of singing that would have seemed absurd to his readers.

None of these references to ballad-making and ballad-singing in earlier days gives the slightest hint, it will be observed, of what may be called co-operative composition. That is, they do not give us any warrant for supposing that songs were made by successive contributions from different members of an assembled group, who shared the pains and pleasures of authorship. On the other hand, nothing whatever is said about composition by individuals. The whole process is ignored. We read of dancing, of singing, of remembrance, but we are left in the dark about the way ballads came into being. We are thus forced to depend, as the basis for any conjectures we may make as to this matter, upon the observation of modern collectors and upon such analogies with the practice of other races as may safely be used.

The evidence from these sources as to co-operative or group composition is not wholly satisfactory, but it comes to this, I think: songs have indeed been thus made, although at all times and in all places individual composition has been the rule. We learn of the Färoese islanders, who have improvised songs in groups, it would appear, since the seventeenth century at least.[2] The quality of their songs, which has been called in question,[3] does not

---

[1] Ed. R. Sievers, *Thomas Deloney*, 1904, p. 195 (*Palaestra*, xxxvi). *Jack of Newbery* seems to have been written in 1596.

[2] See Gummere, *The Popular Ballad*, pp. 24–5, 105.

[3] See Pound, *op. cit.*, pp. 73–5.

greatly matter, since for the moment we are concerned with the habit of co-operative composition rather than with the nature of the words and melodies produced. Closer home to us comes the all too brief entry in Cotgrave:[1] '*Chanson de Robin.* A merrie, and extemporall song, or fashion of singing, whereto one is ever adding somewhat, or may at pleasure add what he list.' It is a thousand pities that Cotgrave did not expand this definition, for clearly he knew some custom of adding stanzas extemporaneously to an existing song, which otherwise lacks record. One must admit the probability that what he had in mind was some kind of game song rather than a ballad; but what he says is at least a hint of a process that may very well have taken place at times in the fashioning or refashioning of narratives.

For we do know that stories in verse have been built up in this way, by contributions from different members of a group, even though they do not happen to be ballads of any intrinsic interest. An instance from Missouri was reported a few years ago by the late Professor Tolman;[2] and examples of such extemporaneous composition among American negroes and the mountaineers of North Carolina have recently been reviewed by Professor Reed Smith in some detail.[3] I am not inclined to stress as evidence of much importance the unquestionable fact that lumbermen in the forests, cowboys on the great ranges, and soldiers have co-operated in the making of narrative songs, for in all these cases the men have certainly been led into the practice by the instinct for social play rather than by a tradition of communal art. The phenomenon has interest, because it shows that even groups which lack a homogeneous background are capable of sharing

---

[1] *A Dictionarie of the French and English Tongues,* 1611.
[2] A. H. Tolman, *Publications of the Modern Language Association,* xlii. 430-1 (1927).
[3] *South Carolina Ballads,* 1928, pp. 20-6, 27-8.

in the composition of verse, but it cannot be said to illustrate very aptly the making of ballads. An analogy from Indian music should be cited by way of showing that, exceptionally at least, co-operative composition is possible among peoples with a primitive background. Miss Densmore reports a song of the Sioux, which was said to have been 'composed recently by several men working together'.[1]

In every case of the sort that has come to my attention, however, there is a lack of the structural organization characteristic of ballads in general. It is apparently easy for a like-minded group, intent on amusement or inspired by a common emotion, to improvise a set of verses about some matter of interest at the moment; but it is not so easy to shape the verses in the mould of the ballad. Songs of labour, we should observe, such as sailors' chanties, often consist of unorganized series of stanzas, which may be indefinitely extended at the will of the singers. Such improvisation as this requires nothing more than the ability to fit words to a given pattern of verse; it does not imply any feeling for structure or style. Chance groups have practised it, while no good evidence appears that even people to whom folk-song has been an inherited art have been able to do much better.

All in all, we are forced to the conclusion that most ballads, both those which have been in circulation in later times and those of earlier date, have been composed by individuals. The qualities they possess with respect to music, to structural organization, and to poetic style are the result of two equally important and inter-related factors: the development, at least as early as the twelfth century, of a traditional art in folk-song, which included the composition of ballads that were sharply focused, dramatic, impersonal; and, secondly, the constant

[1] F. Densmore, *Northern Ute Music*, 1922, p. 26 (Bulletin of the Bureau of American Ethnology, 75).

reshaping of ballads, once they were launched on the stream of oral tradition, by the co-operation of later generations, each of which learned the popular art and passed it on to the generation following. A process like this presupposes, of course, a homogeneous and relatively static population, for any sharp break in tradition might have destroyed the effects of it, as migrations to the colonies and to new urban centres, together with the gradual spread of a literate as opposed to an oral culture, have been by way of doing for the past three centuries. No better evidence for the vitality and value of folk-art could be found than the extraordinary persistence of ballad-singing down to our own time, notwithstanding the adverse influences to which it has been for so long subjected.

Something ought to be said in this connexion of the audience, the circle of listeners to whom ballads have been sung. The extent of their participation must certainly have varied, it seems to me, according to the conditions of performance. The ballad-singer of recent generations has sung privately, at his work, to members of his household, or to small groups of his neighbours. Even such contests as those that used to take place on the borders of Oxfordshire and Gloucestershire, to which reference has already been made,[1] would have been local meetings. On the other hand, we have definite evidence about vagabond minstrels, whose audiences must have been as various as their wanderings. We have good reason to believe, furthermore, that at all times there has been a certain amount of group singing, in which the distinction between performers and listeners would have been altogether eliminated, even though there was a leader. The distinction can never have been a sharp one, in any case, for both audience and singer—or singers—would have been trained in the same craft by

[1] See *ante*, p. 163.

the same traditional means. Even when a minstrel was going through his repertory, singers with some degree of skill must always have been present among the listeners. We cannot know to what extent the attitude of such sympathetic and understanding audiences has affected the course that particular ballads have taken; but we may properly conjecture that their influence has been a conservative one. Once the type was formed, the group would tend to hold it steady. Innovations in form, as well as constant variations, would be made by individuals, but they would be checked by the community of other singers, who constituted the audience.

It seems to me probable that the relatively small number of sea-ballads, to which reference was made earlier in this volume,[1] may be due to the vagabondage of sailors as a class, thus furnishing another example of the operation of the communal processes discussed above. Seamen have always been singers, one knows, and in their chanties they have developed some of the most vigorous folk-songs that have ever been made. That they have sung ballads in the forecastle with equal gusto is certain. Collectors in maritime districts have learned many good things from men who have followed the sea. This does not mean, however, that sailors have been invariably interested in stories about their own craft. More often than not, as their thoughts have turned homeward, they have sung ballads of the land. It does not seem strange, when one considers this, and considers, too, their habitual wanderings and the changes in crews, that they developed no peculiar technique for any kind of folk-song except the chanty. Many of the sea ballads that have been in circulation derive from broadsides made by landsmen, and they have been equally popular ashore and afloat. Child could have added largely to the number of such songs in his list, but may well have felt that their quality

[1] See Chapter III, pp. 56-7.

did not warrant their inclusion. The fact appears to be that seamen have never possessed the kind of communal consciousness, except about songs accompanying specific acts of labour, which has enabled stay-at-home people to perfect the finest ballads by reshaping them under the guidance of traditional art.

Chapter Nine

BALLADS AND BROADSIDES

THOUGH the use has been consecrated by time, the ballad of tradition has, one must admit, only the cuckoo's right to that name. A great deal of confusion would have been avoided if, in the sixteenth century, this way of designating narrative songs in popular circulation had not been adopted. And not until the end of the eighteenth century, indeed, did the traditional ballad come to be so termed at all frequently. In other languages a similar vagueness of nomenclature is found, but none that is quite so unfortunate. The French, the Germans, the Scandinavians have been content to call their ballads 'songs', with or without some modifying element to indicate a connexion with the folk; only the Anglo-Saxons have chosen to adopt a foreign term for a sophisticated product and apply it without discrimination to at least five or six different sorts of verse.

The name originally meant a dance song, as is suggested by its ultimate derivation from the verb *ballare*. After it reached France from Italy and Provence, it became the designation of a conventionalized lyric of a form fixed within narrow limits. Chaucer wrote ballads of this sort, as every one knows, with great success; and it has been practised both in French and English down to our own day. In modern English we have come to distinguish this use of the word by the variant spelling 'ballade'. In the fourteenth century, as is clear from a reference by Chaucer,[1] such ballads were associated with both dancing and singing, although it is equally obvious that Chaucer did not write most of his own for musical accompaniment of any kind. Lydgate used the strict form as the verbal

---

[1] See *The Legend of Good Women*, Prologue A, vv. 199–202.

substance of a masque at Eltham in 1427 or 1428.[1] In this case the verses must certainly have been recited, as must also have been the *balades* in stanzas lacking the final recurrent lines, which he prepared a little later for mummings at Windsor and London.[2]

As the fifteenth century went on, the meaning of the word 'ballad' seems to have been extended to include lyrics in various metrical forms, though always of a sophisticated sort. Apparently the notion of dancing continued to be associated with them, as we can be sure it did on the Continent from the fact that the madrigalists of the late sixteenth century, who borrowed their 'ballet' from the Italian *ballata*, recognized that it was based on a dance song.[3] The ballet is, however, to be distinguished from the ballade of the fifteenth and sixteenth centuries, since it was explicitly a song with a dance rhythm and an elaborate musical refrain to which the syllables *Fa la la* were customarily set.[4] Some of the most notable of the Elizabethan madrigalists, like Morley, used this form.

Until some time in the sixteenth century, clearly enough, the word 'ballad' was not applied to narratives of any kind, but only to various lyrics that were sometimes closely and sometimes only remotely connected with song and dance. By the middle of the sixteenth century, however, 'ballad' had come to mean—among other things—a story told in song. In the words of Professor Baskervill,[5] 'the Stationers' Register leaves no reasonable room for doubt. Almost from the beginning, narratives were freely entered for broadside publication as ballads. While the name at first designated also songs of merely lyric nature, these became increasingly subordinate. The development by the end of the century

[1] See R. Brotanek, *Die englischen Maskenspiele*, 1902, pp. 305–8.
[2] *Op. cit.*, pp. 317–25.
[3] See E. H. Fellowes, *The English Madrigal Composers*, 1921, p. 58.
[4] *Op. cit.*, p. 57.
[5] C. R. Baskervill, *The Elizabethan Jig*, 1929, p. 30.

of a number of compounds like "balladry", "ballad-
ize", and "balladmonger", applicable chiefly to the field
of the broadside ballad, shows the change in meaning as
practically complete.' Why this extension in the use of
the term should have taken place is not so easy to explain. Possibly it came in through the dialogues, set to
music, which became popular about this time. Since
such dialogues were often danced—and acquired the
name jigs thereby [1]—and since the word 'ballad' had
never lost its original connotation of dancing, there may
well have sprung up the fashion of calling any song and
dance of the popular kind a ballad. Dialogues almost
inevitably present a situation, even if only in a rudimentary way, which would make the application of the
term to pure narrative quite natural.

We can be certain, I think, that the kind of narrative
song either composed for broadside production, or very
suitable for printing in that way, was influenced in its
development by what we are calling the ballad of tradition—not then known as a ballad, of course. Professor
Baskervill has recently shown [2] that the literary folk of
London took a warm interest in popular forms between
1550 and 1580. The movement seems to have died out
because it was taken over by the unworshipful lot of
poetasters who provided copy for the printers of broadsides, thus developing the journalistic ballad but bringing all such forms into disrepute. By Shakespeare's day
'ballad' was a term of reproach among the literate, as
we know from the dramatist's numerous and always
contemptuous references. 'An I have not ballads made
on you all and sung to filthy tunes,' says Falstaff; [3] 'I
love a ballad in print, o' life,' says Mopsa, [4] 'for then
we are sure they are true'; and Autolycus responds :
'Here's one to a very doleful tune, how a usurer's wife

---

[1] *Op. cit.*, p. 6.
[2] *Op. cit.*, pp. 30–1.
[3] *1 Henry IV*, II. ii. 48–9.
[4] *Winter's Tale*, IV. iv. 262–70.

was brought to bed of twenty money-bags at a burden.'
'But a month old' was this choice morsel. The narrative ballad was well established, but only for the delight
of the baser sort. We must remember, however, that at
the same time exquisite 'ballets' were being composed
by such men as Thomas Morley, who published a set
in 1595. A fine confusion in nomenclature had been
achieved, which needed only one further step to become
the chaos that has remained to this day to trouble us.

The ballad of popular tradition meanwhile went on
its course, unaffected, as far as one can see, by changing
fashions in lyrical poetry and in the music and dancing that
accompanied it, unaffected also for the time being by the
insidious assault that was to be made on its integrity by
the chapmen, who from London were scattering their
sheets of 'odious ballads' through the countryside.
Journalism had come to birth, and in its lusty infancy
had many of the worst features commonly supposed to
be the product of American enterprise in the later nineteenth century. The ballad of tradition had no name as
yet: Sidney referred to the 'old song of Percy and
Douglas', and Thomas Deloney to *The Fair Flower of
Northumberland* by the same term. It had no name because it was the product of an art that had nothing
whatever to do with fashions at court or in the city.
People went on singing their old songs, sometimes
dancing to them while they sang, or listening to the
humbler sort of minstrel like Sidney's 'blind ¦crowder',
who lacked the sophistication of Autolycus, though for
anything we know he may have been equally weak in
ethics. New songs came into being after the old model,
and were to do so for some time yet, by which good
tales were added to the repertory of the singers. The
ageless and anonymous art of narrative song, which nobody thought of recognizing as an art at all, continued
to flourish.

There would be no excuse, indeed, for including even a brief discussion of broadside ballads in a study of the ballad of tradition if nothing more than names were concerned. The broadside, difficult to define because so various in substance and form, being almost anything in verse that a printer chose to circulate, acquired the name in the sixteenth century and kept it by right of possession as long as publication went on. But something more than a name involves our traditional ballads with those printed sheets. The connexion is threefold, which makes it imperative for us to look carefully at what happened as a result of the circulation of broadsides.

In the first place, the ballad-mongers often set their words to old tunes. Frequently, to be sure, there stood at the top of the page, 'To a pleasant new tune,' or the like, which might mean that a melody had been composed for the occasion, although one suspects that the notoriously unscrupulous publishers of such wares would have been capable of setting a ballad adrift with that caption when no tune had been provided. If the words could be sung at all, they would find a musical accompaniment easily enough among people to whom singing was still a universal accomplishment. More commonly, however, the maker had some tune in mind when he wrote, and sent out the ballad with the proper instructions at its head. There thus came about immediately what one might call an engraftment of new words on traditional tunes. An old song might serve as the accompaniment for half a dozen sets of words, all of them without merit as poetry and many of them vulgarly smart in the journalistic fashion. It should be borne in mind, in this connexion, that the Elizabethans distinguished what they called 'tunes'—simple melodies of popular origin—from 'airs', which were the highly sophisticated products of schooled musicians. Naturally the stall ballads were intended for singing to melodies of the former kind. These tunes were common property, no matter how they originated.

Although we have no record of what happened when the new songs set to old tunes got into circulation, we can very well see what must have occurred. Sometimes the ballad-monger's fabrication would have a brief life and leave the melody to run its course with the older set of words. Sometimes, however, one or another of the various new ballads written to a single old tune must have sunk deep into popular memory and quite ousted the traditional narrative. There can be little doubt that this was the genesis of many a ballad which continued to be in favour with folk-singers down to the time of our modern collectors. *The George Aloe and the Sweepstake* (285) with its successor *The Coasts of Barbary*[1] is an example in point ; and another may be the very far from attractive *Queen Eleanor's Confession* (156), which had a long history despite its theme. Quite possibly, it seems to me—though it be blasphemy to make the suggestion—some of the tales of Robin Hood may have a source of this kind. *Robin Hood and the Tanner* (126), for example, might have begun its course in some such way.[2] It would be most interesting to determine, if we could, how frequently such adoptions took place; but it is impossible to do so, because of the processes of variation that we have studied in an earlier chapter. As soon as a broadside ballad became the property of folk-singers, it would inevitably be subjected to changes such as all songs were constantly undergoing, and would take on in course of time the characteristics of far older productions made in quite other ways by quite other poets. The reason why such ballads lack the dramatic intensity of

[1] See C. J. Sharp, *J. F.-S. S.* v. 262 (1916); F. J. Harvey-Darton, *The Soul of Dorset*, 1922, p. 250; and Barry, Eckstorm, and Smyth, *British Ballads from Maine*, 1929, pp. 413–18.

[2] In addition to Child's version from four stall copies see Sharp, *English Folk-Songs*, i. 8–12; and Davis, *Traditional Ballads of Virginia*, 1929, pp. 393–6.

the best ballads, why they seldom contain a moment of breath-taking emotion or a phrase of magical power, is that they have not been submitted to the full operation of those processes by which traditional songs have at times become great poetry. Or so the case looks to me, though it cannot be satisfactorily proved.

A second connexion between the stall ballad and the ballad of tradition was formed by the habit, into which printers fell, of occasionally printing a song gleaned from oral circulation. Some of the Robin Hood stories, for instance, have been preserved only by this means. We should not know *Robin Hood and Little John* (125) except for broadsides,[1] or *Robin Hood and Allan a Dale* (138). Similarly the admirable *Adam Bell* (116), *Rookhope Ryde* (179), and *Bewick and Graham* (211) have come down to us only in this way. In other cases, our versions of earliest record are from prints, though we also have variants collected from singers of recent times. *Little Musgrave and Lady Barnard* (81), for instance, was licensed for printing three times before the end of the seventeenth century,[2] from 1630 on, and a text represented by an apparently unlicensed broadside in the Pepys collection seems to be quite as old at least; yet nearly fifty variants of the ballad have been garnered from oral tradition.

The circulation of songs in printed texts necessarily dislocated the normal course of things, since it spread them widely in a fixed form and indicated the melodies by which they should be accompanied. In place of the slow processes of dissemination that had been customary, from singer to singer, from older folk to younger, there came in at a single stroke a totally alien process, swift in operation, which could bring the words of a ballad

[1] Fragments, to be sure, have been found by Williams, *Folk-Songs of the Upper Thames*, 1923, pp. 237, 296, and Cox, *Folk-Songs of the South*, 1925, p. 174.
[2] See H. E. Rollins, *Analytical Index to Ballad Entries*, 1924, nos. 1506–8.

into districts where it had been unknown before, and probably confuse the memories of singers in other districts where a tradition had long been established. Thus in a third way broadsides had a marked influence on balladry. Too little has been made of this, I believe, by students of the traditional ballad, though the effect on individual specimens has been admirably investigated.[1]

Since variants that derive ultimately from printed texts are found in the most isolated parts of the United States and Canada, it is clear that broadsides affected an exceedingly widespread area; and since the oral tradition of some of the texts so derived is in itself a long one, it is evident that the influence began a great while ago. There can be no doubt whatever that a pure tradition of oral descent became an impossibility as soon as the purveyors of broadsides had established their trade in the sixteenth century. Contamination, if one choose to regard it as such, became possible in the case of any ballad whatsoever. Since the printing of traditional ballads was sporadic rather than general, the majority of them have never been subject to this artificial interruption of their proper course ; but so many have been affected as to cast suspicion on any specimen that is being studied. The possibility of contamination should always be kept in mind.

As we have noted earlier, the tenacity of popular memory is as extraordinary as its fallibility. Variation appears to be incessant, yet sometimes a text survives almost unaltered the chances of oral repetition for a century and more. The evidence for this rests chiefly upon versions of songs that have in one way or another got into print.[2]

---

[1] See, for example, the illuminating notes of Mr. Barry in *British Ballads from Maine*.

[2] See the history of *Lord Lovel* (75) or *Barbara Allan* (84). Menéndez Pidal has shown traditional versions may sometimes remain unaffected by printed ones. (See *ante*, p. 170.)

It seems to me clear that the effect of circulating them has been to retard variation quite markedly, as if verses one learned directly or indirectly from broadsides and the like made a deeper impression on memory than those learned wholly by ear. One can only wonder whether there has been a feeling for the sanctity of the written word, or whether in some obscure way minds have registered differently verses fixed in print. At all events, it appears that the normal fluidity of alteration has been disturbed whenever publication has taken place.

Apart from the effect on individual ballads of the traditional sort, the circulation of broadsides inevitably produced changes in the art of folk-song as a whole. The rapid adoption of a great number of pieces both lyrical and narrative, some set to old tunes and some to new, and for the most part completely devoid of beauty in form and substance, could not have failed to lower the standards of taste that had been developed. The wonder is that the power of musical and poetical expression among common folk was not altogether destroyed by this, the first assault of many in modern times on the integrity of the traditional art. That it was weakened, there can be no doubt, I believe. There are numerous good ballads from the north that cannot have originated before the seventeenth century, but almost none traceable to districts nearer London. One thinks of *The Fire of Frendraught* (196), *The Bonnie House o Airlie* (199), *The Gypsy Laddie* (200), and *The Baron of Brackley* (203), to name only a few. In a very thoughtful book, published posthumously in 1913, Bryant called attention to this state of things,[1] though he under-estimated the extent to which older ballads survived in the south. It is not a question of a finer development in Scotland than in England, but of an earlier decay in regions nearer London as a result of the infiltration of

[1] *A History of English Balladry*, p. 192.

songs from Grub Street. What appears to have occurred
was a serious, though not mortal, injury to the traditional
art, affecting verse much more profoundly than music
and operating less disastrously in regions that were relatively free from the influence of printed texts.

There could be no better evidence of the vitality of
folk-song than the fact that it survived the cheapening
and deadening effect of broadsides, which for more than
two centuries were hawked about the countryside. We
have to remember, in this connexion, how very few specimens of traditional ballads are extant that antedate this
period. Our studies must largely be confined to specimens as they have been remembered and sung in this
later time, and our judgements are formed upon material
so gathered. The verse and music that have furnished
inspiration and technical guidance to our modern poets
and composers were collected, for the most part, after
the ballad-monger had done his worst. We should not
minimize the evil that he accomplished—certainly not
ignore it, as many students of ballads have done. We
should not forget that a collection like that made by
Child necessarily includes a great number of pieces
either originated by hirelings of the printers or deeply
marked by the influence of their work. At the same
time, having taken these factors into account, we are
justified in saying that folk-song was neither destroyed
nor irretrievably harmed by the flood of new ballads that
poured over the country during the sixteenth, seventeenth,
and eighteenth centuries. One may fairly put it that the
art suffered from a severe case of indigestion, that the glut
of mediocre songs could not be properly absorbed and
adapted to the gracious ways of tradition; but further
than that one cannot go. Not until the spread of primary
education and the conversion of the general public from
oral to visual habits, which took place in the nineteenth
century, was folk-song marked for destruction. And

even now it remains, not altogether dead, in certain remoter parts of the English-speaking world.

It is probable, though I do not see how it can be definitely proved, that balladry of the traditional sort suffered a decline in social esteem with the advent of the broadside. Later collectors have gathered their material for the most part from quite humble folk, or else from persons of higher station who have had the good taste to store their minds with songs learned from more simple people. This cannot be denied. On the other hand, such earlier references to popular songs as we have do not seem to imply that they were the property of the lowest social orders. Sidney, with his 'blind crowder', belonged of course to the higher aristocracy and could have had little intimate knowledge of how things went on in the villages of England. It was inevitable that he should condescend, though he felt his heart moved. The argument of Olrik[1] that the aristocracy of Denmark made the ballad what it was, as well as collected specimens of it, may hold for a country with a simple social organization such as he describes; but in England there can hardly have been so complete a community of interests. Yet the manors and villages of England had a stable and homogeneous population, among whom those higher in station may well have participated as a matter of course in the pleasures of their dependants, and indeed have contributed very notably to the arts of song and dance that were their common property. It is probably safe to assume, therefore, that folk-song did not become a peasant art until the broadside gave balladry a bad name.

No stall ballad is extant that can be dated before the third decade of the sixteenth century. Professor Rollins, who in our time has acquired a greater mastery of such literature than any one else who has worked in the field, sets 1559 and the work of one William Elderton at the

[1] A. Olrik, *Danske Folkeviser i Udvalg*, 3rd ed. (1913), pp. 5, 16–24.

beginning of such balladry,[1] unless we count John Skelton's topical poems as belonging to the *genre*, which is scarcely permissible. About 1535, however, there was printed *Luther, the Pope, a Cardinal, and a Husbandman*, which 'may have been sung',[2] and unquestionably is 'one of the earliest extant broadside ballads'. Later in the century the numbers increased enormously, and throughout the seventeenth century the business of making and selling them flourished beyond all computation. Not until the rise of the news-letter in the eighteenth century did the trade begin to decline. The registers of the Company of Stationers, kept from 1557 to 1709, contain the entries of more than 3,000 ballads, according to the invaluable index compiled by Professor Rollins;[3] and the efforts of the company to make their record complete were by no means successful. Broadsides were also sometimes collected in volumes, after the fashion of miscellanies, which may be illustrated by *A Handful of Pleasant Delights*, first issued in 1566.[4]

The interest of stall ballads lies almost wholly in the picture they give of the way ordinary men looked at life and the events taking place about them. As John Selden wrote, 'Though some make slight of libels, yet you may see by them how the wind sits. As take a straw and throw it up into the air, you shall see by that which way the wind is, which you shall not do by casting up a stone. More solid things do not show the complexion of the times so well as ballads and libels.'[5] They reveal how political occurrences appeared to the observer in the street or on the backstairs, with what interested dis-

---

[1] H. E. Rollins, *A Pepysian Garland*, 1922, p. ix. See also Rollins, *Studies in Philology*, xvii. 199–245 (1920).

[2] See Rollins, *The Pepys Ballads*, i. 3–7 (1929).

[3] 'An Analytical Index to the Ballad Entries in the Registers of the Company of Stationers of London', *Studies in Philology*, xxi. 1–324 (1924).

[4] See Rollins, *A Handful of Pleasant Delights*, 1924

[5] *Table Talk*, lxxx, ed. S. H. Reynolds, 1892, p. 105.

approval the solid citizen regarded criminals, how excited
the populace became at the news of something monstrous
in nature. In the words of Professor Rollins, 'journalistic
ballads outnumbered all other types. Others were ser-
mons, or romances, or ditties of love and jealousy, of
tricks and "jests", comparable to the ragtime, or music-
hall, songs of the present time'.[1] Very seldom do they
rise above the level of capable verse-making, though the
tunes that were in the minds of the scribblers when they
wrote gave their work a lively rhythm.

In considering these ballads as a valuable record of the
time when they appeared, as it is fair to do, there is only
one exception to be taken. The views they express, the
pictures they present, are those of the townsman rather
than that of the countryman. They were written in the
cities—chiefly in London; and, though intended for
distribution throughout the kingdom, they reflect the
interests of the moment in the larger centres. I believe
that this aspect of the matter has never been sufficiently
stressed. Its implications are far-reaching. On the one
hand, they give a partial picture of things: we cannot be
sure that they represent at all correctly the sentiments
of villagers, even though we can be reasonably certain
that they interpret with complete accuracy what town-
dwellers felt. On the other hand, the dissemination of
the sheets must have influenced very strongly the opinions
and the tastes of the rural communities to which they were
brought. In other words, they began that musical hege-
mony of town over country which has been increasingly—
and unfortunately—apparent ever since.

Before the middle of the seventeenth century men of
discernment had come to see the value of broadside
ballads as a record of events and popular notions. I have
quoted John Selden, who was the first great example of
a line of collectors, some of them scholarly like Selden,

[1] *A Pepysian Garland*, p. xi.

some inveterately curious like Pepys, and some merely acquisitive like Bagford, to whom we owe much for their preservation of this fugitive material—and incidentally of many good things like stories of Robin Hood. Selden died in 1654, but was followed by Samuel Pepys, whose magnificent collection was based on that of his predecessor. Pepys—characteristically—arranged his plunder in five volumes, which he bequeathed to Magdalene College, Cambridge, together with the rest of his library, thus securing for them a permanent abode.[1] Pepys had finished making his collection before 1703. It remains one of the greatest ever brought together, containing 1671 ballads, exclusive of duplicates, nearly a thousand of which are unique.

The only rival of Pepys as a collector in his own time was the Oxford antiquary, Anthony Wood, who died in 1695. Wood was less happy than Pepys, however, in the fate of what he garnered, for only 279 items remain in his collection. The evidence is fairly clear that one John Bagford, in the service of Robert Harley, first Earl of Oxford, stole on a grand scale from the Ashmolean Museum, to which Wood had bequeathed his ballads. Harley's acquisitions, before his death in 1724, filled two volumes,[2] while Bagford had three volumes of his own.[3] Towards the end of the eighteenth century, the third Duke of Roxburghe, who at that time owned Harley's collection, added another great volume, largely made up of material likewise abstracted from Wood's papers. Who served the duke in this somewhat ignoble business has not been discovered. Presumably he did not soil his hands by stealing the broadsides for himself any more than did Harley, though the Duchess of Marlborough—

[1] Ed. H. E. Rollins, *A Pepysian Garland*, 1922, and *The Pepys Ballads*, 1929–31, 6 vols., with others to follow.

[2] See *The Roxburghe Ballads*, ed. W. Chappell and J. W. Ebsworth, 1871–97 (Ballad Society).

[3] See *The Bagford Ballads*, ed. J. W. Ebsworth, 1878 (Ballad Society).

had she known—would have been glad to believe the
worst of the latter gentleman. It is amusing to note—to
complete this tale of ancient perfidies—that the contents
of still another volume are suspect, the Rawlinson collection, which was made at about the same time as the
Roxburghe and may well contain things taken from
Wood's papers, and that it in turn has been rifled by a
later thief.[1] The only other collection rivalling in scope
those mentioned above is that formed by Francis Douce
(1757–1834), but there are several minor ones of considerable importance.[2] We ought to note, too, that a large
number of ballads were copied from broadsides, and exist
in manuscript. There is one group of eighty, for example,
in the library of Shirburn Castle, Oxfordshire, which
some one took the pains to put together during the reigns
of Elizabeth and James I.[3]

The activities of copyists and collectors during the
seventeenth and eighteenth centuries furnish the best
possible evidence for the genuine, if perhaps condescending, interest taken in stall ballads by men of education
at the time. No one, indeed, whatever his station, could
well have escaped some knowledge of the ubiquitous
sheets. In Shakespeare's extraordinary memory dozens
must have stuck, along with the country songs he had
learned as a boy. The two kinds were not distinguished
by any one, as we see from the account of Captain Cox
in Laneham's letter from Kenilworth in 1575.[4] That
amateur of popular literature, who loved everything in
print that came to hand, is said to have had ' oversight '
of ' stories ' like *Robin Hood* and *Adam Bell*, as well as of
' a bunch of ballets and songs, all auncient . . . fair

---

[1] See A. Clark, *The Shirburn Ballads*, 1907, p. 5, for an account of these mis-
demeanours.

[2] For example, the Luttrell and the Osterley Park, the latter edited by F. B.
Fawcett, *Broadside Ballads of the Restoration*, 1930.

[3] See A. Clark, *op. cit.*

[4] Ed. F. J. Furnivall, *Captain Cox*, 1871 (Ballad Society).

wrapt up in parchment'. How impossible it must have been to avoid acquaintance with broadsides is shown by Walton in *The Complete Angler*[1] when he makes Piscator say: ' I'll now lead you to an honest ale-house, where we shall find a cleanly room, lavender in the windows, and twenty ballads stuck about the wall.' Two generations later Addison was bearing testimony to the same use of ballads.[2]

With Addison, we begin to find the name ' ballad ' applied not only to broadsides but to the traditional narratives with which the word was destined to be more closely associated as time went on. Although he called *Chevy Chase* a song, in his enthusiastic and somewhat laboured defence of the ' Gothic manner ', he referred to it as ' the favourite ballad of the common people of England '.[3] To him ballads had a certain importance, it is evident, and he gave them his serious attention. In contrast to his attitude was that of the editor—probably Ambrose Philips—of *A Collection of Ballads*, published in 1723–5, which was altogether condescending and feebly jocose. For the most part he printed stall ballads, though he included a few traditional ones, and he gave no hint that he saw any difference between the two sorts. The importance of his three volumes, as has been well observed, lies in this : ' What Addison was in the history of literary criticism of the ballad, this editor was in the history of publication. The one said that the ballads were worth reading ; the other offered them to the curious to be read.'[4]

To Joseph Ritson, near the end of the century, has often been attributed the credit—if there be credit—of reserving the name ' ballad ' for narratives, but impro-

---

[1] Chapter ii.   [2] *Spectator*, no. 85.

[3] *Spectator*, nos. 70, 74. See S. B. Hustvedt, *Ballad Criticism in Scandinavia and Great Britain*, 1916, pp. 65–78, for an account of Addison's criticism and the controversy aroused by it.

[4] Hustvedt, *op. cit.*, p. 105.

perly, as Professor Hustvedt showed in his able volume on *Ballad Criticism*. William Shenstone, the poet, made the point clearly in two letters to Percy in 1761. In the second of these he said : ' It is become habitual to me, to call that a *Ballad*, which describes or implies some action ; on the other hand, I term that a *Song*, which contains only an expression of sentiment.' [1] Doubtless Percy had this distinction in mind when he used, as the running title of the *Reliques*, the heading 'Ancient Songs and Ballads '. In his prefatory essay he distinguished between romances and ballads, but either he had not fully grasped or he did not see fit to accept Shenstone's categories of ballad and song, which were, after all, perfectly arbitrary in view of accepted nomenclature. He was content to employ both terms for narratives like *Chevy Chase*, and in his preface he made an apology ' for having bestowed any attention on a parcel of old ballads '[2] —quite in the pre-Addisonian manner. He did, however, mark a difference in style between ' the more ancient ballads of this collection ' and productions by 'the latter composers of heroical ballads : I mean by such as professedly wrote for the press '.[3]

Ritson went much further, and adopted Shenstone's categories outright, however he came by a knowledge of them. According to his own statement, they appear to have come into general use by this time, which may well have been the case in view of the interest aroused by the *Reliques*. In *A Select Collection of English Songs*, which he published in 1783, he said : ' It may not be impertinent to premise, that, as the collection, under the general title of *Songs*, consists, not only of pieces strictly and properly so called, but likewise, though in great disproportion as to number, of *Ballads* or mere narrative compositions, the word *Song* will, in the course of this

[1] See Hustvedt, *op. cit.*, pp. 160–1.   [2] 2nd ed., 1767, i. XVI.
[3] *Op. cit.*, i. XXXVII.

preface, be almost everywhere used in its confined sense; inclusive, however, of a few modern and sentimental ballads, which no reader of taste, it is believed, will be inclined to think out of place.'[1] He was more explicit and less confusing in a note subjoined to the 'Historical Essay on the Origin and Progress of National Song' that follows his preface : 'With us, songs of sentiment, expression, or even description, are properly termed *Songs*, in contradistinction to mere narrative compositions, which we now denominate *Ballads*.'[2] It is evident that Ritson had no more intention than Percy of reserving the name ballad for traditional narratives in verse, but that he did wish to use it for what he surprisingly calls ' mere narrative compositions' of the popular sort, whatever their origin.

Thomas Gray appears to have been quite alone, throughout the eighteenth century, in comprehending the true value of strictly traditional poetry ; and indeed few commentators have ever understood so well as he the structural merits of such pieces. In saying of *Child Maurice* (83), ' It begins in the fifth act of the play ', he showed a critical acumen that was amazingly far ahead of his age.[3] Not until the nineteenth century, and then only very gradually, did ballads gathered from oral sources, whether recitation or singing, come to be generally regarded as more interesting and valuable than the dubious products of the London hacks. More than forty years after Gray wrote the remarkable words I have quoted, Wordsworth cited a stanza from *The Babes in the Wood*, in his famous Preface to the *Lyrical Ballads*, to illustrate his theory of poetry ; and in his remarks on *Goody Blake and Harry Gill* he showed that he took broadsides as his models.[4] It is not at all strange that differences of

---

[1] Preface, p. ii.   [2] 'A Historical Essay ', p. i, n. 1.
[3] Letter to Mason, June 1757, ed. Tovey, *Letters*, i. 336.
[4] *Prose Works*, ed. W. Knight, i. 69, 71.

opinion have continued ever since as to the beauty of some of the verse included in the *Lyrical Ballads*. Nothing could show Wordsworth's genius in a clearer light than the fact that other pieces in the same volume and in the same strain have the hall-mark of great poetry. But the *Lyrical Ballads* included also, we must remember, Coleridge's *Rime of the Ancient Mariner*, which 'was professedly written in imitation of the style, as well as the spirit of the elder poets', so the preface to the volume informed the public. Although *The Ancient Mariner* owes a good deal to medieval romance, it is even more plainly an adaptation in its rhythmical form and rhetoric of the traditional ballad. All the suggestions Coleridge needed he could have got from Percy's volumes. He and Wordsworth thus differed in what they took from balladry, as they did in so much else. It does not appear that either of them distinguished between kinds, but each simply followed his own bent.

With Scott the case was still different. Saturated in ancient lore of all sorts, he imitated the ballad style as easily as that of medieval romance, and so closely that no one can be quite sure to what extent *Kinmont Willie* is the child of his imagination. The collection of ballads from oral tradition had gone on meanwhile at an ever-increasing pace. Ritson's sour comments on the editorial alterations of Percy, though they did not keep Scott from tampering with the texts he printed in the *Minstrelsy of the Scottish Border*,[1] doubtless helped spread the notion that a song found in oral circulation had peculiar virtues and was worth recovering, however much it might be the duty of an editor to 'improve' its form. Scott was an ardent collector, as every one knows. His boundless enthusiasm, which led him to expand his first scheme for the *Minstrelsy*, did much, and the quiet per-

[1] 1802–3.

sistence of Jamieson [1] in gleaning waifs and strays, helped
a little, to popularize the traditional ballad as distinguished from the product of the stalls. When Keats,
who was of the next literary generation, came to write
La Belle Dame sans Merci, he had absorbed the essential
qualities of the type so completely as to the structure as
well as style that he was able to put them to his own
uses with complete freedom. He did not even find it
necessary to label his poem a ballad. Only a few years
later Motherwell [2] showed by precept and example that
editorial tampering with texts was wrong in principle
and useless in practice. The ballad of tradition had by
this time acquired the sanction of poets and scholars.

Yet the name has never come to mean one thing only.
The poets of the so-called Romantic Period and their
successors have often imitated the traditional ballad,
frequently with great advantage to their work ; they
have used technical devices learned from such ballads to
the enrichment of lyrics that are only to be called ballads
because the term has always been ambiguous ; and they
have made other excellent ballads that may be said
to derive from the broadsides, though so far superior in
literary merit that their origin is not too obvious. There
is no point in trying to rule out of court any of these
kinds. At one time or another so many sorts of verse
have borne the name that it is impossible to restrict its
use in any way. The lover of folk-song may be glad
that increasingly the unmodified word has come to suggest verse narratives moulded by the tradition of
singers, but only because this furnishes an index to a
deeper and wider appreciation of the qualities they possess. To claim more, or desire more, would be foolish.

[1] *Popular Ballads and Songs*, 1806.
[2] *Minstrelsy, Ancient and Modern*, 1827.

Chapter Ten

SOME PHENOMENA OF AMERICAN BALLADRY

IN several ways the traditional ballad, as transplanted to America, deserves special consideration by students of the *genre*. It enables us to see more clearly than we could otherwise do, I believe, certain phenomena of transmission and variation; and it furnishes valuable evidence as to the conditions under which the characteristic features of folk-song may be produced. From no other source have data been gathered that could give us precisely the information which may be gained by analysing the rich store of melodies and texts found in America during the past generation.

The situation is this. In the seventeenth and eighteenth centuries, while the broadside ballad was flourishing in Great Britain but before it had exerted any markedly harmful effects on the musical habits of the people, successive waves of emigration swept overseas, there to intermingle in the formation of the new states. The colonists were humble folk, for the most part, and shared the common heritage of song. Although some of them belonged to peculiar dissenting sects, more given to the singing of psalms than of secular melodies and inclined to discourage frivolous pleasure of every sort, the majority came to America for the very good reason that conditions bore hard on them at home and they hoped to better their lot in the New World. Even the founders of the theocracy of Massachusetts Bay could not well have prospered as they did, had it not been for the worldly immigrants to whom shipbuilding and trade and free land in the forest were attractions that outweighed the possible disadvantages of attendance at the bleak services of the state church. Early New England was dominated by Puritans, but was not altogether inhabited by them. Similarly, the large-minded William Penn did not bar from his colony other folk than Friends, whom he had scandalized his world by joining. As for Maryland, Virginia, and the Carolinas, there was no reason whatever why people should not sing the old songs as they chose.

The phenomenon was a new one. Since the Great Migrations of the fifth century there had been no such movement of races affecting western Europe, and probably never within the compass of recorded history had any people on the move settled in so empty a land as was North America. The Amerindians were too few, too scattered, and too feeble to affect the habits of the conquerors in any but very trivial ways. Representatives of the various stocks of Great Britain were thus uprooted from their familiar environment and flung together under conditions of living that not even hard work for generations could make very similar to those they had left behind. Besides which, many of them at least cannot have wished to reproduce in the Colonies the lives of their fathers. They had turned their backs on repression and poverty; and in the labour of hewing timber, clearing forest land, building houses, mills, and ships, in the excitement of fighting the Red Man and quarrelling with those set in authority over them, they looked to the future rather than the past. The folk-ways that they retained they kept because of the curious instinct for conservation which plays so large a role in human affairs. They continued to sing ballads, as they continued to do a great many other things, because they had always sung them. Custom did not perish without good reason.

In addition to the intermingling of people from various parts of Great Britain, who came to live as neighbours under quite new conditions, the situation was complicated by the infiltration of settlers from Ireland and the Continent. New York had been founded by the Dutch, who remained to dominate the colony after it passed to the rule of the English Crown; before 1700 large numbers of French Huguenots had scattered themselves up and down the seaboard; there were Swedes in Delaware; in Pennsylvania Germans from the Palatinate and adjacent regions settled in solid groups, which have retained their special characteristics until our own day; and the Irish from Ulster made their presence felt by their numbers and energy both north and south.

From the beginning there was thus a mixed population in the colonies, each section of which had a different background of tradition in the arts as well as in other social activities. Yet English was the dominant language, soon accepted by all save the Pennsylvania Germans; and with the language the various elements accepted the ways of the settlers from England and Scotland, though always with minor local modifications wherever some alien strain was at all powerful. Sectional differences also appeared very soon, which were due to the varying conditions of the colonies, each very jealous of its integrity and each far more isolated than could have been the case on a more thickly settled continent.

The conditions under which folk-song had to survive, if it survived at all, were therefore unlike those under which it had previously developed, and unlike in a number of ways. Instead of being cultivated by a static, homogeneous population, it had to live among people flung together in quite new groups, who had been uprooted from their old environments and were, moreover, subject to nomadic impulses to move ever farther from the seaboard, conquering the forest as they went. That they remembered their old songs at all is an interesting index of the vitality of the art at the time of the early settlements.

It should not be forgotten that a similar state of things came into being in French Canada, with the single important difference that in Quebec the population was solidly French instead of being a mixture of various stocks. Since the French retained their language and racial identity even after the English conquest, the folk arts were not subjected there to quite the same influences as in the colonies that became the United States or in the Maritime Provinces. The problems presented by the folk-lore of French Canada are exceedingly interesting, but they are somewhat less complex than those of English-speaking America, inasmuch as they have to do with a homogeneous rather than a mixed population in a new environment.[1] The closest analogy to this state of things would be found in Australia and New Zealand, which were settled almost exclusively from Great Britain and Ireland. As far as I know, the balladry of neither country has ever been adequately investigated, though studies ought to be made if the possibility of them has not already been lost for all time.

Latin America furnishes still another state of things, since the aboriginal stocks there became the basis of new races with a considerable infusion of European blood. From Mexico southward, Spanish and Portuguese were accepted as the dominant languages, and with them the culture of the Iberian peninsula, although parts of Brazil and Argentina have come nearer in recent times to reproducing the conditions of racial mixture that have prevailed in the United States. The study of folk-song in all these countries is still in its infancy, and offers very interesting possibilities for the future if workers can be found while there is yet time. Excellent versions of Spanish ballads, it should be noted, have been collected in Mexico.

[1] See the excellent book by M. Barbeau and E. Sapir, *Folk-Songs of French Canada*, 1925.

The collecting that has been done with so much enthusiasm in the United States and eastern Canada since the early years of this century has provided a mass of material for investigation that enables us to draw the conclusions at which I have hinted in the opening paragraph of this chapter. Although no discriminating person can maintain that American versions of traditional ballads are so good as the more attractive versions found in the British Isles, as far as texts are concerned, they are not at all inferior musically, and they show such interesting adaptations to new conditions with regard to the stories they tell that their somewhat rough texture can easily be forgiven. I do not mean that some American survivals have not delightful qualities of verse; but for the most part, it cannot be denied, there has been an even more marked deterioration of the lyrical element than has been the case in Great Britain. Structure and rhythm have endured the shock of transplanting much better than diction.

In this connexion, it must be remembered, however, that ballad collecting was delayed in the United States and Canada long past its due time. Child printed very few variants from America, for no one had then made any systematic attempt to find them.[1] Whatever could have happened to destroy or spoil the ancient songs had occurred before the effort was made to save them. They had been transplanted to an alien country, they had been confused by the mixture of stocks, and they had been subjected in certain regions to the supposedly inimical influences of a primary school system of long standing. Indeed, an examination of ballads from the coast of Maine and New Brunswick makes one doubt whether popular education is quite such a menace to folk-song as we have always been led to believe.[2] Possibly an

[1] Child issued a circular of appeal in 1881, but got few results. See S. B. Hustvedt, *Ballad Books and Ballad Men*, 1930, pp. 217–18.

[2] See Barry, Eckstorm, and Smyth, *British Ballads from Maine*, 1929.

intelligent respect for tradition and a settled habit of life for a good many generations in isolated communities may have counterbalanced the effect of sound elementary teaching. In any case, it has now been proved that ballads may survive quite as well among people of native intelligence and genuine, if limited, education as among the mountaineers of the southern Appalachians, who were left stranded by the tide of migration long ago in a region that gave them no chance to rise above pioneer conditions. The notable fact is that ballads are still sung in so many parts of the United States. Although collecting did not begin until folk-song was supposed to be dead, ballads have been found in more than half of the States of the Union, as well as in New Brunswick, Nova Scotia, Prince Edward Island, and Newfoundland.

In publishing his admirable collection of *South Carolina Ballads*,[1] Professor Reed Smith recently computed the number of songs from Child's list that have survived in America as ninety-five, or about one third, 'allowing', as he said, 'for the existence of nine or ten ballads in oral tradition which as yet are undiscovered and unrecorded'. Probably the ratio he established will not be markedly altered by future collecting, although it must be noted that thirteen specimens more came to light in the following year through the publication of *British Ballads from Maine*, making a total of 108. As it happens, Greig's remarkable collection of Aberdeenshire ballads contains precisely the same number. In a word, about as many ballads have remained alive down to our day in America as in Scotland or England, which is not a little surprising in view of the dislocation they have endured.

American singers have not confined themselves to the canon that Child set up, any more than their cousins in Great Britain have done. Eighteen of the fifty-five speci-

[1] 1928, pp. 78, 169–74.

mens in *English Folk-Songs from the Southern Appalachians*, which were classified by Sharp as ballads, do not appear in Child's collection. The actual state of things is even more strikingly revealed if one looks at a volume containing songs of American origin as well as songs that have crossed the Atlantic. There are something like 120 ballads, for example, in Professor Cox's *Folk-Songs of the South*, only thirty-four of which are versions of specimens found in Child. For reasons I have stated in earlier chapters, one cannot safely be altogether dogmatic in classifying certain songs; but the figures I have given will serve as a rough indication of what Professor Cox's book contains. Three-quarters of the narrative songs he has included—quite properly—are not found in Child's collection. Without much doubt, this proportion represents with some degree of accuracy the repertory of singers in other regions than West Virginia. As one would expect to be the case, most of these ballads, in so far as they are of British origin, can be traced to broadsides, for oral tradition long ago adopted the product of the London makers as its own. Between forty-five and fifty of the songs Professor Cox printed come from this source. Thirty-four others, as I make the count, are American in origin, not to mention a few specimens that have been very freely adapted after their migration to America.

A collection of this kind does not differ notably in content, it will be observed, from those made by equally eclectic standards in Great Britain, except in the one respect that it includes American songs. But are there, indeed, American ballads that belong in the same category with British ballads? The question confronts us and demands an answer, as soon as we look at such a volume as the one we have been analysing. We cannot hesitate to admit, I believe, that a great many songs of American origin exist, which have quite as good right to the title of ballad as a great many in the English and Scottish collections. In both cases, the words of these songs go back, for the most part, to broadsides, and were the work of insignificant versifiers; but they have been accepted by oral tradition and have been submitted for a limited time to the influences of that tradition. We may, of course, call them ballads in the historic sense of the term, but we may go farther and say that they are ballads in so far as they have been modified by the processes of popular transmission. There is no reason to think that these processes have not operated in America as they have done in the mother country, though it is quite possible that they have worked less effectively. I have shown with some care in an earlier chapter that, to keep our thinking clear, we must not confuse the problem of the origin of the ballad type with the origin of individual ballads. The latter may be anything that chance decrees. The important thing to discover about any particular song is not where and how it started—though this may be both interesting and valuable—but what has happened to it since it was launched on the tide of oral tradition.

Let us grant at once that ballads of American origin have not gone very far in structure and texture towards the form of the European traditional ballad. Most of them betray the hands of their makers, who were either journalistic scribblers, hacks in the employ of broadside and song-book publishers or theatrical managers, or else country folk in whom the impulse to compose lingered though the art of composition had perished. With some few exceptions, they are no better and not much worse than similar ballads that got into circulation in Great Britain after the chapman had pursued his nefarious activities for a couple of centuries. Since very few American songs have survived that originated before the early nineteenth century—in only one case can an earlier date be proved[1]—they have been in circulation for a relatively short time and under lamentably bad conditions. Originating among folk of heterogeneous stock and traditions, diffused by print and by settlers on the move to new homes on the frontier, they could not well have become things of grace and beauty. They are often vigorous in action, they tend to present an incident in sharp focus, they preserve the old habit of semi-dramatic narration with an abundance of dialogue; but they have not the restrained emotional tensity or the unconsciously poetic language of the traditional ballad in its better state. They are sentimental instead of being poignant with feeling, as is of course true of balladry wherever it has been affected by the disruptive influences of modern times.

Apart from their interest as documents of social history, which is considerable, these American ballads are important because they give evidence even more clearly than do British songs, that the habit of singing and power of adaptation persist even after what we may call the communal discipline of taste has gone. The importance of this communal discipline on the processes by which the European ballad came to be what it was in the fifteenth and sixteenth centuries is made quite evident by what has happened in default of it. As long as there were homogeneous communities with relatively static populations, not easily affected by influences from outside, a tradition of good artistry had a chance to develop and to continue. Whatever their native gifts, those who handed on ballads were trained singers, trained as only the few are likely to be under other conditions. If not musically educated, they were at least musically

[1] Miss Pound, *American Ballads and Songs*, 1922, p. xxii, makes the statement: 'Nothing indigenous lives from colonial times, so far as is known'. On the same page, however, she calls attention to *Springfield Mountain* as a 'still recognizable piece from the eighteenth century'. See *J.A.F.-L.* xiii. 105–12, for its supposed origin in Massachusetts.

skilled, which comes to the same thing in practice. Their training was the more effective because it was a communal matter. Every one learns easily, in any society, the things that are common knowledge. There is every reason to believe that under such conditions, individual ballads rather consistently improved in form and texture as they circulated, instead of deteriorating in quality. It is not too much to believe that the average folk-song may have been a finer product in the sixteenth century than in the thirteenth. As conditions changed—in England through the operations of the ballad-monger, in America through the variety of causes already sketched—the effective power of taste declined. The old ballad texts tended to degenerate in quality, though an occasional variant appeared that showed improvement in one detail or another, while new songs from the manufacturers of such things changed only very slowly towards such a norm as they would have approached in earlier times. What I have called the communal discipline of taste no longer held sway, though something of the old tradition survived in exceptionally gifted individuals. More and more, folksong was driven back into remote quarters or was preserved by families to whom it became a sort of heirloom.[1] Yet the impulse to make songs and to transmit them orally, with the necessary consequence of almost incessant variation, did not die out.

This impulse was apparently stronger in America during the nineteenth century than it was in Great Britain, perhaps because life was more exciting. At all events, ballads somehow came into being and were widely disseminated, reproducing in a rough-and-ready fashion the history of popular songs in the Old World. The extensive group in which John Henry and John

[1] See the valuable observations recorded in *British Ballads from Maine*, pp. 489-95.

Hardy appear as the heroes presents an interesting case in point, and deserves serious consideration on the part of any one interested in ballads of whatever kind. This material has recently been made the subject of a study by Professor Johnson,[1] whose conclusions have an interest beyond that of his immediate theme. *John Henry* has to do with the prowess of a negro, who—in most versions—died while attempting to compete by hand with a steam drill. The legend about him seems to have originated somewhat more than sixty years ago, and 'is now known in one form or another to about nine-tenths of the negro population ',[2] not to mention its wide circulation among white people. ' Whether John Henry was a flesh-and-blood man or not,' says Professor Johnson,[3] ' there are thousands of Negroes who believe that he was, and many of them can give the intimate details of his career.' A persistent tradition has associated him with the construction of a tunnel on the Chesapeake and Ohio Railroad in West Virginia during the years 1870 to 1872 ; but the evidence that has been presented for his existence and for the reality of his exploit is far from satisfactory. It is significant for all legend-making, however, that many white men, as well as the Negroes to whom he is a hero, have no doubts about him. The ballad is sung with the assumption that the core of it is true history.

The matter is complicated by the second ballad mentioned above, that of *John Hardy*. About the actuality of John Hardy himself there is no doubt whatever. He was a West Virginia Negro, who killed a man in a crap-game and was hanged for murder at Welch, McDowell County, in January 1894.[4] Probably because he was a

---

[1] G. B. Johnson, *John Henry. Tracking down a Negro Legend*, 1929.
[2] *Op. cit.*, p. 3.
[3] *Op. cit.*, p. 8.
[4] *Op. cit.*, p. 57. See J. H. Cox, *Folk-Songs of the South*, pp. 175-7.

powerful creature and came to a spectacular end, he was somehow associated in the popular mind with John Henry of earlier fame. The similarity of the names was undoubtedly a factor in the confusion. The ballad about Hardy, which cannot be tracked to a definite source any more than can *John Henry*, pictures him as a ' desperately bad ' man, who kills in a spirit of bravado and dies to a sentimental strain. The versions of this song multiplied, as did those of *John Henry*, until it came to be known throughout the southern Appalachian region within a few years, though it has apparently not spread quite so widely as the earlier song.

Inevitably, since the heroes of the two ballads were confused with one another, mixed versions appeared. Until Professor Johnson made his study, it was indeed not clear that the two were separate in origin rather than divergent forms of the same story. Even with this question settled, it is impossible to keep them altogether apart, for stanzas occur that appear to be common property. The result is a bewildering set of variants with complexities of relationship as baffling as any found in our oldest ballads. For example, each hero has been provided with a woman to lament his death. In some versions of John Henry she can ' drive steel like a man ', usually doing so when the champion ' lay sick on his bed '; but often she is only an admiring spectator of his prowess, as in the following stanza :

> John Henry, he had a woman,
> Her name was Mary Magdalene.
> She would go to the tunnel and sing for John,
> Just to hear John Henry's hammer ring.

In many variants of both ballads two stanzas quite obviously borrowed from *The Lass of Roch Royal* are worked into the text, having as little to do with the story in the one case as in the other. Certain versions of both ballads, again, open with a prophetic utterance of which the following is a specimen :

> John Henry was a little boy,
> Sittin' on his mama's knee.
> Said, 'The Big Bend Tunnel on the C. and O. Road
> Gonna cause the death of me, Lawd, Lawd.'

We may surmise that this belongs to *John Henry* rather than to *John Hardy*; but we cannot be sure, for the vagaries of transmission have played strange tricks with both songs. It is interesting to note that the tunes to which they are sung are quite distinct, and appear never to interchange.[1]

The two ballads at which we have just been looking, though widely known among singers of the white race, belong more particularly to the Negroes; which introduces a complication of American balladry that has not yet been mentioned but is nevertheless of great importance. As slaves and as freemen, Negroes have been living in America almost from the beginning of the European settlements. They are a musically gifted race, with somewhat remarkable powers of mimicry; they have, moreover, lived in close association with white people, despite all social barriers, either as domestic servants or as farm labourers. It was inevitable that they should take over the songs of their employers as they adopted so many other things, good and bad, varying them in accordance with their own instincts and ideas. They are still singing some of the oldest of British ballads in forms of their own devising.

No one can at present be quite certain to what extent Negro music has an African basis, though it is impossible to deny some influence on tone and rhythm.[2] In any event, the melodies which in our day have had a marked

---

[1] See Johnson, *op. cit.*, p. 66.
[2] See the judicious remarks of N. I. White, *American Negro Folk-Songs*, 1928, pp. 19-26.

effect on musical taste have come into being by a process of adaptation. They are what Negroes have made of the white man's music. In the same way, they have not only changed the words of old folk-songs to suit themselves but have made new ones. Whether or no *John Henry* be of Negro composition—and I believe it is, despite the broadside discovered by Professor Johnson[1]—other ballads must certainly be. *The Boll Weevil*[2] is an example in point, a wholly indigenous product and as good a popular ballad as has sprung up in a great while. The form it takes of a conversation between a farmer and his insect enemy is very similar to that of *Riddles Wisely Expounded*, to which Child gave the first place in his list, and it is quite free from the taint of the broadside, which cannot be said of many ballads of American origin. What it lacks, as do all Negro ballads, is organization, which accounts for the extreme variability of the stories they tell. As Professor White has put the matter: 'There is hardly any such thing as a stanza belonging particularly to one song and to that alone. Generally speaking, practically any stanza is at home in practically any song.'[3] The confusion that results from such freedom of treatment can be seen in *John Henry* and *John Hardy*. The songs of white men have never varied so widely and so swiftly, we can be sure, as these have done.

Such fluidity would not be possible, furthermore, if the Negroes did not improvise with the greatest ease. For their power of doing this the evidence is unexceptionable.[4] *Frankie and Albert*, with its many titles and multitudinous stanzas,[5] illustrates very well the extra-

---

[1] *Op. cit.*, pp. 84–5, 88–90.

[2] See D. Scarborough, *On the Trail of Negro Folk-Songs*, 1925, pp. 77–9.

[3] *Op. cit.*, p. 26. See also D. Scarborough, *op. cit.*, pp. 74–5.

[4] See, for example, Scarborough, *op. cit.*, pp. 75–6, and R. Smith, *op. cit.*, pp. 20–6.

[5] See Cox, *op. cit.*, pp. 218–20 ; White, *op. cit.*, pp. 214–16 ; Scarborough, *op. cit.*, pp. 79–85 ; Odum and Johnson, *The Negro and his Songs*, 1925, pp. 228–9.

ordinary fecundity of a theme in their hands. In a case of this sort, it has been easier for them to make new verses than to remember old ones. Better than any other singers, who have been carefully observed, they show the power of instantaneous response to a stimulus of any kind, and a very general habit of composition under stress of excitement. In many respects what the Negroes have done in adapting old songs to their uses and making new ones on the same general model is the most interesting thing in American balladry. To a very large extent illiterate until of late, gregarious and imitative of habit, possessed of an excellent sense of rhythm and beautiful voices, till this last generation not nomadic, they have reproduced certain of the conditions that are most suitable for the development of folk-song. It is a thousand pities that systematic study of their music did not begin a generation or two earlier.

Two other groups of American singers, in both cases occupational, furnish evidence of peculiar interest as to the ways of narrative song in oral circulation. In neither case has anything developed that is important for the craft of balladry, since the groups have been too shifting and evanescent to permit it. Their ballads are useful chiefly as showing how easily songs become traditional and scatter themselves about with wide variations; but they serve admirably for this purpose. Nothing could better illustrate the effect of oral transmission on songs, whatever their origin, or show more clearly that an established tradition of taste and native art is necessary for the production of ballads that have interest otherwise than as material for social history.

For a comparatively brief period the cowboys of the Great Plains lived under conditions that were altogether suitable for the dissemination of songs and in some respects for the creation of them. While the ranges lasted, the men formed a large group with homogeneous interests and occupations, though they were recruited from all parts of the United States and many foreign lands. They were almost all young men, too, and in the leisure of bunk-house or encampment fell naturally into song. Although they lived much in isolated groups or rode solitary, they crossed the trails of many of their fellows on their long drives from the feeding-grounds of the Rio Grande to those of the North. Stories and songs thus travelled far and fast. The combination of circumstances was extraordinary—probably never duplicated elsewhere. The cowboy was forced by his work both into solitude and intimate gregariousness, with the result that he took on very quickly specialized characteristics, no matter what his previous environment had been. The cowboy of legend, who shot straight, rode as hard as he drank, and held rigidly to a code of his own devising, is simply a romanticized version of a real creature.

Perhaps if the homesteader had not come in and destroyed the ranges, the cowboys might have developed something in balladry that would have been distinctive in form as well as in content. *The Old Chisholm Trail*[1] and *The Lone Star Trail*[2] seemed to be tending in that direction, as did a few other popular pieces. But the cowboy had a brief existence as a type, and could not well have done more than he did: sing lustily with variations whatever caught his fancy. Certain of the songs to which he gave currency have a rich pungency of their own, whatever their origin. *The Buffalo Skinners*,[3] for example, is as forthright as *Hobie Noble*. It has to be admitted, however, that things as good as this are rare. The cowboys were quite content with adaptations of sentimental ditties, which doubtless amused them, though

---

[1] See J. A. Lomax, *Cowboy Songs and other Frontier Ballads*, 1910, pp. 58–63.

[2] See Lomax, *op. cit.*, pp. 310–13 ; C. Sandburg, *The American Songbag*, 1927, pp. 266–7.

[3] See Lomax, *op. cit.*, pp. 158–63 ; Sandburg, *op. cit.*, pp. 270–2.

the cheap and obvious emotion was somehow gratifying to their instincts. Other youths than cowpunchers have been known to indulge themselves in maudlin sentiment with an ironic twist. In general, these songs of the plains and the frontier, while they furnish an admirable index to the high spirits as well as the youthful melancholy of the men who sang them, to the invincible courage and other attendant virtues that were bred by a life of hard reality, lack the qualities that are acquired by ballads long circulated among people with a real tradition of craftsmanship in verse and music. Oral transmission appears to have given some of them a rough vigour of phrase, but that is all. In the history of balladry they are important as showing that groups of individuals fortuitously gathered to share a common life outside lettered circles will fall back on old habits of entertainment, and will be able to impart some colour of that life to their songs, but cannot thereby achieve what in earlier times was brought to pass through the slow development of tradition.

The ballads of the lumberjack furnish evidence of much the same sort. In the isolation of the great woods from Maine to British Columbia men have long been getting comfort and pleasure by singing, and they have built up an extensive repertory. It used to be the case that a man who had the voice and temperament to be a leader was sought after for every crew, since employers well understood what mischief could be worked by the cold solitude of the forest. The lumberjacks have never confined themselves to songs of their own craft, any more than the cowboys did, but they have liked to celebrate certain incidents in the heroic manner; and they have created one legendary figure who belongs to American mythology as much as John Henry. There is no worthy ballad of this Paul Bunyan, as it happens; which illustrates the limitations of balladry in these latter times, for the imagination that went to his making worked as soundly as popular fancy has ever done.

The story of lumbering operations in America is, of course, a tale of extravagant devastation, with the chief point of attack for ever moving westward as the forests have been ravaged of their virgin growth. But the movement has been slow. The day of the shanty-boy in Maine is just over, and he would be singing now in Washington if conditions of lumbering had not altered. To some extent he is still doing so all along the northern frontier, one gathers, though in diminishing volume. The lumberjack's trade has always been a peculiar one in that it has been seasonal. Countrymen from the Maritime Provinces and New England, together with French Canadians, have made up the crews in the east, and in summer they have had other occupations. Their common interests have extended from the first snowfall to the end of the spring drives. In so far, therefore, as their songs had to do with their craft, they were concerned with events of the winter and the spring. No more than the cowboys, but for different reasons, did the lumberjacks develop anything new in the form of their ballads. The interest lies in the extent to which certain specimens reflect the bold spirit of men in action. There is something heroic about the best of them, though little enough of grace.

The nature of the ballads developed in the great woods can be well illustrated from *The Jam on Gerry's Rock*,[1] which has had an amazing popularity. It tells how Young Munroe, a foreman, met his death while breaking a log-jam of a Sunday morning. That is all, but it 'moves the heart', as Sidney's was moved by the song of Percy and Douglas. Where the ballad originated is past finding out, though there has been a curious tendency on the

[1] See Eckstorm and Smyth, *Minstrelsy of Maine*, 1927, pp. 82-90; F. Rickaby, *Ballads and Songs of the Shanty-Boy*, 1926, pp. 11-14, 192-3; Sandburg, *op. cit.*, pp. 394-5.

part of lumbermen to localize their songs. In Maine they have positively known the time and place of the accident, and in Michigan they have been equally sure of where and when it happened.[1] The testimony of the opposed witnesses must be thrown out of court, but it indicates most interestingly the firm belief of the true ballad-singer in the reality of his tale. While songs like this remain alive, balladry is not yet dead.

[1] See the judicious discussion in Eckstorm and Smyth, *op. cit.*, pp. 176–98.

APPENDIX

SPECIMEN BALLADS OF AMERICAN ORIGIN

SPRINGFIELD MOUNTAIN

This version was printed by P. Barry, *Journal of American Folk-Lore*, xviii. 296 (1905), as contributed by 'L. W. H., Cambridge, Mass., in whose family it has been traditional for three generations'.

1. On Hoosic Mountain there did dwell
   A hawk-eyed youth I knowed full well.

     Ri too ral loo, ri too ral lay,
     Ri too ral loo, ri too ral lay.

2. One day this John he did go
   Down to the meadow for to mow.

3. He had not mowed nigh half a field,
   When a pesky sarpent bit his heel.

4. He riz his scythe, and with one blow,
   He laid that pesky sarpent low.

5. He took it up into his hand,
   And kerried it to Molly-i Bland.

6. 'Oh, Molly-i, Molly-i, here you see
   The pesky sarpent what bit me.'

7. 'Oh, John!' said she, 'Why did you go
   Down to the meadow for to mow?'

8. 'Oh, Molly-i, Molly-i,' John he said,
   '"Twas Father's hay, which had got to be mow-ed!'

9. He riz his heel into her lip,
   The pesky pizen for to sip.

10. And heving there a hollow tooth,
    The pizen took upon them both.

11. Their bodies now are 'neath the sod,
    Their souls, I trust, are jined to God.

POOR OMIE

From Campbell and Sharp, *English Folk-Songs from the Southern Appalachians*, 1917, pp. 228–9. Sung by Hilliard Smith at Hindman, Kentucky. By courtesy of G. P. Putnam's Sons, Publishers, New York and London.

1. 'You promised to meet me at Adams's spring;
   Some money you would bring me, or some other fine thing.'

2. 'No money, no money, to flatter the case,
   We'll go and get married, it will be no disgrace.

3. 'Come jump up behind me and away we will ride
   To yonder fair city; I will make you my bride.'

4. She jumped up behind him and away they did go
   To the banks of deep waters where they never overflow.

5. 'O Omie, O Omie, I will tell you my mind;
   My mind is to drown you and leave you behind.'

6. 'O pity! O pity! Pray spare me my life,
   And I will deny you and not be your wife.'

7. 'No pity, no pity, no pity have I;
   In yonder deep water your body shall lie.'

8. He kicked her and stomped her, he threw her in the deep;
   He jumped on his pony and rode at full speed.

9. The screams of poor Omie followed after him so nigh,
   Saying: 'I am a poor rebel not fitten to die.'

10. She was missing one evening, next morning was found
    In the bottom of Siloty below the mill dam.

11. Up stepped old Miss Mother, these words she did say:
    'James Luther has killed Omie and he has run away.

12. 'He has gone to Elk River, so I understand,
    They have got him in prison for killing a man.'

13. They have got him in Ireland, bound to the ground;
    And he wrote his confession and sent it around.

14. 'Go hang me or kill me, for I am the man
    That drowned little Omie below the mill dam.'

THE JAM ON GERRY'S ROCK

From Eckstorm and Smyth, *Minstrelsy of Maine*, 1927, pp. 88–90. Collected at Mattawamkeag, Maine. By courtesy of Mrs. Fannie H. Eckstorm and Miss Mary W. Smyth.

1. Come all of you brave shanty boys, wherever you may be,
   I pray you pay attention and listen unto me,
   Concerning six brave Canadian boys, so manfully and brave,
   Breaking a jam on Gerry's Rock they met a watery grave.

2. It being on Sunday morning, the truth you shall hear,
   Our logs were piled up mountain high, we could not keep them
   clear;
   The foreman says: 'Turn out, my boys, without no dread or
   fear,
   We'll break the jam on Gerry's Rock and for Logantown we'll
   steer.'

3. And some of them were willing, whilst others did stand back,
   For to work upon a Sunday they did not think 'twas right,
   Whilst six of those brave shanty boys did volunteer to go
   To break the jam on Gerry's Rock, with their foreman young
   Munroe.

4. They had not been on the jam long when the boss to them did
   say:
   'I would have you be on your guard, for the jam will soon
   give way.'
   And scarcely had he spoke those words, when the jam did
   break and go,
   Carrying off those six brave shanty boys and the foreman
   young Munroe.

5. When the rest of those brave shanty boys sad tidings came to hear,
   For to search for their dead bodies to the river they did steer,
   And amongst those reckless bodies to their sad grief and woe,
   All cut and mangled on the beach was the head of young
   Munroe.

6. They raised it from the watery grave, combed down his raven
   hair;
   There was one fair form among them whose groans did rent
   the air,

[There was one fair form among them], a girl from Sidney town,

Whose groans and cries did rent the skies for her lover who was drowned.

7. They buried him quite decently, being on the first of May;
   It's come all of you brave shanty boys and for your comrade pray.
   They engraved it on a tree close by his grave doth grow,
   His age—his name—the drowning of that hero young Munroe.

8. Miss Carro was a handsome girl, likewise [the] Rogueman's friend,
   Her mother was a widow, lived by the River Glenn,
   And the wages of her own true love the boss to her did pay,
   And a little subscription she secured from the shanty boys next day.

9. Miss Carro did not long survive to her sad grief and woe,
   In a space of six months after Death called on her to go,
   And her request was granted to be buried with young Munroe.

10. Now it's come all of you brave shanty boys, who'd like to come and see
    A little mound by the river side, where grew a hemlock tree.
    The shanty boys they cut their woods—two lovers they lie low;
    There lies Miss Carro in her grave and her foreman young Munroe.

THE WRECK ON THE C. AND O., or GEORGE ALLEY

From J. H. Cox, *Folk-Songs of the South*, 1925, pp. 229–30. Secured from a sister of George Alley in West Virginia. The wreck on the Chesapeake and Ohio Railroad took place on 23 Oct. 1890. By courtesy of Professor John H. Cox.

1. Long come the F. F. and V., the fastest on the line,
   Running on the C. and O. Road, thirty minutes behind the time;

When she run into old East Sewell, quartered on the line,
There to receive orders: 'tis Hinton, behind time.

   Chorus.

  Many a man's been murdered by the railroad,
    By the railroad, by the railroad;
  Many a man's been murdered by the railroad,
    And laid in his lonesome grave.

2. When at Hinton she made her stop, the engineer was there;
George Alley was his name, with his curly golden hair;
And his fireman, Jack Dickinson, was standing by his side,
Ready to receive his orders and in his cab to ride.

3. Georgia's mama came to him, with a bucket on her arm:
'Pray to God, George, my dear son, be careful how you run;
Many a man has lost his life, trying to make up lost time;
If you'll run your engine right, you'll get there just in time.'

4. 'Dear mama, your advice is good; to it I will take heed;
But my engine she's all right, and I know that she will speed;
It's over the road I mean to fly with speed unknown to all;
When I blow at the Big Bend Tunnel, you'll surely hear my call.'

5. Said George to his fireman: 'A rock ahead I see;
I tell you death is awaiting there, to snatch both you and me;
From this cab you now must fly, your darling life to save;
I want you to be an engineer, when sleeping in your grave.'[1]

6. 'No, no, George! I cannot go, I want to die with you.'
'No, no, Jack! that will not do! I'll die for me and you.'
From this cab poor Jack did fly; New River it was high;
As he struck the water, old No. 4 flew by.

7. Up the road she darted; upon the rock she crashed;
Upside down his engine turned, and upon his breast it smashed;
His head upon the firebox door, the burning flames rolled o'er;
'I'm glad I was born an engineer, to die on the C. & O. Road.'

---

[1] An obvious error for 'when I'm sleeping in my grave'.

8. The people to the engine run, to see the engineer;
   Georgia said, 'God bless you, friends! You'll surely find me
   here.'
   There was never a braver man than Georgia Alley born
   To die upon the C. & O. Road, one reckless July morn.

9. The doctor said, 'Now Georgia, my darling boy, be still;
   Your precious life may yet be saved, if it is God's blessed
   will.'
   'No, no, Doc! I want to die so free;
   I want to die with my engine, One Hundred Forty-three.'

THE BUFFALO SKINNERS

From J. A. Lomax, *Cowboy Songs and Ballads*, 1910, pp. 158-61. By courtesy
of Mr. Lomax.

1. Come all you jolly fellows and listen to my song,
   There are not many verses, it will not detain you long;
   It's concerning some young fellows who did agree to go
   And spend one summer pleasantly on the range of the buffalo.

2. It happened in Jacksboro in the spring of seventy-three,
   A man by the name of Crego came stepping up to me,
   Saying, 'How do you do, young fellow, and how would you
   like to go
   And spend one summer pleasantly on the range of the buf-
   falo?'

3. 'It's me being out of employment,' this to Crego I did say,
   'This going out on the buffalo range depends upon the pay.
   But if you will pay good wages and transportation too,
   I think, sir, I will go with you to the range of the buffalo.'

4. 'Yes, I will pay good wages, give transportation too,
   Provided you will go with me and stay the summer through;
   But if you should grow homesick, come back to Jacksboro,
   I won't pay transportation from the range of the buffalo.'

5. It's now our outfit was complete—seven able-bodied men,
   With navy six and needle gun—our troubles did begin;
   Our way it was a pleasant one, the route we had to go,
   Until we crossed Pease River on the range of the buffalo.

6. It's now we've crossed Pease River, our troubles have begun.
   The first damned tail I went to rip, Christ! how I cut my thumb!
   While skinning the damned old stinkers our lives wasn't a show,
   For the Indians watched to pick us off while skinning the buffalo.

7. He fed us on such sorry chuck I wished myself most dead,
   It was old jerked beef, croton coffee, and sour bread.
   Pease River's as salty as hell fire, the water I could never go,—
   O God! I wished I had never come to the range of the buffalo.

8. Our meat it was buffalo hump and iron wedge bread,
   And all we had to sleep on was a buffalo robe for a bed;
   The fleas and gray-backs worked on us, O boys, it was not slow,
   I'll tell you there's no worse hell on earth than the range of the buffalo.

9. Our hearts were cased with buffalo hocks, our souls were cased with steel,
   And the hardships of that summer would nearly make us reel.
   While skinning the damned old stinkers our lives they had no show,
   For the Indians waited to pick us off on the hills of Mexico.

10. The season being near over, old Crego he did say
    The crowd had been extravagant, was in debt to him that day,—
    We coaxed him and we begged him and still it was no go,—
    We left old Crego's bones to bleach on the range of the buffalo.

11. Oh, it's now we've crossed Pease River and homeward we are bound,
    No more in that hell-fired country shall ever we be found.
    Go home to our wives and sweethearts, tell others not to go,
    For God's forsaken the buffalo range and the damned old buffalo.

JESSE JAMES

From C. Sandburg, *The American Songbag*, 1927, pp. 420–21. It should be known that Jesse James was shot while living under the name of Howard. By courtesy of Harcourt, Brace & Co., Publishers, New York.

1. It was on a Wednesday night, the moon was shining bright,
      They robbed the Glendale train.
   And the people they did say, for many miles away,
      'Twas the outlaws Frank and Jesse James.

         Jesse had a wife to mourn all her life,
            The children they are brave.
         'Twas a dirty little coward shot Mister Howard,
            And laid Jesse James in his grave.

2. It was Robert Ford, the dirty little coward,
      I wonder how he does feel,
   For he ate of Jesse's bread and he slept in Jesse's bed,
      Then he laid Jesse James in his grave.

3. It was his brother Frank that robbed the Gallatin bank,
      And carried the money from the town.
   It was in this very place that they had a little race,
      For they shot Captain Sheets to the ground.

4. They went to the crossing not very far from there,
      And there they did the same ;
   And the agent on his knees he delivered up the keys
      To the outlaws Frank and Jesse James.

5. It was on a Saturday night, Jesse was at home
      Talking to his family brave,
   When the thief and the coward, little Robert Ford,
      Laid Jesse James in his grave.

6. How people held their breath when they heard of Jesse's
      death,
      And wondered how he ever came to die.
   'Twas one of the gang, dirty Robert Ford,
      That shot Jesse James on the sly.

7. Jesse went to his rest with his hand on his breast.
    The devil will be upon his knee.
He was born one day in the county of Clay,
    And came from a solitary race.

THE OLD CHISHOLM TRAIL

From J. A. Lomax, *Cowboy Songs and other Frontier Ballads*, 1910, pp. 58–61. By courtesy of Mr. Lomax.

1. Come along, boys, and listen to my tale,
    I'll tell you of my troubles on the old Chisholm trail.

      Coma ti yi youpy, youpy ya, youpy ya,
      Coma ti yi youpy, youpy ya.

2. I started up the trail October twenty-third,
    I started up the trail with the 2-U herd.

3. Oh, a ten dollar hoss and a forty dollar saddle,—
    And I'm goin' to punchin' Texas cattle.

4. I woke up one morning on the old Chisholm trail,
    Rope in my hand and a cow by the tail.

5. I'm up in the mornin' afore daylight
    And afore I sleep the moon shines bright.

6. Old Ben Bolt was a blamed good boss,
    But he'd go to see the girls on a sore-backed hoss.

7. Old Ben Bolt was a fine old man
    And you'd know there was whiskey wherever he'd land.

8. My hoss throwed me off at the creek called Mud,
    My hoss throwed me off round the 2-U herd.

9. Last time I saw him he was going cross the level
    A-kicking up his heels and a-running like the devil.

10. It's cloudy in the West, a-looking like rain,
    And my damned old slicker's in the wagon again.

11. Crippled my hoss, I don't know how,
    Ropin' at the horns of a 2-U cow.

12. We hit Caldwell and we hit her on the fly,
    We bedded down the cattle on the hill close by.

13. No chaps, no slicker, and it's pouring down rain,
    And I swear, by god, I'll never night-herd again.

14. Feet in the stirrups and seat in the saddle,
    I hung and rattled with them long-horn cattle.

15. Last night I was on guard and the leader broke the ranks,
    I hit my horse down the shoulders and I spurred him in the
    flanks.

16. The wind commenced to blow, and the rain began to fall,
    Hit looked, by grab, like we was goin' to lose 'em all.

17. I jumped in the saddle and grabbed holt the horn,
    Best blamed cow-puncher ever was born.

18. I popped my foot in the stirrup and gave a little yell,
    The tail cattle broke and the leaders went to hell.

19. I don't give a damn if they never do stop;
    I'll ride as long as an eight-day clock.

20. Foot in the stirrup and hand on the horn,
    Best damned cowboy ever was born.

21. I herded and I hollered and I done very well,
    Till the boss said, 'Boys, just let 'em go to hell.'

22. Stray in the herd and the boss said kill it,
    So I shot him in the rump with the handle of the skillet.

23. We rounded 'em up and put 'em on the cars,
    And that was the last of the old Two Bars.

24. Oh it's bacon and beans most every day,—
    I'd as soon be a-eatin' prairie hay.

25. I'm on my best horse and I'm goin' at a run,
    I'm the quickest shootin' cowboy that ever pulled a gun.

26. I went to the wagon to get my roll,
    To come back to Texas, dad-burn my soul.

27. I went to the boss to draw my roll,
    He had it figgered out I was nine dollars in the hole.

28. I'll sell my outfit just as soon as I can,
    I won't punch cattle for no damned man.

29. Goin' back to town to draw my money,
　　Goin' back home to see my honey.

30. With my knees in the saddle and my seat in the sky,
　　I'll quit punching cows in the sweet by and by.

　　　　Coma ti yi youpy, youpy ya, youpy ya,
　　　　Coma ti yi youpy, youpy ya.

THE LONE STAR TRAIL

From J. A. Lomax, *Cowboy Songs and other Frontier Ballads*, 1910, pp. 310–13.
By courtesy of Mr. Lomax.

1. I'm a rowdy cowboy just off the stormy plains,
　　My trade is girting saddles and pulling bridle reins.
　　Oh, I can tip the lasso, it is with graceful ease;
　　I rope a streak of lightning, and ride it where I please.
　　My bosses they all like me, they say I am hard to beat;
　　I give them the bold standoff, you bet I have got the cheek.
　　I always work for wages, my pay I get in gold;
　　I am bound to follow the longhorn steer until I am too old.

　　　　Ci yi yip yip yip pe ya.

2. I am a Texas cowboy and I do ride the range;
　　My trade is cinches and saddles and ropes and bridle reins;
　　With Stetson hat and jingling spurs and leather up to the
　　　　knees,
　　Gray backs as big as chili beans and fighting like hell with fleas.
　　And if I had a little stake, I soon would married be,
　　But another week and I must go, the boss said so to-day.
　　My girl must cheer up courage and choose some other one,
　　For I am bound to follow the Lone Star Trail until my race
　　　　is run.

　　　　Ci yi yip yip yip pe ya.

3. It almost breaks my heart for to have to go away,
　　And leave my own little darling, my sweetheart so far away.
　　But when I'm out on the Lone Star Trail often I'll think of
　　　　thee,
　　Of my own dear girl, the darling one, the one I would like
　　　　to see.

And when I get to a shipping point, I'll get on a little spree
To drive away the sorrow for the girl that once loved me.
And though red licker stirs us up we're bound to have our
fun,
And I intend to follow the Lone Star Trail until my race is
run.

> Ci yi yip yip yip pe ya.

4. I went up the Lone Star Trail in eighteen eighty-three;
   I fell in love with a pretty miss and she in love with me.
   'When you get to Kansas write and let me know;
   And if you get in trouble, your bail I'll come and go.'
   When I got up in Kansas, I had a pleasant dream;
   I dreamed I was down on Trinity, down on that pleasant
   stream;
   I dreampt my true love right beside me, she come to go my
   bail;
   I woke up broken hearted with a yearling by the tail.

> Ci yi yip yip yip pe ya.

5. In came my jailer about nine o'clock,
   A bunch of keys was in his hand, my cell door to unlock,
   Saying, 'Cheer up, my prisoner, I heard some voice say
   You're bound to hear your sentence some time to-day.'
   In came my mother about ten o'clock,
   Saying, 'O my loving Johnny, what sentence have you got?'
   'The jury found me guilty and the judge a-standin' by
   Has sent me down to Huntsville to lock me up and die.'

> Ci yi yip yip yip pe ya.

6. Down come the jailer, just about eleven o'clock,
   With a bunch of keys all in his hand the cell doors to unlock,
   Saying, 'Cheer up, my prisoner, I heard the jury say
   Just ten long years in Huntsville you're bound to go and
   stay.'
   Down come my sweetheart, ten dollars in her hand,
   Saying, 'Give this to my cowboy, 'tis all that I command;
   O give this to my cowboy and think of olden times,
   Think of the darling that he has left behind.'

> Ci yi yip yip yip pe ya.

STAGOLEE

From H. W. Odum, *Journal of American Folk-Lore*, xxiv. 288 (1911), and Odum and Johnson, *The Negro and his Songs*, 1925, pp. 196–7, as sung in Mississippi, Louisiana, and Tennessee. By courtesy of Professor Howard W. Odum.

1. Stagolee, Stagolee, what's dat in yo' grip?
   Nothin' but my Sunday clothes, I'm goin' to take a trip.

   O dat man, bad man, Stagolee done come.

2. Stagolee, Stagolee, where you been so long?
   I been out on de battle fiel' shootin' an' havin' fun.

3. Stagolee was a bully man, an' ev'ybody knowed,
   When dey seed Stagolee comin', to give Stagolee de road.

4. Stagolee started out, he give his wife his han':
   'Good-bye, darlin', I'm goin' to kill a man.'

5. Stagolee killed a man an' laid him on de flo',
   What's dat he kill him wid? Dat same ole fohty-fo'.

6. Stagolee killed a man an' laid him on his side.
   What's dat he kill him wid? Dat same ole fohty-five.

7. Out of house an' down de street Stagolee did run,
   In his hand he held a great big smokin' gun.

8. Stagolee, Stagolee, I'll tell you what I'll do,
   If you'll git me out'n dis trouble, I'll do as much for you.

9. Ain't it a pity, ain't it a shame?
   Stagolee was shot, but he don't want no name.

10. Stagolee, Stagolee, look what you done done,
    Killed de best ole citerzen; now you'll hav' to be hung.

11. Stagolee cried to de jury: 'Please don't take my life,
    I have only three little children an' one little lovin' wife.'

JOHN HENRY

From G. B. Johnson, *John Henry. Tracking down a Negro Legend*, 1929, pp. 91-5. Contributed by a man in Illinois, who had been a 'rambler' all his life. He regarded this version as coming from Virginia and West Virginia. By courtesy of Professor Guy B. Johnson.

1. Lissen to my story;
   'Tis a story true;
   'Bout a mighty man,—John Henry was his name,
   An' John Henry was a steel-driver too—
   Lawd,— Lawd,—
   John Henry was a steel-driver too.

2. John Henry had a hammah;
   Weighed nigh fo'ty poun';
   Eb'ry time John made a strike
   He seen his steel go 'bout two inches down,
   Lawd,— Lawd,—
   He seen his steel go 'bout two inches down.

3. John Henry's woman, Lucy,—
   Dress she wore was blue;
   Eyes like stars an' teeth lak-a marble stone,
   An' John Henry named his hammah 'Lucy' too,—
   Lawd,— Lawd,—
   John Henry named his hammah 'Lucy' too.

4. Lucy came to see him;
   Bucket in huh han';
   All th' time John Henry ate his snack,
   O Lucy she'd drive steel lak-a man,—
   Lawd,— Lawd,—
   O Lucy she'd drive steel lak-a man.

5. John Henry's cap'n Tommy,—
   V'ginny gave him birth;
   Loved John Henry like his only son,
   And Cap' Tommy was the whitest man on earth,—
   Lawd,— Lawd,—
   Cap' Tommy was th' whitest man on earth.

6. One day Cap' Tommy told him
   How he'd bet a man;
   Bet John Henry 'd beat a steam-drill down,
   Jes' cause he was th' best in th' lan',—
   Lawd,— Lawd,—
   'Cause he was th' best in th' lan'.

7. John Henry tol' Cap' Tommy;
   Lightnin' in his eye;
   'Cap'n, bet yo' las' red cent on me,
   Fo' I'll beat it to th' bottom or I'll die,—
   Lawd,— Lawd,—
   I'll beat it to the bottom or I'll die.

8. 'Co'n pone's in my stomach;
   Hammah 's in my han';
   Haint no steam-drill on dis railroad job
   Can beat "Lucy" an' her steel-drivin' man,
   Lawd,— Lawd,—
   Can beat "Lucy" an' her steel-drivin' man.

9. 'Bells ring on de engines;
   Runnin' down th' line;
   Dinnah's done when Lucy pulls th' c'od;
   But no hammah in this mountain rings like mine,—
   Lawd,— Lawd,—
   No hammah in this mountain rings like mine.'

10. Sun shined hot an' burnin'
    Wer'n't no breeze at-tall;
    Sweat ran down like watah down a hill
    That day John Henry let his hammah fall,—
    Lawd,— Lawd,—
    That day John Henry let his hammah fall.

11. John Henry kissed his hammah;
    White Man turned on steam;
    Li'l Bill held John Henry's trusty steel,—
    'Twas th' biggest race th' worl' had ever seen,—
    Lawd,— Lawd,—
    Th' biggest race th' worl' had ever seen.

12. White Man tol' John Henry,—
    'Niggah, dam yo' soul,
    You might beat dis steam an' drill o' mine
    When th' rocks in this mountain turn to gol',—
    Lawd,— Lawd,—
    When th' rocks in this mountain turn to gol'.'

13. John Henry tol' th' white man;
    Tol' him kind-a sad:
    'Cap'n George, I want-a be yo' fr'en;
    If I beat yo' to th' bottom, don't git mad,—
    Lawd,— Lawd,—
    If I beat yo' to th' bottom don't git mad.'

14. Cap' Tommy sees John Henry's
    Steel a-bitin' in;
    Cap'n slaps John Henry on th' back,
    Says, 'I'll give yo' fifty dollars if yo' win,'
    Lawd,— Lawd,—
    I'll give yo' fifty dollars if yo' win.'

15. White Man saw John Henry's
    Steel a-goin' down;
    White Man says,— 'That man's a mighty man,
    But he'll weaken when th' hardes' rock is foun',—
    Lawd,— Lawd,—
    He'll weaken when th' hardes' rock is foun'.'

16. John Henry, O John Henry,—
    John Henry's hammah too;
    When a woman's 'pendin' on a man
    Haint no tellin' what a mighty man can do,—
    Lawd,— Lawd,—
    No tellin' what a mighty man can do.

17. John Henry, O John Henry!
    Blood am runnin' red!
    Falls right down with his hammah to th' groun',
    Says, 'I've beat him to th' bottom but I'm dead,—
    Lawd,— Lawd,—
    I've beat him to th' bottom but I'm dead.'

18. John Henry kissed his hammah;
    Kissed it with a groan;
    Sighed a sigh an' closed his weary eyes,
    Now po' Lucy has no man to call huh own,—
    Lawd,— Lawd,—
    Po' Lucy has no man to call huh own.

19. Cap' Tommy came a-runnin'
    To John Henry's side;
    Says, 'Lawd, Lawd,—O Lawdy, Lawdy, Lawd,—
    He's beat it to th' bottom but he's died,—
    Lawd,— Lawd,—
    He's beat it to th' bottom but he's died.'

20. Lucy ran to see him;
    Dress she wore was blue;
    Started down th' track an' she nevvah did turn back,
    Sayin', 'John Henry, I'll be true—true to you,—
    Lawd,— Lawd,—
    John Henry, I'll be true—true to you.'

21. John Henry, O John Henry!
    Sing it if yo' can,—
    High an' low an' ev'ry where yo' go,—
    He died with his hammah in his han',—
    Lawd,— Lawd,—
    He died with his hammah in his han'.

22. Buddie, where'd yo' come from
    To this railroad job?
    If yo' wantta be a good steel-drivin' man,
    Put yo' trus' in yo' hammah an' yo' God,—
    Lawd,— Lawd,—
    Put yo' trus' in yo' hammah an' yo' God.

FRANKIE AND ALBERT

From C. Sandburg, *The American Songbag*, 1927, pp. 76–7. By courtesy of Harcourt, Brace and Co., Publishers, New York.

1. Frankie and Albert were sweethearts, everybody knows,
   Frankie spent a hundred dollars just to get her man some clothes;
   He was her man, but he done her wrong.

2. Frankie went down to the corner, took along a can,
    Says to the lovin' bartender, 'Has you seen my lovin' man?
        He is my man, but he's doin' me wrong.'

3. 'Well, I ain't gonna tell you no story, ain't gonna tell you
    no lie,
    Albert went by 'bout an hour ago, with a girl called Alice
    Fry;
        He was your man, but he's doin' you wrong.'

4. Frankie's gone from the corner, Frankie ain't gone for fun,
    Underneath her apron she's got Albert's gatlin' gun;
        He was her man, but he done her wrong.

5. Albert sees Frankie comin', out the back door he did scoot,
    Frankie pulled out the pistol, went roota-de-toot-toot-toot.
        He was her man, but she shot him down.

6. Frankie shot him once, Frankie shot him twice,
    Third time she shot him the bullet took his life;
        He was her man, but he done her wrong.

7. When Frankie shot Albert, he fell down on his knees,
    Looked up at her and said, 'Oh, Frankie, please,
        Don't shoot me no mo', don't shoot me no mo'.

8. 'Oh, turn me over, doctor; turn me over slow,
    Turn me over on my right side, 'cause the bullet am hurtin'
    me so.
        I was her man, but I done her wrong.'

9. Now it's rubber-tired carriages, decorated hack,
    Eleven men went to the graveyard, and only ten come back;
        He was her man, but he's dead and gone.

10. Frankie was a-standin' on the corner, watchin' de hearse
    go by,
    Throwed her arms into the air, 'Oh, let me lie
        By the side of my man, what done me wrong.'

11. Frankie went to the graveyard, bowed down on her knees,
    'Speak one word to me, Albert, an' give my heart some ease.
        You was my man, but I done you wrong.'

12. Sheriff arrested Frankie, took her to the county jail,
    Locked her up in a dungeon cell, and throwed the keys
    away.
    She shot her man, said he done her wrong.

13. Judge tried lil' Frankie, under an electric fan;
    Judge says, 'Yo' free woman now, go kill yourself anothah
    man.
    He was yo' man, now he's dead an' gone.'

THE BOLL WEEVIL

From D. Scarborough, *On the Trail of Negro Folk-Songs*, 1925, p. 78. From
Houston, Tex. The boll weevil began its depredations on cotton about 1895.
By courtesy of Professor Dorothy Scarborough.

1. Oh, have you heard de latest,
   De latest all yore own?
   All about de Boll Weevil
   Whut caused me to lose mah home?

2. First time ah saw de Boll Weevil
   He was settin' on de squah.
   Next time ah saw dat Weevil
   He was settin' everywhah,
   Jes' a-lookin' foh a home,—lookin' foh a home!

3. Fahmah say to de Weevil,
   'Whut makes yore head so red?'
   Weevil say to de fahmah,
   'It's a wondah ah ain't dead,
   Lookin' foh a home, lookin' foh a home!'

4. Nigger say to de Weevil,
   'Ah'll throw you in de hot sand.'
   Weevil say to de nigger,
   'Ah'll stand it lak a man.
   Ah'll have a home, ah'll have a home!'

5. Says de Captain to de Mistis,
   'Whut do you think ob dat?
   Dis Boll Weevil done make a nes'
   Inside mah Sunday hat;
      He 'll have a home,—he 'll have a home!'

6. Ef you wanta kill de Boll Weevil
   You betta staht in time.
   Use a little sugar
   An' lots o' turpentine,
      An' he 'll be dead,—an' he 'll be dead.

SELECTED BIBLIOGRAPHY

To serve as an introduction to study of ballads. British and American books with melodies are indicated by an asterisk (*). Older collections winnowed by Child are not listed.

COLLECTIONS

BRITISH AND AMERICAN

*S. Baring-Gould and H. F. Sheppard, *Songs of the West*. 4 parts. London, 1889–91. Revised and enlarged by C. J. Sharp, 1905.

* —— *A Garland of Country Song*. London, 1895.

*P. Barry, F. H. Eckstorm, and M. W. Smyth, *British Ballads from Maine*. New Haven, Conn., 1929.

*L. E. Broadwood, *English Traditional Songs and Carols*. London, 1908.

* —— and J. A. Fuller-Maitland, *English County Songs*. London, 1893.

*J. C. Bruce and J. Stokoe, *Northumbrian Minstrelsy*. Newcastle, 1882.

*O. D. Campbell and C. J. Sharp, *English Folk-Songs from the Southern Appalachians*. New York, 1917.

*F. J. Child, *English and Scottish Popular Ballads*. 5 vols. Boston, 1882–98. As a widely representative collection, the indispensable basis for all study of British ballads. Bibliography virtually complete down to 1898.

*W. Christie, *Traditional Ballad Airs*. 2 vols. Edinburgh, 1876–81.

*J. C. Colcord, *Roll and Go. Songs of American Sailormen*. Indianapolis, Ind., 1924.

J. H. Combs, *Folk-Songs du Midi des États-Unis*. Paris, 1925.

*J. H. Cox, *Folk-Songs of the South*. Cambridge, Mass., 1925.

*A. K. Davis, Jr., *Traditional Ballads of Virginia*. Cambridge, Mass., 1929.

F. H. Eckstorm and M. W. Smyth, *The Minstrelsy of Maine*. Boston, 1927.

*G. Eyre-Todd, *Ancient Scots Ballads*. London, 1895.

C. J. Finger, *Frontier Ballads*. Garden City, N.Y., 1927.

C. H. Firth, *Naval Songs and Ballads*. London, 1908.

*H. H. Flanders and G. Brown, *Vermont Folk-Songs and Ballads*. Brattleboro, Vt., 1931.

*G. Greig, *Folk-Song of the North-East*. 2 series. Peterhead, 1909–14.

*_The Journal of American Folk-Lore_. New York, 1888–

*_The Journal of the Folk-Song Society_. 7 volumes. 1899–1926.

*A. Keith, *Last Leaves of Traditional Ballads and Ballad Airs, collected in Aberdeenshire by the late Gavin Greig.* Aberdeen, 1925.

*F. Kidson, *Traditional Tunes.* Oxford, 1891.

*J. A. Lomax, *Cowboy Songs and Other Frontier Ballads.* New York, 1910.

*J. McGill, *Folk-Songs of the Kentucky Mountains.* New York, 1917.

*W. R. Mackenzie, *Ballads and Sea Songs from Nova Scotia.* Cambridge, Mass., 1928.

*R. Maver, *Genuine Scottish Melodies*, ed. G. Alexander. 2 vols. Edinburgh, 1866.

H. W. Odum and G. B. Johnson, *The Negro and his Songs.* Chapel Hill, N.C., 1925.

L. Pound, *American Ballads and Songs.* New York, 1922.

*E. P. Richardson, *American Mountain Songs.* New York, 1927.

*F. L. Rickaby, *Ballads and Songs of the Shanty-Boy.* Cambridge, Mass., 1926.

*C. Sandburg, *The American Songbag.* New York, 1927.

H. C. Sargent and G. L. Kittredge, *English and Scottish Popular Ballads, edited from the Collection of Francis James Child.* Boston, 1904. Contains one or more versions of all save four of the 305 ballads printed by Child.

*D. Scarborough, *On the Trail of Negro Folk-Songs.* New York, 1925.

*C. J. Sharp, *American English Folk-Songs.* 1st series. New York, 1918.

* —— *English Folksongs.* Selected edition. 2 vols. London, 1920.

*—— *Folk-Songs of England.* London, 1908–12. I. *Folk-Songs from Dorset*, by H. E. D. Hammond. II. *Folk-Songs from the Eastern Counties*, by R. V. Williams. III. *Folk-Songs from Hampshire*, by G. B. Gardiner. IV. *Folk-Songs from Various Counties*, by C. J. Sharp. V. *Folk-Songs from Sussex*, by W. P. Merrick.

*—— *One Hundred English Folksongs.* London, 1916.

*—— and C. L. Marson, *Folk-Songs from Somerset.* 5 series. London, 1904–9.

H. W. Shoemaker, *Mountain Minstrelsy of Pennsylvania.* Philadelphia, 1931.

F. Sidgwick, *Popular Ballads of the Olden Time.* 4 series. London, 1903–12.

R. Smith, *South Carolina Ballads.* Cambridge, Mass., 1928.

*W. B. Whall, *Sea Songs and Shanties.* Rev. ed. London, 1926.

N. I. White, *American Negro Folk-Songs.* Cambridge, Mass., 1928.

A. Williams, *Folk-Songs of the Upper Thames.* London, 1923.

*L. Wyman and H. Brockway, *Lonesome Tunes. Folk-Songs from the Kentucky Mountains.* New York, 1916.

CELTIC

L. A. Bourgault-Ducoudray, *Trente mélodies populaires de la Basse-Bretagne*. Paris, 1885.

J. F. Campbell, *Leabhar na Feinne. Heroic Gaelic Ballads*. London, 1872.

P. W. Joyce, *Old Irish Folk Music*. London, 1909.

F. M. Luzel, *Gwerziou Breiz-Izel. Chants populaires de la Basse-Bretagne*. 2 vols. Lorient, 1868–74.

—— *Soniou Breiz-Izel. Chansons populaires de la Basse-Bretagne*. 2 vols. Paris, 1890.

G. Petrie, *The Complete Collection of Irish Music*. London. 1902.

FRENCH

D. Arbaud, *Chants populaires de la Provence*. 2 vols. Aix, 1862–4.

M. Barbeau and E. Sapir, *Folk Songs of French Canada*. New Haven, Conn., 1925.

C. Beauquier, *Chansons populaires recueillies en Franche-Comté*. Paris, 1894.

J. F. Bladé, *Poésies populaires en langue française, recueillies dans l'Armagnac et l'Agenais*. Paris, 1879.

—— *Poésies populaires de la Gascogne*. 3 vols. Paris, 1881–2.

Champfleury (J. Fleury). *Chansons populaires des provinces de France*. Paris, 1860.

T. F. Crane, *Chansons populaires de la France*. New York, 1891.

G. Doncieux and J. Tiersot. *Le Romancéro populaire de la France*. Paris, 1904.

J. Fleury, *Littérature orale de la Basse-Normandie*. Paris, 1883.

E. Gagnon, *Chansons populaires du Canada*. 5th ed. Montreal, 1908.

J. M. Gibson, *Canadian Folk Songs*. London, 1927.

M. Haupt, *Französische Volkslieder*. Leipzig, 1877.

L. Pineau, *Le Folk-lore de Poitou*. Paris, 1892.

E. Rolland, *Recueil de chansons populaires*. 6 vols. Paris, 1883–90.

J. Tiersot, *Chansons populaires recueillies dans les Alpes françaises*. Grenoble, 1903.

—— *Mélodies populaires des provinces de France*. 4 series. Paris, 1887–94.

J. B. T. Weckerlin, *L'ancienne chanson populaire de France*. Paris, 1887.

SCANDINAVIAN

A. P. Berggreen, *Svenske Folke-Sange og Melodier*. Vol. iii of the editor's *Folke-Sange og Melodier, fædrelandske og fremmede*. 2nd ed. Copenhagen, 1860–71.

S. Bugge, *Gamle norske Folkeviser*. Christiania, 1858.

E. G. Geijer and A. A. Afzelius, *Svenska Folkvisor.* New ed. by R. Bergström and L. Höijer. 3 vols. Stockholm, 1880.

S. Grundtvig and A. Olrik. *Danmarks gamle Folkeviser.* 6 vols. Copenhagen, 1853–1920.

V. U. Hammershaimb, *Færösk Anthologi.* 2 vols. Copenhagen, 1891.

T. Laub, *Danske Folkeviser med gamle Melodier.* 2 parts. Copenhagen, 1899–1904.

L. M. Lindeman, *Ældre og nyere norske Fjeldmelodier.* Rev. ed. 2 vols. Christiania (1878).

J. M. Moe and I. Mortenson, *Norske Fornkvæde og Folkevisur.* Christiania, 1877.

A. Olrik and I. A. Falbe-Hansen, *Danske Folkeviser i Udvalg.* 1st coll., 2 vols., 3rd ed. Copenhagen 1913. 2nd coll. 1909.

A. Olrik, *Nordisk Aandsliv.* New ed. Copenhagen, 1927.

L. Pineau, *Le romancero scandinave.* Paris, 1906.

R. C. A. Prior, *Ancient Danish Ballads.* 3 vols. London, 1860.

E. M. Smith-Dampier, *Danish Ballads.* Cambridge, 1920.

E. Wigström, *Folkdiktning. Visor, Sägner, Sagor.* Copenhagen, 1880.

—— *Skaonska Visor, Sagor, och Sägner.* Lund, 1880.

GERMAN

P. Alpers, *Die Alten niederdeutschen Volkslieder.* Hamburg, 1924.

—— *Das deutsche Volkslied.* Nürnberg (1925).

—— *Hannoversche Volkslieder.* Frankfurt am M., 1927.

F. M. Böhme, *Altdeutsches Liederbuch.* Leipzig, 1877.

—— *Deutscher Liederhort.* 3 vols. Leipzig, 1893–4.

—— *Volksthümliche Lieder der Deutschen.* Leipzig, 1895.

F. W. von Ditfurth, *Deutsche Volks- und Gesellschaftslieder des 17. und 18. Jahrhunderts.* Nördlingen, 1872.

H. Frischbier, *Preussische Volkslieder in plattdeutscher Mundart.* Königsberg, 1877.

—— and J. Sembrzycki, *Hundert ostpreussische Volkslieder in hochdeutscher Sprache.* Leipzig, 1893.

A. Hruschka and W. Toischer, *Deutsche Volkslieder aus Böhmen.* Prague, 1888–9.

J. Lewalter, *Deutsche Volkslieder in Niederhessen.* 5 parts. Hamburg, 1890–4.

R. von Liliencron, *Die historischen Volkslieder der Deutschen vom 13. bis 16. Jahrhundert.* 5 vols. Leipzig, 1865–9.

E. Meier, *Schwäbische Volkslieder.* Berlin, 1855.

C. Mündel, *Elsässische Volkslieder.* Strasbourg, 1884.

L. Parisius, *Deutsche Volkslieder mit ihre Singweisen, geistliche Lieder und Balladen, in der Altmark und im Magdeburgischen.* Magdeburg, 1879.

A. Reifferscheid, *Westfälische Volkslieder.* Heilbronn, 1879.

A. Schlossar, *Deutsche Volkslieder aus Steiermark.* Innsbruck, 1881.

L. Tobler, *Schweizerische Volkslieder.* 2 vols. Frauenfeld, 1882–4.

—— *Das Volkslied im Appenzellerlande.* Zurich, 1903.

E. H. Wolfram, *Nassauische Volkslieder.* Berlin, 1894.

DUTCH AND FLEMISH

J. A. Alberdingk-Thijm, *Gedichte uit de verschillende Tijdperken der Noord- en Zuid-nederlandsche Literatuur.* 2 vols. Amsterdam, 1850–2.

J. A. and L. J. Alberdingk-Thijm, *Oude en nieuwere Kerstliederen.* Amsterdam, 1852.

L. de Baecker, *Chants historiques de la Flandre.* Lille, 1855.

E. de Coussemaker, *Chants populaires des Flamands de France.* Gand, 1856.

Hoffman von Fallersleben, *Niederländische Volkslieder.* 2nd ed. Hanover, 1856.

A. Lootens and J. M. E. Feys, *Chants populaires flamands.* Bruges, 1879.

SPANISH AND PORTUGUESE

M. Aguilo y Fuster, *Romancer popular de la terra catalana.* Barcelona, 1893.

Ali-Ben-Noab-Tun, *Romancer popular catala.* Barcelona, 1900.

T. Braga, *Romanceiro general.* Coimbra, 1867.

—— *Cancioneiro popular.* Coimbra, 1867.

A. Duran, *Romancero general.* 2 vols. Madrid, 1849–51.

F. R. Marin, *Cantos populares españoles.* 5 vols. Seville, 1882–3.

R. Menéndez Pidal, *Flor nueva de romances viejos.* Madrid, 1928.

M. Milá y Fontanals, *Romancerillo catalan.* 2nd ed. Barcelona, 1882.

S. Roméro, *Cantos populares do Brazil.* 2 vols. Lisbon, 1883.

F. J. Wolf and C. Hofmann, *Romances viejos castellanos.* Ed. M. Menéndez y Pelayo. 3 vols. Madrid, 1899.

ITALIAN

M. Barbi, *Poesia popolare pistoiese.* Florence, 1895.

G. Bernoni, *Canti popolari veneziani.* Venice, 1872.

—— *Nuovi canti popolari veneziani.* Venice, 1874.

—— *Tradizioni popolari veneziane.* Venice, 1875.

G. Bolza, *Canzoni popolari comasche.* (Sitzungsberichte der kaisl. Akad., Phil.-hist. Classe, liii.) Vienna, 1867.

A. Casetti and V. Imbriani, *Canti popolari delle provincie meridionali*. 2 vols. Turin, 1871–2.

C. Nigra, *Canti popolari del Piemonte*. Turin, 1888.

G. Pitrè, *Canti popolari siciliani*. 2nd ed. 2 vols. Palermo, 1891.

L. Sinigaglia, *Vecchie Canzoni popolari del Piemonte*. Leipzig, 1914–28.

ROUMANIAN

V. Alecsandri, *Ballades et chants populaires de la Roumanie*. Paris, 1855.

E. C. G. Murray, *The National Songs and Legends of Roumania*. London, 1859.

LITHUANIAN

A. Leskien and K. Brugman, *Litauische Volkslieder und Märchen*. Strasbourg, 1882.

SLAVIC

A. Chodźko, *Les chants historiques de l'Ukraine*. Paris, 1879.

I. F. Hapgood, *The Epic Songs of Russia*. New ed. London, 1915.

L. A. Magnus, *The Heroic Ballads of Russia*. London, 1921.

W. R. S. Ralston, *The Songs of the Russian People*. London, 1872.

A. Rambaud, *La Russie épique*. Paris, 1876.

G. Rosen, *Bulgarische Volksdichtungen*. Leipzig, 1879.

A. Waldau, *Böhmische Granaten. Czechische Volkslieder*. 2 vols. Prague, 1858–60.

GREEK

L. M. J. Garnett, *Greek Folk-Songs from the Turkish Provinces of Greece*. London 1885.

A. Passow, *Carmina popularia Græciæ recentioris*. Leipzig, 1860.

B. Schmidt, *Griechische Märchen, Sagen und Volkslieder*. Leipzig, 1877.

MAGYAR

B. Bartók, *Das ungarische Volkslied*. Berlin, 1925.

—— *Hungarian Folk Music*. Trans. M. D. Calvocoressi. Oxford, 1931.

GYPSY

H. von Wlislocki, *Volksdichtungen der siebenbürgischen und südungarischen Zigeuner*. Vienna, 1890.

CRITICISM

It should be remembered that some of the most valuable studies of balladry as an art, as well as of individual ballads, are to be found in the books listed above.

P. Barry, 'The Origin of Folk-Melodies', *Journal of American Folk-Lore*, xxiii. 440–5 (1910).

P. Barry, 'The Transmission of Folk-Song', *ibid.* xxvii. 67–76 (1914).

C. R. Baskervill, *The Elizabethan Jig.* Chicago, 1929.

P. F. Baum, 'The English Ballad of Judas Iscariot', *Publ. Mod. Lang. Ass.* xxxi. 181–9 (1916).

A. Beatty, 'Ballad, Tale, and Tradition', *ibid.* xxix. 473–98 (1914).

M. W. Beckwith, 'The English Ballad in Jamaica: A Note upon the Origin of the Ballad Form', *ibid.* xxxix. 455–83 (1924).

H. M. Belden, 'Popular Song in Missouri—The Returned Lover', *Arch. f. d. Studien der neueren Sprachen*, cxx. 62–71 (1908).

—— 'Boccaccio, Hans Sachs, and The Bramble Briar', *Publ. Mod. Lang. Ass.* xxxiii. 327–95 (1918).

F. E. Bryant, *A History of English Balladry.* Boston, 1913.

W. H. Clawson, *The Gest of Robin Hood.* Toronto, 1909.

E. Flügel, 'Zur Chronologie der englischen Balladen', *Anglia*, xxi. 312–58 (1899).

G. H. Gerould, 'The Ballad of the Bitter Withy', *Publ. Mod. Lang. Ass.* xxiii. 141–67 (1908).

—— 'The Making of Ballads', *Modern Philology*, xxi. 15–28 (1923).

R. Graves, *The English Ballad.* London, 1927.

R. L. Greene, *The English Carol before 1550.* Dissertation. Princeton University, 1929. (On deposit in the University Library.)

F. B. Gummere, *Old English Ballads.* Introduction. Boston, 1894.

—— *The Beginnings of Poetry.* New York, 1901.

—— *The Popular Ballad.* Boston, 1907.

—— 'Primitive Poetry and the Ballad', *Modern Philology*, i. 193–202, 217–34, 373–90 (1904).

—— 'The Ballad', *Cambridge History of Literature*, ii. 449–74. Cambridge, 1908.

W. M. Hart, 'Professor Child and the Ballad', *Publ. Mod. Lang. Ass.* xxi. 755–807 (1906).

—— *Ballad and Epic.* Cambridge, Mass., 1907.

T. F. Henderson, *The Ballad in Literature.* Cambridge, 1912.

A. Heusler, *Lied und Epos.* Dortmund, 1905.

S. B. Hustvedt, *Ballad Criticism in Scandinavia and Great Britain.* New York, 1916.

—— *Ballad Books and Ballad Men.* Cambridge, Mass., 1930.

G. B. Johnson, *John Henry. Tracking Down a Negro Legend.* Chapel Hill, N.C., 1929.

W. P. Ker, 'On the History of the Ballad', *Proc. of the Brit. Acad.*, iv. 1910.

—— 'On the Danish Ballads', *Scottish Hist. Rev.* i. 357–78 (1904), v. 385–401 (1908).

L. McWatt, *The Scottish Ballads and Ballad Writing*. Paisley, 1923.

J. Meier, *Kunstlied im Volksmunde*. Halle, 1906.

R. Menéndez Pidal, Series of studies in *Revista de filología española*, i.
357–77; ii. 1–20, 105–36, 329–39; iii. 233–89 (1914–16);
vii. 229–338 (1920).

—— *Poesía popular y Poesía tradicional en la literatura española*.
Oxford, 1922. Reprinted in *El Romancero Teorias e investigaciones*.
Madrid, n.d.

—— *Poesía juglaresca y juglares*. Madrid, 1924.

—— 'Romances y baladas', *Modern Human. Research Ass*. i. 1–17 (1927).

S. G. Morley, 'Spanish Ballad Problems', *Univ. of California Publ. in
Modern Philology*, xiii. 207–28 (1925).

K. Nessler, *Geschichte der Ballade Chevy Chase*. Berlin, 1911 (Palaestra
cxii).

W. W. Newell, 'Individual and Collective Characteristics in Folk-Lore',
Journal of American Folk-Lore, xix. 1–15 (1906).

L. Pound, *Poetic Origins and the Ballad*. New York, 1921.

—— 'The Term: Communal', *Publ. Mod. Lang. Ass*. xxxix, 440–54
(1924).

H. E. Rollins, 'An Analytical Index to the Ballad Entries in the
Registers of the Company of Stationers', *Studies in Philology*, xxi.
1–324 (1924).

C. J. Sharp, *English Folk-Song: Some Conclusions*. London, 1907.

F. Sidgwick, *The Ballad*. London (1914).

J. O. H. R. Steenstrup, *The Medieval Popular Ballad*. Trans. E. G.
Cox. Boston, 1914.

A. Taylor, 'Das Schloss in Oesterreich', *Modern Lang. Notes*, xlii.
222–8 (1927).

J. Tiersot, *Histoire de la chanson populaire en France*. Paris, 1889.

A. H. Tolman, '"Mary Hamilton"; the Group Authorship of Ballads',
Publ. Mod. Lang. Ass. xlii. 422–32 (1927).

N. I. White, *American Negro Folk-Songs*. Cambridge, Mass., 1928.

L. C. Wimberly, *Minstrelsy, Music, and the Dance in the English and
Scottish Popular Ballads*. Univ. of Nebraska Stud. in Lang., Lit.,
and Criticism, no. 4. *Death and Burial Lore in the* ——. *Ibid.*
no. 8. Lincoln, Neb., 1921, 1927.

—— *Folklore in the English and Scottish Ballads*. Chicago, 1928.

INDEX OF BALLAD TITLES

GENERAL INDEX